Telling Our Selves

Oxford Studies in Anthropological Linguistics
William Bright, General Editor

Telling Our Selves

Ethnicity and Discourse
in Southwestern Alaska

CHASE HENSEL

New York   *Oxford*
Oxford University Press
1996

Oxford University Press

Oxford New York
Athens Auckland Bangkok
Calcutta Cape Town Dar es Salaam Delhi
Florence Hong Kong Istanbul Karachi
Kuala Lumpur Madras Madrid Melbourne
Mexico City Nairobi Paris Singapore
Taipei Tokyo Toronto

and associated companies in

Berlin Ibadan

Copyright © 1996 by Chase Hensel

Published by Oxford University Press, Inc.
198 Madison Avenue, New York, New York 10016

Oxford is a registered trademark of Oxford University Press, Inc.

Library of Congress Cataloging-in-Publication Data
Hensel, Chase.
Telling ourselves : ethnicity and discourse in southwestern Alaska / Chase Hensel.
    p   cm. – (Oxford studies in anthropological linguistics : 5)
ISBN 0-19-509476-X – ISNB 0-19-509477-8 (pbk.)
1. Yupik Eskimos – Social conditions 2. Yupik Eskimos – Ethnic
identity. 3. Yupik languages – Alaska – Bethel. 4. Subsistence
economy – Alaska – Bethel. 5. Ethnicity – Alaska – Bethel.
6. Discourse analysis, Narrative – Alaska – Bethel. 7. Sex role –
Alaska – Bethel. 8. Gender identity – Alaska – Bethel. 9. Bethel
(Alaska) – Economic conditions. 10. Bethel (Alaska) – Social
conditions. I. Title. II. Series.
E99.E7H467 1996
305.8'009798'4—dc20   95-31923

1 2 3 4 5 6 7 8 9

Printed in the United States of America
on acid-free paper

Preface

My mom said she tried to help my grandma [cut king salmon for dry-ing] as my grandma grew older, but my grandma always said, "You're gonna butcher the fish, you're gonna butcher them, you're gonna mess them up." . . . And she wouldn't let my mom help. And my mom said . . . soon after my grandma died, within a couple of years I'd say, when she went to make her first flat fish, which is the more elaborate bunch of cutting that you have to do, she stood there at her table, with no help, and made the cuts. And she said it was as if my grandma's hand was on her hand. . . . And I'm thirty-eight, and I have friends who have just taken up the knife, and had the same thing happen that happened to my mom.

With these words Janet Shantz of Bethel, Alaska, linked the "Yup'ik part" of who she is with the generational recycling of women at the fish-cutting tables. This central, repeated enactment of ethnicity through the catching and processing of subsistence foods was to be described in nu-merous interviews with the residents of this mixed Native and non-Native community. It is the thesis of this book that talk about ethnicity and subsistence, as well as the doing of subsistence activities, are all interlinked forms of practice. In the interweaving of these strands, eth-nicity is constantly re-created. Although ethnicity is overtly constructed in terms of either/or categories, the discourse of Bethel residents suggests

that their actual concern is less with whether one is Native or non-Native than with how Native one is in a given context.

This book, then, examines discourse strategies used by individuals in their self-definitions. This occurs in a conversational setting where ethnicity is both implicitly and explicitly contested. In this sense I have tried to combine the insights of sociolinguistics with broader anthropological concerns. While the book is ethnographic, it is not "about Eskimos." Rather, it is about how Bethel residents use similar forms of discourse to strategically validate disparate identities. In this context, in the Yup'ik Eskimo heartland, subsistence is the focus of peoples' interactions regardless of their ascriptive ethnicity. Even people who spend little time in subsistence activities spend a great deal of time in subsistence talk. In short, unlike traditional ethnographies, which focus on traditions and consequently tend to reify the past (especially in studies of hunter-gatherers), this ethnography focuses on contemporary preoccupations. The ethnographic description becomes a device for preserving and explicating the opulent polysemy of situated talk.

The book begins with a general ethnographic description of the area and builds in complexity until the final chapter, at which point it is possible to see the subtlety with which strategic moves are used in actual discourse. Chapters are interspersed with composite accounts of my own participation in subsistence activities.

Chapter 1 reviews the ethnographic background and recent history of the area. Chapter 2 introduces the practical and ideological dimensions of contemporary subsistence. Together these chapters suggest that subsistence discourse displays an overlay of associations with tradition, gender role ideology, and concerns over contemporary regulation of subsistence activity.

Chapters 3 and 4 explore subsistence activities and discourse as markers of ethnic identities and social boundaries. In particular, chapter 4 elaborates the ways in which subsistence discourse can substitute for the actual activities it references.

Chapter 5 considers socioeconomic change and its differential effects on Yup'ik male and female gender roles. I suggest that for women engagement in Western wage-work most calls their ethnicity into question, while for men wage-work primarily challenges their proper performance of gender roles. These concerns only become evident through a close reading of men's and women's discourse.

Chapter 6 looks not at hunting, fishing, and processing but at eating and the enjoyment of the harvest. I argue that talk about food is yet another way to mark one's identity. Like talk about subsistence activities, talk about food not only takes place in the absence of its referents but may also be heightened by their absence.

Chapter 7 reexamines several discourse samples and places them in a theoretical perspective informed by practice theory, family systems theory, and sociolinguistics. I suggest that anthropological theory may be advanced by combining elements of these three approaches. Such a theoretical synthesis is based on the primacy of interaction. In this light, discourse can be seen as a fundamental form of practice.

I have developed these ideas through a lively interchange with a number of people. The list of those I wish to thank seems daunting, particularly since some of them might be embarrassed to see their names in print. It includes all the people who agreed to be interviewed or were interested in discussing these issues—those who are named in the text and those who chose to remain anonymous. In a larger sense, I would like to thank all the people who have, in myriad ways, enriched my life in the Yukon-Kuskokwim Delta. I hope that my appreciation for them comes through in this book.

Earlier versions of this manuscript benefited from close readings by Mary C. Pete, John Gumperz, Nelson Graburn, Lilly Wong Fillmore, James H. Barker, and David Smith. Robin Barker, Kathy Forbes, and Sara Miller all reviewed and commented on chapter 5. Anthony Woodbury, William Bright, Barbara Bodenhorn, David Marshall, and Willem de Reuse provided helpful comments in the revision stages. Throughout the entire process, Phyllis Morrow commented on drafts, debated theoretical and ethnographic issues, and provided encouragement. Thank you all.

Final preparation of the manuscript was made possible during a research year at the Scott Polar Research Institute and the department of social anthropology, Cambridge University. My particular thanks to Barbara Bodenhorn, Marilyn Strathern, Piers Vitebsky, William Mills, and Stephen Wells for their collegiality and consideration. My thanks also to Catherine Byfield for editorial assistance.

Research conducted in 1992 was funded by a Dissertation Improvement Grant from the National Science Foundation, Divisions of General Anthropology and Polar Programs #BNS 9103347. A portion of the support from National Science Foundation grant #OPP-9322092 (Arctic Social Sciences, Division of Polar Programs) allowed me to reconceptualize chapter 7.

Contents

Telling Our Selves

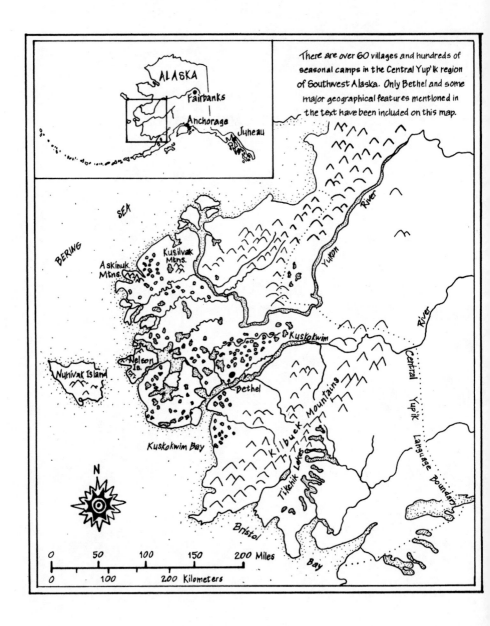

There are over 60 villages and hundreds of seasonal camps in the Central Yup'ik region of Southwest Alaska. Only Bethel and some major geographical features mentioned in the text have been included on this map.

ALASKA
Fairbanks
Anchorage
Juneau

BERING SEA

Askinuk Mtns.
Kusilvak Mtns.
Yukon River
Central Yup'ik Language Boundary
River
Kuskokwim
Nelson Is.
Nunivak Island
Bethel
Kilbuck Mountains
T'Kenik Lakes
Kuskokwim Bay
Bristol Bay

N

| 0 | 50 | 100 | 150 | 200 Miles |

| 0 | 100 | 200 Kilometers |

Introduction

OVERVIEW

This book examines the subsistence discourse and practices of Central Alaskan Yup'ik Eskimos[1] (hereafter Yupiit, the plural of Yup'ik) and non-Natives[2] in Southwestern Alaska. Subsistence discourse is a dynamic arena of social action in which identities and ideologies are constructed and negotiated. It ranges from informal exchanges in which subsistence is the perennial topic to formal public hearings on various governmental and commercial aspects of subsistence, wildlife, and their regulation. I suggest that their discourse is itself a vital form of practice and that through this situated discourse personal, ethnic, and gender identities are constructed, negotiated, and publicly validated. For Yupiit, talk about subsistence both presupposes traditional subsistence ideologies and serves as a locus of social and political negotiation. Concurrently, subsistence activity and discourse have also become a key arena in which Euro-Americans—many new to Southwestern Alaska—have sought to achieve and validate a "local" identity, modeled on Yup'ik subsistence practices or Euro-American perceptions of them. But as with new kinds of Yup'ik subsistence identity, the practice and achievement of this Euro-American local identity differs widely among individuals. Briefly, I will argue that subsistence is the central focus in the intellectual material, and spiritual culture of both historic and contemporary Yup'ik society. The values associated with subsistence have become key symbols of Yup'ik ethnic, social, and spiritual identity, particularly as traditional subsistence practices and Yup'ik identity are challenged and threatened in what is effectively a postcolonial setting. The symbolic importance of subsistence as an ethnic marker has been heightened most obviously for those Yupiit heavily involved in the cash economy and in continuous contact with Euro-Americans. Subsistence discourse is privileged over the actual practices of hunting, fishing, gathering, and processing because it is constantly available for strategic use in ways in which the physical practices of subsistence are not.

Detailed analysis of subsistence talk of any kind reveals such negotiation in action and hence permits inferences about speakers' underlying assumptions and the connotative meanings attached to the practices invoked in discourse. Of special interest are instances of interethnic miscommunication (see Example 4 in chapter 7) since they demonstrate the failure of particular (usually tacit) assumptions of interpretations to be shared or understood. When subsistence talk is involved, these miscommunications provide key evidence for both implicit assumptions about subsistence and identity held by Natives and non-Natives and for the kinds of strategic moves speakers make in these areas. The high frequency of such strategic moves and the variability with which non-Natives have acquired new structures (in this case, new ways of understanding and interacting) also allow larger issues of structuration to be addressed in this setting.

This question—how structures (Giddens 1979, 1984), or what Bourdieu (1977, 1990; Bourdieu and Passeron 1977) calls "habitus," are learned, maintained, and changed—is the major theoretical focus of this book. I will argue (in chapter 7) that such structures are homologous with what sociolinguists (Gumperz and others) have called contextualization conventions and with what psychologists (Hoffman, Auerswald) in family systems theory (also called the ecological approach) have called family roles. Conceiving of structures in this way considerably strengthens structuration theory, since the sociolinguistic and psychological approaches are inherently dynamic and have focused on interaction, thereby providing models of sedimentation, maintenance, and (slow) change. This recognition also provides a better theoretical basis for making generalizations from micro- to mezzo- to macrolevel groups. A more interactionally based approach provides a way of examining what *is* shared, with generalizations valid to the extent that structures *are* actually shared at different levels.

The approach is also important for linguistic anthropology and sociolinguistics, because it explicitly recognizes discourse as among the most, if not *the* most, important form of practice, *and* it suggests ways in which language may be studied more fruitfully. In the dominant sociolinguistic paradigm (the variationist paradigm of Labov and others), language is viewed as a dependent variable, based upon other social "facts" of the conversants (ethnicity, class, gender, status) or of the situation (setting). Language use is describable to the extent that such dependencies can be discovered. I follow Gumperz, Gal, and others in suggesting that the social "facts" of conversants are potentially fluid and open to negotiation, and that language usage is both a forum for, and a tactic of, such negotiation. While the "facts" and setting of an interaction provide the raw material from which various sorts of strategic moves may be fashioned, language usage is, in principle, autonomous. Participants' literal messages are simultaneously the vehicle for a variety of strategic moves, which are signaled through the usage of particular words, referents, dialects, and registers. Such moves are more powerful because they are generally implicit, relying upon shared referents of stories, genres, settings and worldview—what I would call shared structures. I have been particularly interested in the ways in which image and identity are manipulated by the shifting of frames in interaction (à la Goffman), as well as how members of different groups use the same discourse to different ends. However, such strategies are difficult to "capture," that is, to identify convincingly, and it is difficult to describe their saliency. I suggest that one approach is to identify a key discourse arena (in this case subsistence) and examine transcripts of conversations. Within a given discourse arena, there are likely to be recurrent routines linked to particular strategies, and more broadly to local social and ideological concerns. However, making such linkages requires significant ethnographic depth. In sum, this study examines language as practice—strategic moves in real conversation—but argues that, like any other form of practice, such strategies rely upon locally situated shared conventions of interpretation.

While the issue of structuration forms the primary theoretical focus of this work, it is also important to studies of gender and economic anthropology. Ethnicity and gender are examined as inter-articulating categories, which are more achieved than ascribed. This inter-articulation means that, for instance, particular practices may call one's gender or ethnicity into question. Which of these is called into question seems to differ for women and men, and relates to differing ideologies of gender role fulfillment, as well as differing gender histories under colonialism.

In relation to economic anthropology, this book argues that for many people subsistence is not exclusively or even primarily an economic activity. Because of the increasing importance of subsistence as a symbolic activity, it is likely that at least some types of subsistence activities may become more, rather than less, important over time.

Like many other contemporary ethnographers, I seek to make this work polyvocalic: while it remains mostly my own words, I have included relatively long transcript selections. These words are in many ways my primary data. As such they should be available to reinterpretation by others. Further, like uncropped photographs, larger chunks of speech provide assurance that words are not taken out of context. They also allow interviewees to speak for themselves. This method respects speakers in a fashion that is locally appropriate in the Yup'ik area, a place where one is taught to listen without interrupting.

This book is posited upon the idea that understanding language as practice requires in-depth cultural as well as linguistic understanding, that context is vital to both analysis and comprehension. This includes not only the historical and contemporary setting but also a variety of issues that may potentially impinge upon the sort of strategic moves people may be making in discourse. That is, for a particular field of discourse, one must identify what is contested or taken for granted, and by whom; what can be gained or may be lost; and how and why this particular field of discourse has become marked—why it is important. In effect, then, an ethnography is required to understand the use of language as practice. Therefore, the book begins with a generally standard ethnographic description, building in complexity until the final chapter, where it is possible to see the subtlety with which strategic moves are used in actual discourse. To bridge the distance between analysis and experience, chapters are interspersed with accounts (in italics) of actual subsistence activities. All of these accounts are to some extent composites of my own experiences as participant-observer, written in the style of, and partially taken from, field notes. These accounts progress through the seasons in a calendrical cycle.

WHY BETHEL?

Bethel is an exemplary place to examine issues of discourse and identity. Here the first world meets the third, a border town between Euro-America and "Yup'ik-land" that is in a constant state of flux. With the exception of a few old Bethel families, everyone is a migrant, either from the surrounding Yup'ik villages or from elsewhere in the state, nation, or world. Population changes are so rapid that identities must be constantly reenacted and re-created: there is little stasis. Questions of identity, of who and how to be, face everyone. Yupiit have been, to various degrees, colonized mentally as well as economically and socially. Consequently, they need to construct a positive image of themselves that is also worth emulating. I suggest that they do this through interaction. For non-Native immigrants, on the other hand, the problem is how to adapt to a new social, cultural, and physical environment, and how to construct and convey a symbolic image that is in accord with these adaptations and adoptions. To the extent that Bethel, being neither city nor Yup'ik village, fits almost no one's previous identity, an interactional focus allows one to examine what happens in this process of bicultural accommodation.

SUBSISTENCE AND DISCOURSE

As currently used, the word "subsistence" itself has two separate meanings. The local meaning refers to the actual activities of hunting, fishing, gathering, processing, and sharing. Presently, in the Bethel area, virtually all Yupiit and most non-Natives are involved in these subsistence activities, and discourse about subsistence is a conversational staple for both groups. The second meaning of subsistence is a legal one. In this sense, "subsistence" has inclusionary and exclusionary elements (now under review), dictating who can pursue certain activities, when, and by what means. The legal definition has widely differing implications for Native groups, rural non-Natives, and urban non-Natives. Activities that were formerly unregulated, undefined, and largely ignored by regulatory agencies are now the focus of position papers and court battles, embroiled in issues of legally defined residence, ethnicity, and Native sovereignty. In the larger Alaskan context, the subsistence battle might be viewed as a struggle against the expropriation of Native resources by non-Natives, while in the Bethel context, Natives and non-Natives have similar legal access to the majority of species harvested, and resource conflicts have not been particularly divisive, although they may become more so in time.[3] I will suggest that the battle over subsistence rights and usage also concerns the expropriation of Native images/identities by non-Natives. This attempt at image appropriation is found in both urban and rural contexts, but seems more contested in urban ones.

SUBSISTENCE AS AN ECONOMIC ACTIVITY?

The most common way to "explain" subsistence has been economic (Wolfe 1979, Fienup-Riordan 1983b [partially], Jorgenson 1990), even though many statements by Native people contain at least an implication, and often an outright denial, of economic primacy. Perceiving cultural systems solely in economic terms requires either completely overextending the meaning of economics to include all issues of power and control, or reducing life to a balance sheet.[4] This is possible only if larger cultural issues and meanings are ignored. The writer and anthropologist Richard K. Nelson once described how an economic approach might appear if applied to non-Native culture:

> Imagine that you set out to determine what Christmas means to people. First you added up the costs of all the presents, and of all the food eaten, all of the gas costs and the wear and tear on everyone's cars, perhaps the incremental cost of everyone's clothes, and then you said that that was Christmas. You'd have missed the point entirely. (notes from a conversation, March 1987)

Nelson's description highlights what is wrong with economically oriented subsistence research: it tries to equate the value of having Aunt Suzy present at the Christmas table with the fair value of the car mileage that brought her, or the cost of the mashed turnips that a particular family "needs" on the Christmas Eve table even though no one eats them.

Arvin Dull, a Yup'ik man of bicultural background who is the manager of a bank in Bethel, gave the following response to a question about the importance of subsistence.[5]

> It's the reason we live in Bethel rather than in Anchorage or Fairbanks. It's not just to save money either. We'd do things we are doing, even if it costs *more* money than buying things at the store. I mean, take moose hunting. It costs a thousand dollars to go moose hunting. . . .
>
> I know one guy, an Eskimo, who says moose hunting is too expensive, that he'll buy his moose at the store, but he's definitely in the minority.[6]
>
> It has emotional value as well. Like when we have someone over and they eat our fish and when they find out that we put it up they go, "Wow, you guys do all that stuff and have time to put up fish too." And it makes you feel good. (notes from a conversation, June 24, 1991)

When I (= C) handed him (= A) an interview consent form, he responded:

> A: In looking at this, I find it's very interesting that you put down [that] the federal government and state government only look at subsistence as a way of saving money. That's hardly true at all. You can save

money by fishing. If you have a big freezer, and you load up your freezer, you could save money that way.

But if you're going goose hunting and moose hunting, it usually costs a lot of money to go, especially for people in Bethel. To go goose hunting by boat, you have to go by boat or charter a plane and fly out and do your hunting. It costs money for gas, [and] of course all the costs associated with your equipment, shells, food that you have to take with you when you go hunting.

So, if you put everything on paper, and did some number crunching, you'd find that it cost more to go out and catch the animal that you wanted to catch, and do your subsistence hunting, than it was to go to the store and catch, I mean, go to the store and buy the food. And it's probably cheaper to go and buy a chicken than it is to go out to the wild and catch a goose.

C: And that's not even counting your hours of work.

A: Yeah, the time. I'm able to sit down and think about the economics of subsistence hunting and fishing, because that's what I do for a living. That's my job you know, banking and uhm.

C: You cost stuff out all the time.

A: But subsistence hunting and fishing for me is what people traditionally say, it's a way of life. It's my way of life, and I fit right in. It's my way of life too. I could afford to buy anything in the store but I just prefer to eat subsistence-caught food, and that's what my family eats. We eat moose, caribou, ducks, geese, fish, ptarmigan, you name it, beaver, seal.

The neat thing about subsistence fishing—especially fishing—is I do that after work, or on weekends. And then my family can come with me, so we're all together. The boys like to club the fish when we pull them into the boat, so it's kind of a family affair.

When we get to the fish camp the family's together. The wife and I are cutting fish, and the boys are packing water, and stirring brine, or exploring in the trees, in the woods, what little short trees we have. They're always able to find a nest with little eggs or birdies in it. . . .

You get not only food from subsistence hunting and fishing, but of course, like I mentioned to you before, you get the psychological benefits of producing your own food. You know what you produced. You know what's in it.

You feel good when your friends come over to eat, and they enjoy what you produced, and in making the food you get exercise. You got to go out in the boat, and you got to fish. As I told my wife this spring, I said I can't wait for fishing because I need the exercise.

People that hunt and fish subsistence, for a way of life, if you see them, you know that they're healthy people, because they have to work for what they get. Even a lot of the foods that they eat, they have strong jaws. You go to the coast . . . .

C: Oh, you see those coast people who eat dried seal all the time.

A: Yeah, they have big jaws because of the muscles, and when you have bigger jaws, it kind of pulls the skin, right? And so they have less wrinkles. *[Laughs]*

And of course I think a lot of men would go absolutely crazy out here if it weren't for hunting and fishing. I mean, what do you do in the winter time in Bethel, Alaska? I mean, there's no bowling, there's no malls to go to, no theater, so what do men do? They go ptarmigan hunting, fox hunting, jackrabbit hunting, or ice fishing.

So they're busy doing that, they're busy fixing their little hooks and stuff, or cleaning their guns, or modifying their guns, or looking for a new gun to use for hunting or working on their snow machine, or getting their boat ready for the next year.

It's just a different way of life, it's a busy way of life, but it keeps you going, you don't sit idle. . . .

And taking [the] kids out and doing hunting and fishing, it brings the family closer together, so subsistence hunting does a lot for people, a lot of things, more things than they realize. [It] brings the family together. It teaches them something, gives them exercise, gives them nutrition. In most cases they save money.

And then [there is] the psychological part of it. Especially working all day long, even professional people in Bethel. Since it's a hub of fifty-seven villages, a lot of professional people live in Bethel.

After they've been here at least one season, even if they don't have a boat, motor, snow machine or something like that to get out, they'll have it the next year, or at least one of those things. Because their friends will take them out and let them try ice fishing, drift netting, or ptarmigan hunting, and they'll more or less become addicted to at least one of those things. And they'll want to go out, and instead of bothering their friends, they'll want to have their own things to go out with.

And the professional people find that it's better than psychotherapy. They're able to go out, and catch fish, and while they're catching fish it's so exciting and fun that they forget about all the problems

> at work. And I know a lot of professional people in Bethel are under
> a lot of stress, doctors, lawyers, state administrative people, you name
> it. (transcript of an interview, June 24, 1991)

The attitudes expressed by Mr. Dull are widely shared in this part of Alaska. I have used several sections from transcripts of interviews with him, not because he is expressing a unique viewpoint but because he so succinctly expresses this shared viewpoint.

Similarly, women value subsistence for more than its economic importance. In another interview, a Yup'ik woman professional highlighted the importance of subsistence to her:

> You know I have had some really good offers, more money and advancement if I would move to Anchorage or Juneau, but I've wanted to stay here so that I could continue to do subsistence.
>
> One time when my supervisor was out from Anchorage, and we were having her over to dinner, and serving her moose, [dried king salmon] strips, salmonberry and blueberry pie. I told her how important it was for me to be able to eat this food, and hunt and fish. I thanked her for all her help with my career, but told her that I wanted to stay here. (notes from an interview, July 1991)

Although these two people explicitly addressed the multiple values of subsistence, more often they are taken for granted. In Bethel, conversational references to subsistence are almost continual, and its obviously fundamental importance is taken for granted. This very importance, coupled with my long-term residence and relationships, made it somewhat difficult to obtain explicit statements of that importance: people knew that I had been actively involved in subsistence and assumed a shared understanding of its importance. For example, when I visited a local Yup'ik man active in church affairs, I tried to steer the conversation toward the spiritual importance of subsistence. He was untypically direct when he said, in effect, "Look, you know it's important, and I know it's important. Why belabor the obvious?" What *he* wanted to talk about was the likelihood of civil disobedience if subsistence rights were curtailed.

Subsistence activities are important to non-Natives as well, as is evident from the following comments by Mike Coffing:

> I wouldn't be, I wouldn't live, I couldn't live, I wouldn't feel, say, really whole or really at peace with any place that I couldn't go out and harvest resources. And I guess maybe associated with harvesting resources for me, and maybe other people too, is [a] kind of exploring,

getting out and seeing, going places, and doing things outside. Just being kind of involved in [the natural world?]. It's difficult to put in words, being involved in things that I like to do outside, that get you out of the house, [instead of] sitting watching TV, and waiting for something else to happen, but doing it, and being physical about it. (transcript of an interview, July 2, 1991)

Much of the power of subsistence clearly derives from its connections with the past or, more accurately, with several visions of the past that differ for Yupiit and non-Natives. In this respect, subsistence in Bethel parallels Anthony Cohen's description of traditional crofting activity on Whalsay, an island in the Shetlands:

Of all Whalsay milieux apart from the kirkyard, the croft is the supreme repository of the past, and the instrument which connects past and present most tangibly. To borrow Geertz's term (1971:27), it provides Whalsay people with a "sentimental education" into the meanings of "being Whalsa. . . ."

The croft, then, condenses the past through the landscape itself, and through its associations with the natural calendar; with community; with an earlier mode of subsistence and the ideal of self-sufficiency. It evokes the astonishing breadth of skill, the ingenuity and stamina necessary for physical survival in "daa old days." It may even be that it suggests an orientation to values somehow more substantial, more genuine, than those of the materialistic, debt-burdened tax benefit–maximizing present. . . . In this respect, it is the very *ir*rationality of crofting in economic terms which provides its attraction. It provides relief from the pressure associated with modern fishing, not because it is *un*economic, but because it is *non*economic; it belongs to a quite different realm of discourse. (1986:109, emphasis in original)

DECONSTRUCTING THE ECONOMIC ANALYSIS OF SUBSISTENCE

Researchers seem to persist in this Procrustean economic reductionism largely because of their ethnocentric preoccupations with economic value. Funding agencies also support this approach.

Most researchers (like most nonrural Alaskans, and, in general, most Americans) have had limited personal experience living in a so-called subsistence economy. Though researchers may have studied subsistence (professionally), few grew up on a break-even farm or ranch; indeed, given the twin pressures of taxes and agribusiness, such farms and ranches are rare. Their personal experience is with a compartmentalized world, where one set of activities—work—is clearly economic, another set religious, another social, and so on, and they bring this bias into the professional arena as well. Obviously, activities can cross from one realm to another; for example, baking a cake for a fellow employee's office birthday party is social, unless it's for one's supervisor, where it might be somewhat economic. The cultural assumption (which may also be a consciously chosen intellectual position) is that these realms—vocation and avocation—are separate and usually dichotomized. Many researchers divide Yup'ik activities into economic and noneconomic spheres. Once this is done, the (usually unconscious) assumption is that everything within the economic sphere should make rational economic sense: behavior should ultimately result in a net profit.

Within mainstream Euro-American culture, this rule is usually unconsciously applied the other way. If an activity does not show a profit, it is thought to be a hobby or recreation. This is even enshrined in the tax code: in order to remain a legitimate deduction, a business must show a profit one year out of five. Bicycling is clearly recreational activity for most people. If someone spends a thousand dollars on a bicycle, that is the purchaser's privilege. On the other hand, if that same person is a bicycle messenger, people would be interested to know whether riding a thousand-dollar bicycle is cost-effective, given the risk of theft, accidents, and normal wear and tear. If something is an economic activity, it needs to make economic sense; conversely, if it does not make economic sense, it is not an economic activity.

I have heard non-Native trappers in Fairbanks sum up their winter by saying, "We made enough to cover gas and expenses." This informs the listener that the trapping was not for profit but for other reasons. Trapping may have been deeply meaningful to the speakers, but they put it outside the realm of "work" in the usual sense of significant income-generating activity.

In terms of subsistence economics, an additional theoretical problem is that in the Bethel area, subsistence foods have yet to be fully monetized. That is, many things have yet to become fully convertible to and from money. Legal complications aside, many subsistence products, particularly delicacies or rare items, are virtually impossible to buy. They are unavailable for money. Few subsistence products have commercially available equivalents. The exceptions include commercially caught local fish such as salmon and whitefish, locally made smoked salmon strips, and commercial reindeer as a substitute for wild caribou. Even with these, however, most people would prefer the wild foods from their own area. All other substitutes are really not equivalents. People judge them to be inferior on the basis of taste, texture, amount of fat, and possible presence of pollutants.

The lack of a ready market (and the general legal separation of commercial and subsistence realms) is coupled with the fact that most families produce only what they need—there is little surplus production.[7] Still, economic theory would predict that scarcity should increase prices, not make things completely unavailable; while this can be described as supply being inelastic to demand, this very inelasticity should raise warning flags that subsistence is not strictly, or even primarily, an economic activity. Like crofting on Whalsay, its primary importance is that it provides an arena, a focus, and a mechanism through which people can construct a symbolic dialogue of ethnicity and identity. This arena is especially important given the general power differential that characterizes colonized and peripheral settings. Other researchers working in the Arctic have also stressed the importance of the symbolic aspects of subsistence (Graburn 1971; Freeman 1985, 1988). In this study, however, these aspects will be examined in depth.

NEGOTIATED GENDER AND ETHNICITY

Such settings as Bethel call for a new treatment of ethnicity: ethnicity as a negotiated category. In bicultural situations where members of both groups are acculturating, and some people are bicultural as well, ethnicity is less an ascriptive category (Goffman 1959, 1963) than a constantly negotiated and reenacted identity; that is, it is less a matter of pigmentation than portrayal. This is clearest at the middle of the bicultural continuum, where people of bicultural background can claim legitimacy in either group, but it applies to the rest of this continuum as well. The local conception suggests that ethnicity exists on a continuum, with descriptive placement based on symbolic portrayals of cultural allegiance. These include language use and interactional style, subsistence activities, diet, clothing, and religious activity. At issue is not "is she white?" but "how white is she?" Certain actions are marked ethnically and serve to identify their actors, rather than the reverse. A subsidiary theme of this manuscript is to wed the insights of practice theory to the study of ethnicity, in order to portray this strategic enactment of ethnicity. The approach recasts ethnicity as a continuously negotiated interchange in which participants construct and maintain images of themselves, rather than presenting it as a static system of labels; ethnicity is "for" something, rather than "as" something. This focuses attention on the dynamic and interactional nature of boundary markers. The methodology and conclusions are widely applicable to other studies of ethnicity and boundary markers.

Although I began this study with a sense that subsistence practices and discourse were more important to Yup'ik men than to Yup'ik women, I was soon disabused of this notion. I came to recognize that Yup'ik men and women have been unequally affected by Western "development," and that differential outmarriage and emigration are sequelae of this differential history and cultural patterns that favor women's involvement in the labor force. These differences also affect which aspects of one's identity are highlighted through subsistence practices. For men, subsistence most importantly validates gender identity and role fulfillment, and ethnicity secondarily. For women, the situation is reversed: subsistence primarily validates ethnic identity, and gender identity, secondarily. These identities—masculinity for Yup'ik men and ethnicity for Yup'ik women—are the ones most likely to be challenged.

MUTUAL INFLUENCES

Some major trends in ethnographic description may be clarified by asking, "Who is influencing whom, and which influences are the proper subject of anthropological inquiry?" Seen in this light, traditional ethnographies portray an isolated "other" untainted by outside forces, concepts, or cultures. In juxtaposition, many acculturation studies focus on the effects of the hegemonic culture on that "other"; the extent to which the Natives do or do not "go white." Alternatively, books intended for a general readership portray the reverse, the effects of the "other" on a member of hegemonic culture; whites "go Native." More recent self-reflective works in anthropology have partially combined these viewpoints by including the anthropologist's reflections on her own acculturation to the exotic; "the anthropologist goes self-consciously Native."

My approach has been to portray both sides: the acculturation of non-Natives to Yup'ik culture, and that of Yupiit to Euro-American culture. This does for subjects what postmodernist anthropologists have done for themselves—allowing people to voice the changes they perceive themselves to have undergone. Although the effects of Euro-American culture on Yupiit are more obvious, the effects of Yup'ik practices, beliefs, and worldview on non-Natives have also been profound. At the least, even non-Natives whose hunting and fishing practices are noncongruent with Yup'ik ones often cast their practices in Yup'ik terms. At the most, some non-Natives have internalized aspects of Yup'ik beliefs as well as practices.

FIELDWORK

For this project, I returned to Bethel for two months of fieldwork in the summer of 1991. Because of my previous experience in the area, I was able to define many of the issues in advance. I arrived with a series of hypotheses, some of which turned out to be correct, some not. I relied primarily on participant observation and on conversations to illuminate these issues; these were supplemented by interviews, some of which were recorded.

In the course of the project, I fished and processed fish, visited, steambathed, and attended meetings of the Kuskokwim River Salmon Management Working Group. I placed less importance on interviews: in general this is not a productive approach with Yupiit, though it was a straightforward process with non-Natives. The Yupiit I interviewed were people who either had expressed an interest in the project or who seemed likely to be interested in some particular aspect(s) of subsistence. They were all people with whom I was acquainted beforehand.

The non-Natives I interviewed were mostly people with whom I had at least a nodding acquaintance. I interviewed a range of subsistence users, from one person who did no subsistence whatsoever, though he said he was usually given some moose or caribou most years, to people for whom subsistence was a major focus. Interviews were conducted wherever the interviewees chose: at their home, on the porch, outside, at my apartment, or at their office. Interviews ranged in length from five minutes to more than three hours.

I had initially planned to make audio recordings of free conversations about subsistence with both Yupiit and non-Natives, in both English and Yup'ik, as well as to conduct interviews in both languages. This plan seemed perfectly reasonable at the University of California, Berkeley, but on arriving back in Bethel it immediately seemed much less so. I realized that such recordings would be seen as an imposition by most Yupiit, at least partly because of the implication that by allowing themselves to be recorded they were potentially claiming "expert" status (Mather 1985). My sense was that with Yupiit who were English dominant, the recording process was more familiar and less problematic, but I chose to be cautious in also asking to audiotape them. I extended this same caution to the use of people's names. I maintained their anonymity unless they seemed quite unconcerned about being cited, and I also felt that they would not regret seeing their comments in print. All quotations, both from transcripts and notes, were sent, in context, back to the interviewees for their approval.[8]

This project therefore relies not on the wider range of taped material initially planned but on a combination of reconstructions of interviews and conversations (generally written down shortly afterward) and audiotaped material. These tapes include a few interviews with English-dominant Yupiit, interviews with non-Natives, and a large corpus of tapes of Yupiit and non-Natives in public meetings. All quotations in the text are marked either as transcripts (of interviews or public meetings) or notes. All interviews occurred in Bethel unless otherwise noted.

This study uses discourse not only to examine speakers' strategic moves but also as a source of ethnographic data. As such, it constantly shifts back and forth between discourse and ethnography rather than focusing solely or even primarily on the microscopic analysis of linguistic and paralinguistic features. Transcripts are presented in a simple format, as are notes of conversations. Generally speaking, such notes are used to add texture to the ethnographic description, supplementing data from actual transcripts. While transcripts are preferable to field notes as a source of data, some of the most interesting comments were made when the tape recorder was off, perhaps partly *because* the tape recorder was off. This no doubt also reflects speakers' sense of the power and possible usage of situated discourse.

1

Ethnographic Background and Post-Contact History of the Area

JIGGING FOR PIKE

It is a cold day in early March—ten degrees Fahrenheit, but with only a light breeze. My wife (Phyllis Morrow) and I have been invited to go pike fishing with a friend. The night before he had gassed up the snow machine and we had checked our lures and tackle. While we were talking he also gave his ice chisel a few licks with a file. Now, after breakfast, we help load the sled with the chisel, a shovel, a small axe, the lures and twine, some jigging sticks, a box of shells for the shotgun, less a few in his pockets, some extra clothing, a gunnysack, some dried fish, buttered pilot crackers, and a half-gallon thermos of tea. My wife climbs on top of this load, and I ride behind on the runners.

We bump off across the tundra and down to the river as the sun starts to come over the horizon, big and blood red. The ice is smooth and fast. Even with a fur ruff on my parka I am glad I have put on a face mask. The trick to pulling a sled is to drive so that it always stays behind you, and never threatens to pass the snow machine or pendulum erratically from side to side on the glassy ice. This responsibility is shared with the person riding the sled runners, who is expected to crouch and lean to help stabilize the sled.

Where there is snow or hoarfrost on the ice, or on shortcuts through frozen marshes, this is not too difficult. On the glare ice, refrozen after last week's rain, it is considerably harder. But we never pass the snow machine or turn over, although a few times the sled hangs out at ninety degrees, sliding down the river sideways. We have no problems with fresh overflow, although we go through several areas where there are thin layers of ice with air pockets, where overflow has frozen and then the water between the ice layers has drained out before freezing solid.[1]

We arrive at the mouth of the Johnson River early enough to claim some holes someone else has dug on another day, so that we don't have to dig through the winter's accumulated five or six feet of ice. Instead, a few quick jabs of the chisel break through to water. It takes only a few minutes to set up: one person uses the sled as a windbreak, another the snow machine. We sit on pieces of cardboard.

Time passes slowly. Other people arrive by snow machine, car, and truck. We sit, or eventually lie, on the ice. For this sort of fishing you hold a small stick one and one half to two feet long in one hand and jerk up on it every few seconds. Tied to the end of the stick is enough twine to reach through the ice. At the bottom is a large and somewhat heavy lure, which may or may not be baited. Pike eyeballs work well. We jig steadily, looking out at the huge flat expanse of river, at the distant rise of tundra, and the blue sky. Every once in a great while one of us gets a bite, or a fish. The sun arcs higher in the sky, hot on our faces, soporific. Lying there on the smooth ice in our warm clothes, heliotropic as Arctic poppies, ruffs like petals, it is hard to stay awake. My jigging slows down considerably, but I manage to convince myself that this is only another technique, as twice I spasm to wakefulness with a fish on the line. After a long while the tide changes, and we all start catching. First one, then two, and eventually around twenty pike, mostly sixteen to twenty-four inches, but one smaller one and two close to three feet long. When pulled out into the cold they flop around until rapped on the head with the jigging stick. Then they slowly open their mouths and freeze, jaws agape.

The others are doing similarly. For a while we all start jigging with a stick in each hand. It gets exciting when you have two bites at once from adjacent holes. Then the fishing slows down again. We eat lunch. One of the things we learned early on is that sandwiches, apples, and carrots aren't much good frozen solid. Not surprisingly, the easiest things to eat are also the most traditional for the area. Dried fish is great. There is too little water in it to really freeze. The oil solidifies but doesn't get really hard, and as someone told me once, "It's got the right octane rating for the climate." Some akutaq (literally a "mixture," most frequently a mixture of whipped shortening, sugar, and berries) would have gone down well, but we didn't have any to bring. The prebuttered crackers and tea are wonderful.

Other people don't seem to be catching much either, some pack up and leave. Our friend decides to go see if there are any tracks along the band of willows. Sometimes one can find a snowshoe hare or a flock of ptarmigans. He spends an hour wending his way through the willow thickets, along dried-up sloughs and across expanses of frozen swamp. When he returns he says he saw one set of fox tracks, but gave up on them when they crossed a slough now filled with fresh overflow from the last high tide. We had continued to fish, but didn't catch anything while he was gone. The consensus seems to favor going home, so we load the now-frozen pike in the gunnysack, put the gear on a sled, and head back to the village we are living in.

Unloading is even quicker than loading. We take a couple of the larger fish to eat fresh, the rest go onto our friend's porch from where they will later be thawed and filleted, then hung and dried.

INTRODUCTION

The area where Central Alaskan Yup'ik Eskimo is the indigenous language extends from Norton Sound to the Alaskan Peninsula. The Yukon-Kuskokwim (Y-K) Delta is a subset of this larger area and includes the deltas of these rivers and the adjacent coastline. Roughly the same area is included in the Alaska Native Claims Settlement Act (ANCSA) regional profit corporation (Calista), and the regional nonprofit corporation, the Association of Village Council Presidents, Inc. (AVCP). Thus, in the literature the terms "Y-K Delta," the "Calista region," and the "AVCP region" are often used interchangeably. This region is approximately the size of the state of Oregon, with a population of roughly twenty-one thousand living in about fifty villages (Alaska Department of Labor 1991).

This study focuses primarily on Bethel, the lower Kuskokwim River, and the adjacent coastline. This area is also the linguistic heartland of Central Yup'ik. It includes most of the villages where children enter school speaking Yup'ik as a first language.

GEOLOGY AND TOPOGRAPHY OF THE YUKON-KUSKOKWIM DELTA

Extending through the vast alluvial lowlands of the delta are a few volcanic uplands, such as Nelson and Nunivak Islands, and the Askinuk and Kusilvak Mountains. The lowlands have been built up through the slow accumulation of sand and silt dropped as the Yukon and Kuskokwim Rivers decelerate en route to the sea. This process is ongoing. The rivers still carry a heavy load of sediment, the spoils of innumerable glaciers at their headwaters. Most of the land is very flat; a few feet of elevation may mark the boundary of major drainages. Much of the surface is covered with water: large lakes and ponds, rivers, streams, and meandering sloughs. Lakes are generally shallow, and many are filled with aquatic weeds in late summer.

The region is bounded to the north by hills and to the south by mountains, some glaciated. In these mountains glacial lakes (including the Tikchik Lakes) lie at the headwaters of many of the numerous rivers that flow north and west into the Kuskokwim River and Bay, and south and west into Bristol Bay.

The vegetation is predominantly tundra, although spruce is found inland along waterways, and birch, alder, and willow occur sporadically, growing increasingly decumbent near the coast. The tundra is covered with a host of small perennials. Many of these—such as blueberry, bearberry, and lowbush cranberry—fruit in profusion in favorable years. The tundra thaws shallowly each spring, and is soon covered with miniature panoramas of flowers, as well as lichens and mosses.

The gradation from dry tundra to lake or river is gradual and fluctuates depending on snow melt, rainfall, and storm surges. Marshes, bogs, and seasonal swamps are common. The brackish intertidal areas seem to be particularly fertile and are important spawning grounds and winter refuges for a number of fish species. Because of sediment loads, river depth is dependent largely on current. Slow waters are shallow, fast waters deep. Tidal sections of rivers and sloughs tend to be even broader and shallower, with a deeper channel constantly reexcavated as the tide changes.

WILDLIFE

The Y-K Delta supports limited numbers of moose, musk oxen, and caribou, as well as brown and black bears, wolves, and wolverines. Much more common are small mammals including Arctic and red foxes, tundra and snowshoe hares, beaver, otter, mink, and muskrat. Sea mammals, often seasonally abundant, include beluga whales, walrus, bearded, ringed and spotted seals, and sea lions.

Fish is the mainstay of most local diets, however. Commonly harvested fish include saltwater species such as herring, saffron cod, and halibut, and anadromous and freshwater species such as salmon, trout, pike, whitefish, blackfish, loche (burbot), sheefish, grayling, smelt, and needlefish.

Geese, ducks, cranes, and swans, along with sea birds and bird eggs, are also seasonally important, although declining populations and multiparty agreements—such as the Yukon Delta Cooperative Goose Management Plan—have led to at least temporarily reduced reliance on some species.

This is only a partial listing of the more important animals and fish. Many villages harvest other species that are abundant locally or are occasionally available in their particular area, such as gray whale.

Aside from berries and greens, much of this richness is not directly apparent to the eye. The migrating salmon that fill drift and set gill nets each year become visible only when brought to the surface. Most water is so opaque that one can see only a few inches into it. It is possible to feel the presence of fish through line or net, but seeing them often occurs only after they are lifted from the water. To many newcomers, used to the ordering of agriculture and to appraising with the eye, the area can look bleak, especially in winter. At this time, the wealth of fish and furbearers such as otter, beaver, and the mink for which the delta is famous are hidden beneath the snow and ice.

The expanse of sky almost overwhelms the eye. There are no big trees to block the view, and often no distant mountains visible to give one a sense of scale and meaning. The broad expanses of river and lake tease one's vision outward, toward the edge, toward the point where earth and sky merge. And sometimes, in the winter, when the wind blows up the snow, that point is only a few yards off. Yet there are other days when it seems one can see forever, and the mottled oranges and vermilions of the tundra cry out to be recorded, painted, photographed, and remembered. In the short nights of early summer, the cacophony of romancing waterbirds can make it difficult to sleep. Nature is almost profligate with migrating fish one season, almost barren at another. It is an environment that rewards foresight, wisdom, and flexibility. Successful hunters, fishers, gatherers, and processors all grow to their craft over many years.

LOCAL VILLAGES

The majority of delta residents live in villages of 250 to 750 people (see Barker 1993 for wonderfully evocative photographs of Yup'ik people, villages, and subsistence activities). In these villages, the population is skewed in the direction of the young, with more than half of the Yup'ik population under fifteen. Population growth rates exceed two percent annually in some villages (Mary Pete, personal communication). As one would expect, given this rate of population increase, families are large, with five to eight children seemingly the norm. It is only in the past thirty to forty years that child mortality figures have decreased, and there are only a few signs of any impending demographic transition. Partially counterbalancing this natural increase is the considerable emigration to regional centers such as Bethel, to urban Alaska, and to the lower forty-eight states. There is also return migration. Young women are more likely to emigrate and to marry out, creating a pronounced gender imbalance among unmarried adults in some villages (Coffing 1992:41, Levin 1991:68–69, Hamilton and Seyfrit 1993).

In most villages, almost all permanent non-Yup'ik residents are public school teachers and their families. Teachers vary widely in age, from newly certified to retirement age. They vary less in class and ethnicity; most come from middle- to lower middle-class Euro-American backgrounds. Some are married, with or without children, others are single. The number of years each teaches in a particular village varies tremendously. Many stay only one or two years, others may spend a decade or more. Some teachers become at least somewhat integrated into the local community, others remain very separate.

Other non-Yupiit include clergy, magistrates, and the occasional in-marrying spouse. Most villages have churches of at least two denominations: church activities play an important role in many peoples' lives. The lower Kuskokwim area was missionized first by Russian Orthodox, then by Moravians and Catholics. Recently there is a growing Pentecostal movement as well.

There are few year-round jobs available in most villages, apart from teaching. Generally, there are jobs for two or three health aides, a janitor and maintenance person at the school, one or two people who operate the generator, and a few clerks and teachers' aides. Most adults, including those with jobs, are involved year-round in subsistence, although such activity is highest from March through November. For most residents, income-producing work is usually only available seasonally, consisting of commercial fishing and the occasional construction jobs in the summer, and trapping in the winter.

All permanent villages in the lower Kuskokwim now have airstrips, although deep mud at breakup often temporarily closes some strips. Villages are not connected by road except for a few connected in winter, when ice roads can be plowed on the rivers. Otherwise, travel is by air, boat, snow machine, or three- and four-wheel all-terrain vehicles.

Air travel in small planes between villages requires patience and flexibility. The near constant winds and the frequency of fog, rain, and drifting snow make piloting difficult and schedules often irrelevant.

Travel by boat requires knowledge and skill: sandbars change, channels open and close, the tides rasp at the shore, smoothing and widening. Frequent high winds and accompanying waves limit boat travel as well.

All-terrain vehicles are used on the snow and ice in the winter, and on village roads, beaches, and the tundra in the summer. They are especially useful in villages where the airport is located some distance away from the settlement. In such villages they are used throughout the year to haul passengers and freight to and from the airport.

Summer travel, except by plane, is usually slow and indirect, following meandering sloughs, lakes, and shallow shortcuts between deep water channels. In winter, travel is faster and more direct, but it is still easy to become disoriented, and overflow—water on top of the ice—is a frequent hazard.

From a distance, many villages, particularly those without trees, give a sense of having just been placed there. They look as if they had been delivered by helicopter, like an instant stage set for a television commercial. Their layouts vary tremendously. Some are tightly clustered into a band on limited higher ground overlooking a river or slough. More commonly, there will be several smaller clusters, often of closely related families whose ties go back to a former, now uninhabited village. In some villages, such clusters may extend for several miles to take advantage of scattered spots of non-flooding land.

Housing varies from small, low-ceilinged houses built not long after World War II to large new multiroom dwellings elevated on six-foot pilings to protect the tundra from melting and slumping away. The older houses were owner-built, either from lumber milled in Alaska or from lumber shipped up from Seattle. Most of the newer houses are built by crews of local men, employed under federal or state grants. While there are some prefabricated houses, most are built on site from plywood and dimension lumber.

Around many houses are a number of essential outbuildings: steambath, smokehouse, storage shed, and drying racks. Although most houses are painted, often in bright colors, wind, rain, and snow quickly fade the paint, and new buildings age rapidly. New houses typically have bathrooms with tubs and showers, but few villages have year-round water systems, so that the bathroom fixtures reflect regulation more than reality. Many villages do have seasonal water systems that deliver water to central points during the summer, and to a washeteria building for washing and showers. In the winter, people melt ice for drinking water; in the summer most prefer rainwater to the heavily chlorinated piped water.

Public structures typically include a new or relatively new state school building, which dwarfs everything else in the village, an old Bu-

reau of Indian Affairs school building and staff quarters, a village corporation–owned store, a National Guard armory, a clinic, a washeteria,
and one or more churches. Most villages have an Alaska Village Electri-
cal Cooperative (AVEC) generator, which provides electricity of varying
reliability. Generally there are also one or more locally owned stores.
The smallest of such stores consist of a few goods stacked against one
wall of someone's living room. The largest are well stocked and have
additional warehouses. In addition, there may be a large Alaska Native
Investment Cooperative Association (ANICA) store, often co-owned
with the Alaska Native Claims Settlement Act (ANCSA) village
corporation.

Villages coalesced at their present locations for a variety of reasons.
Many villages are situated to take advantage of salmon or herring runs,
whitefish, pike, and sea mammal migrations, or blackfish stocks. Others
are located in a "compromise" position, between where the logic of subsistence usage would put them and where an agency or institution was
willing to put a church or school, or where a trader set up shop.

Prior to the establishment of permanent villages, most Yupiit moved
to several camps throughout the year. They returned to a winter village
only in the darkest months, which was also the ceremonial season. Like
the land itself, the location of villages has been, and remains, fluid. A
village may grow in new directions as houses are moved across the river
to gain year-round access to a new airport. In the recent past, two new
villages have been formed as parts of one or more villages moved en
masse to another location.

BETHEL

Bethel is the transportation and administrative center of the region. It
was officially founded in 1885 by Moravian missionaries, although there
was already a trading post at this site, run by a Russian Finn (Lenz
1985). It was not a traditional winter village site. Now, more than a
hundred years later, Bethel's function is most easily understood by
thinking of the delta as a colony, with Bethel as the capital city. It has
the regional hospital, the regional jail, the college, the school district
offices, and the court. The barge lines and airlines are based there, as
well as the salmon processors and the local fishermen's cooperative.

Bethel (its name chosen by bibliomancy) spreads out along the
Kuskokwim on the first significantly high ground the Moravians reached
as they paddled up the river. The oldest part of town lies right along the

river. There are a number of new subdivisions, resulting from land claimed through ANCSA. There are also three areas of high-density housing: the Alaska State Housing Authority housing (ASHA), the trailer court, and the fairly new (1990) low-income housing.

From the air, Bethel's buildings give the impression of having been tossed down temporarily—like multicolored dice—along roads of drifting silt. Adding to this impression of impermanence is the bright yellow hospital building on stilts, known locally as the Yellow Submarine, and the single remaining obsolete White Alice radar screen, which looks like a giant drive-in movie screen.[2]

Bethel's population is roughly two-thirds Yupiit and one-third non-Native, with a total population of around 4,700. The Yup'ik population includes some "old" Bethel families, many considerably intermarried with non-Natives, and immigrants from throughout the delta, who have moved to Bethel for a variety of reasons, including employment, health care, education, and proximity to relatives. For some Yupiit, Bethel may be a first stop on the way to somewhere else in Alaska, or to the lower forty-eight states. Other Yupiit move back to Bethel from elsewhere. For many, it is a satisfactory compromise between living in a village and living in a larger and more distant urban center. It is possible to maintain intense ties with one's natal village through frequent visits and frequent hosting. For many it is also possible to participate in subsistence in Bethel and in a "home" village as well, by timing vacations or time off with peak subsistence seasons.

While the vast majority of Alaska Native residents are Yupiit, there are some people in Bethel who identify themselves as Athabascan Indians, as well as a few members of other Native American groups. U.S. Census Bureau data do not distinguish among these groups. Generally, in ordinary conversations in Bethel, non-Native and non-Yup'ik are used interchangeably.

There is variation in background among the non-Native population of Bethel as well. Non-Natives come to Bethel from all over, although primarily from the lower forty-eight states and from other parts of Alaska. They come from rural, suburban, and urban environments. They represent a cross section of Americans, with the exception that many non-Native migrants to Bethel are recruited on the basis of professional qualifications and degrees, and there is proportionately greater migration from colder (and nearer) areas of the United States , such as the upper Midwest and the Pacific Northwest. The net effect of these factors is that proportionately fewer Blacks (0.8%), Hispanics (less than 0.4%), and Asians (1.6%) migrate to Bethel than appear in the general U.S. population (Jane Elam, Bethel city clerk, personal communication, March 19, 1992).

Compared to the Yup'ik population in Bethel, there is a much higher turnover among non-Natives. There are a number of reasons for this. The environment is extremely different from anywhere in the lower forty-eight states. The cold, wind, isolation, and perceived barrenness take a toll on many. Another factor is that many non-Natives come to Bethel because they are recruited for professional positions, as doctors, public defenders, teachers, and administrators. In many of these positions they are chronically overworked, and after one, two, or four years they look for more sustainable work elsewhere. Partially overlapping with this group are those who move to Bethel to make a grubstake, working long hours and spending as little as possible, so that in two to four years they can go back "home" to buy the house, the land, or the business that motivated them to come to Alaska in the first place. Perhaps the majority come because Bethel promises an adventure; it usually delivers.

Subsistence in Bethel

One of Bethel's virtues is that it is possible to do a variety of subsistence activities in the immediate vicinity. According to Arvin Dull,

> I think one of Bethel's best-kept secrets is [that] you could just step out from work, walk to your house, change your clothes, hop in the boat, and throw out a net, all in ten or fifteen minutes. If you want to go ptarmigan hunting in the winter, you just hop on your snow machine and drive out one or two miles. In five or ten minutes you're hunting and catching ptarmigan. (transcript of an interview, June 25, 1991)

Many people, Native and non-Native, also maintain a fish camp somewhere along the nearby river, or on a slough. Dull explains that "in a lot of cases we'll just park the boat right by our house. If we have to go to the fish camp to start our smoker, everything is so close" (transcript of June 25, 1991 continued). Because it is possible to fish close to Bethel, many people are able to put up significant quantities of fish, despite the fact that they fish primarily on weekends and after work.

Subsistence is one of a number of activities that crosscut cultural and ethnic lines. Almost everyone is involved with members of the other culture in some aspects of their lives: work, hobbies, organizations, church. Such contacts may be shallow or deep. One non-Native, Martha Scott (= M), described her perception of these interactions:

M: There's a lot of people that are that way [who never get involved in subsistence] who, in many strange ways, are on their way somewhere else.

C: Not really here?

M: Well, either literally, here for two years to make a lot of money. Or mentally, it's mostly *Kass'aqs* [non-Natives] that I'm talking about, who tolerate being here.

And they might even like being here, but, just like you're asking me how this fits my image, they have a certain image that has to feel comfortable to them too. And that might mean a VCR, David Letterman, chicken-and-beef-and-potatoes kind of image.

To survive in this area you have to be mentally healthy, and you have to be able to make that happen for yourself. There's not a whole lot of distractions here. You've got to kind of make that happen in your home. Frankly, I've been surprised at some of the people who have stayed. I've really kind of admired them for their inability to get into what I see as what's actually happening here. And to keep mentally healthy.

I see those people having real problems making what I would call *contacts of integrity* with people who make this their home. They're kind of oblivious to that lack of connection because the people who stay here, by and large, are Yup'ik, and they're very polite. (transcript of an interview, July 12, 1991; emphasis added)

Bootleggers, Discos, and Sin

Bethel's local reputation as a wide-open town is not totally undeserved. Although most of the surrounding villages have elected to ban the possession, importation, and sale of alcoholic beverages through the so-called Local Option law, Bethel voters have resisted pressures to either "go dry," matching the surrounding villages, or "go wet," which was the situation prior to 1975, when there was a liquor store and bars. Now it is often referred to as "damp." It is legal to buy limited quantities of alcoholic beverages elsewhere and import them, or have them shipped in, but it is not legal to sell them in Bethel. Contravening this ordinance is a seemingly limitless supply provided by bootleggers. Typically they order liquor from Anchorage at a cost of less than ten dollars per bottle and sell it for sixty dollars per bottle. A large proportion of these bootleggers are alcoholics themselves and sell primarily to friends and acquaintances to support their own addictions. Some sophisticated and well-organized bootleggers sell to almost anyone, and reportedly make thousands of dollars per week. One somewhat effective response to these professional bootleggers was a change in the law against bootlegging. A first conviction is now a misdemeanor, and a second conviction is a felony. Potential profits are no longer totally out of proportion to the risks (Craig McMahon, Bethel magistrate, personal communication, March 19, 1992).

Even with this change, and constant sting operations and convictions, it remains very easy to buy alcohol in Bethel. A visit to one of the discos or a ride with most cab drivers will provide either an opportunity for a buy or the location where a "jug" may be purchased.

Drugs, including cocaine, are also a problem in Bethel, as periodic arrests, seizures, and statements by recovering users attest. Until fairly recently (1991), possession of small amounts of marijuana in the home was legal under Alaska statutes, but it has now been recriminalized.

Some of the social costs of substance abuse in Bethel are starkly evident; others are not. Rates of accidental death from exposure, drowning, or vehicle or hunting accidents are far higher than national averages, as are rates of suicide and homicide (Marshall 1992). The less visible costs are those paid by the children, parents, and partners of substance abusers. These costs include fetal alcohol syndrome and fetal alcohol effects, as well as mental, physical, and sexual abuse and neglect.

There are a variety of support institutions, including an alcohol treatment center, the State of Alaska's Department of Family and Youth Services, and a state-funded shelter program, which also provides counseling services and reentry training. In the current budget climate, all such agencies are overworked and understaffed for the tasks confronting them.

The preceding description makes Bethel sound like an exciting and vivid mixture of good and bad. Many find that living there enriches their lives. There *are* problems, but there are also few precedents to constrain creativity in dealing with those problems, and little entrenched hierarchy. While substance abuse is a major problem in both the Native and non-Native community, there are also many people who lead sober and productive lives. The fact that Bethel is a bilingual and bicultural community[3] makes life more interesting and thought-provoking for many of its residents. The relative isolation and harshness of the environment combine to force an unusual interdependence among people, and to compel them to recognize this interdependence. This is a new experience for many non-Natives, often cherished in retrospect. It is common for non-Native former Bethelites to reminisce about the intense sense of community they shared in Bethel, and the absence of which they regret in their present lives elsewhere.

SUBSISTENCE: PAST, PRESENT, AND FUTURE

I was struck anew in the summer of 1991 by how powerfully the metaphor of local control and local reliance is evinced in some Y-K Delta meals. One afternoon my sons and I had stopped in to visit at a Yup'ik friend's fish camp near Bethel. When we arrived, the men were just returning from fishing. After helping to carry the fish to the waiting wheelbarrow, I wound my way back through the tents, sheds, and smokehouses to the family's cook tent.

We were invited to eat, and we sat down around a low table in a large white canvas wall-tent. As we caught up on the news, we ate from a sampler of local spring delicacies. We had dried pike dipped in seal oil, its taste and texture a little like the dried squid so prized in Asia. We had dried smoked whitefish—delicate, with an almost coconut oil smell—and some of the last of the previous year's dried smoked king and chum salmon, tangy now after long storage. We ate dried seal with seal oil, rich and oceany, and herring that had been dried and then preserved in seal oil. We ate cooked marsh marigold greens, vaguely like bean sprouts, also dipped in seal oil.

Moving on to the next course, we ate *akutaq*—locally called Eskimo ice cream—made with salmonberries and crowberries, a delicacy that most resembles a slightly sweet frosting loosely binding a mass of sweet and tart berries. There were also freshly made circles of fry bread—like doughnuts, but flatter and with smaller holes. Finally, satiated to the bursting point, we drank a combination of black and Labrador tea (*Ledum ledum* sp.). Labrador tea tastes like the tundra smells when you walk on it—resinous, sharp and clean, like an unknown conifer.

It was a wonderful meal, a gourmet repast shared with good friends. In a more analytic sense it was also a singular meal in comparison with the diet of most Americans and indeed most Alaskans. Virtually everything was locally caught and processed. All the fish and the seal were caught by either my host's immediate family or by more distant relatives. The same was true of the greens, berries, and "tundra tea." The only foods that weren't local were the fats used in the *akutaq* and fry breads, the flour, salt, sugar, and black tea. The closest most Americans ever come to this sort of involvement in all stages of the harvesting and preparation of their own food is when, if they have a garden, they eat a salad dinner of vegetables they have grown. Such a meal is usually considered worth remarking on as an example of how unusually successful their gardening has been.

This was a typical meal in the Y-K Delta, unusual only because of the variety of fish and meat available. Normally one might have two or three choices. The reliance on locally caught and processed foods was expected. Food comes from the land and waters, not—except for certain staples and Western luxuries—from the store.

It is also worth noting that my hosts were college educated and have professional jobs. They eat subsistence foods not because they cannot afford to do otherwise but out of choice: "We are used to that food and we can't do without it. A lot of people can't find jobs for one reason or another, and they always fish. Everybody does it. But those of us who are working still have the need for the food" (Tiny Jack, in Lenz 1985:173). Often, as was previously mentioned in the introduction to this chapter, it is more costly to secure some types of subsistence foods than their store-bought "equivalents," except that there are no equivalents for many of these foods. Nothing one can buy in a store can replace, for example, seal oil.

Historic Subsistence Uses in the Yukon-Kuskokwim Delta

In comparison with other Arctic areas, there is an unusual amount of information about the Y-K Delta in the immediate postcontact period. We owe this to the massive and sensitive documentation provided by a young ornithologist at the Smithsonian Institution. E. W. Nelson's official charge (from the U.S. Army Signal Service) was to make a daily record of the weather at St. Michael, a former Russian trading post on the northern edge of the delta. His unofficial charge (from Spencer Baird, assistant director of the Smithsonian) was to collect ethnographic and natural history specimens, and to record as much as possible about the culture of the indigenous peoples. The thoroughness and relative sensitivity of the resultant monograph is astounding. The Yup'ik writer and researcher Elsie Mather said that Nelson "gave pretty accurate descriptions as an outsider to our culture" (Mather 1995:25).

It is almost tautology to say that Yup'ik people were completely reliant on local subsistence products at contact (Collins 1982). The Moravian missionary and teacher John Henry Kilbuck, himself a Delaware Indian, described this subsistence focus:

> As with most other races, the Yupiat [Yupiit] are engaged in a constant struggle to make a living—that is to provide food and clothing for the

body, and to do this every man is a hunter and fisherman—for there is no other pursuit that will gain the prime object of keeping alive. (Kilbuck, in Fienup-Riordan 1988:6)

There was extraregional trade, but it seems to have been restricted to trading furs for luxury items such as the white skins of reindeer fawns, for fancy parkas, and metal for toolmaking. There was also interregional trade in surplus subsistence products. This included the exchange of coastal products such as seal and beluga oil, and bearded seal skin for inland products such as carved wooden bowls and caribou skins (Nelson 1899). In general, subsistence needs were met within the local area, with an annual cycle based on a series of short- to medium-distance (less than 100 km) migrations.

Subsistence needs could be met in the local area at least in part because the delta provides a much richer environment, in comparison with other Eskimo areas farther north, with a greater variety of resources. As one would expect, it also supported a much denser human population than more northern environments (Ager 1982). Famines were unusual, but not unknown. The period in early spring prior to the beginning of seal hunting and fish migrations was often a lean time.

This relatively dense population was primarily fed, and sometimes clothed as well, through fishing. The general Yup'ik term for food *(neqa)* is also the word for fish. This reflects a dietary truism. Fish, including herring, salmon, blackfish, tomcod, whitefish, pike, sheefish, smelt, needlefish, halibut, and flounder, were staples. Many of these species remain staples today. In the 1890s Nelson recorded that the densest population occurred not, as one would expect, along the coast or the major rivers, but was situated in the lowlands between the Kuskokwim and Yukon, where stocks of blackfish were both abundant and reliable (1899).

At contact, fish were taken in gill and dip nets, by jigging with lures, by spearing, and in a variety of different-sized wooden splint fish traps. Fish were eaten fresh and preserved by splitting and drying, fermenting, and freezing. Fish skins were used for making rain gear as well.

Calorically second in importance for most villages were sea mammals, particularly bearded and harbor seals, walrus, and beluga whales. The meat and blubber were eaten fresh, and also dried and rendered for later consumption. Firearms were becoming increasingly common in the Y-K Delta in Nelson's time, but they had not completely replaced traditional methods of killing game. Sea mammals were taken with guns and harpoons from kayaks, and by nets, as well as occasionally with clubs. The only exception to these methods was the prohibition of the use of firearms or other metal weapons and tools for beluga, because it was believed to be offensive to the spirit of the belugas (Fitzhugh and Kaplan 1982:70). Beluga whales were often taken in large numbers in drives. They would be herded up a small coastal river with a sandbar at its mouth and held there until they were stranded by the outgoing tide.

Caribou had been of near equal importance for inland villages, but they were virtually extinct in the Y-K Delta by Nelson's time.[4] (Musk oxen became extinct in the Y-K Delta in prehistoric times and were reintroduced in the 1930s. Moose were just beginning to spread throughout the area in Nelson's time.) Previously, caribou had been taken with guns, bows and arrows, and snares and surrounds, as well as with lances from kayaks.

Brown bears were also of significant economic importance to inland villages, perhaps of more importance than can be recovered. Unfortunately, Nelson (and others who wrote about the area in the early contact period) spent relatively little time in areas that are prime brown bear habitat. However, contemporary elders who lived or spring-camped in the mountains south of the Kuskokwim comment on an increased reliance on brown bear for meat in the past because of low numbers of available moose and caribou. For these people, brown bears seem to have been the most symbolically important animal as well.

Efficient techniques of capture have long been highly valued. There has been a significant bias toward devices that capture animals and fish in the absence of the hunter, such as nets, fish traps, traps, and snares, as well as ones such as bows, bolas, and spear-throwers *(atlatl)*, which multiply the hunter's power, strength, or effective range. The same is true of transportation technology. Kayaks appear to have been adapted to cope with local conditions, particularly sea ice (Hensel n.d.). Efficiency, here as elsewhere, could spell the difference between life and death.

TRADITIONAL HOUSING AND GENDER ROLES

Traditionally, women and children lived in multigenerational households in smaller houses, while men and older boys lived in the men's house *(qasgiq)*.[5] There was a clear demarcation of male and female space. There were the women's houses where men would visit in the evening after everyone was asleep. Ideally they were supposed to return to the men's house before morning. There were also the men's houses where women brought food and attended ceremonies.

Men's houses were typically large (from twenty to thirty feet square, and up to twenty-five feet from floor to ceiling) subterranean structures of heavy logs covered with sod. The floor was covered with wood except for a removable center section where the fire pit and winter entrance were located. This center section was used as the hearth for firebathing, with the passageway then serving as an air intake. A small porch served as a windbreak to the summer entrance, which came directly through one wall. In winter, a coldtrap-style entrance was used, consisting of a tunnel from the porch to the center of the men's house floor. This tunnel entrance also served as an air intake for the fire when firebathing. There was a bench around the perimeter of the room about three feet high, and sometimes an additional one another three feet higher. A rectangular hole in the roof (approximately four feet by six feet, to six feet by six feet, normally covered with gutskin) served as a smokehole/skylight, entry and exit for large manufactures such as sleds, kayaks, and fish traps, and as an exit for corpses. The women's houses were much smaller versions of the men's houses. They typically had low ceilings, with a platform area on one or both sides of a central fire pit.

A central daily event in men's lives was the firebath, which was like a sauna with intense radiant heat. Ideally men firebathed twice a day, morning and evening. To prepare a firebath, the gutskin window was removed, the center flooring was taken up to reveal the fire pit, and thin splints of wood were piled in the fire pit and lit. The smoke was often intense at first, but it lessened as the fire burned and the draft improved. Bathers usually breathed through a bundle of fine wood shavings to filter out the smoke and cool the air. After the heat died down, the men would exit to roll in the snow or immerse themselves in a nearby lake or stream. The gut window would then be replaced and the building would retain the heat for several hours (Nelson 1899; Kilbuck, in Fienup-Riordan 1988). Kilbuck described the firebath:

> The heat is sometimes so intense as to blister the ears—before perspiration takes place. When the wood is dry and piled properly—there is quick combustion with a minimum amount of smoke, and the bathers in the midst of such enjoyment—set up a lamentation which is so like the howling of a pack of huskies or wolves. This lamentation is for the dead because they are missing such a luxurious sweat-bath. (in Fienup-Riordan 1988:20)

There was a stark contrast between the men's house, which under ideal conditions was heated twice daily, and the women's houses, which were heated very occasionally, and used clear ice for their windows, rather than gut. Tom Imgalrea of Chevak describes such a house:

> When the roof was covered on the inside
>   with built-up frost,
> they assembled wood
> below
> for a fire. . . .
>
> Well now,
> they used to cover their clothes
> when the melting frost from the roof
>   was dripping.
>
> After the dripping stopped,
> but before the embers burned out
> in the fireplace
> below,
> they covered the smoke window.
>
> And as soon as the window was covered,
>   the house was warm.
>
> Whenever it got cold in the evening,
> black lumps of ice formed
> where the drips had landed
> on the sod
> down on the floor.
>
> And the lumps of ice
> grew in height there on the floor,
> and were black in color;
> just as black
> as the ceiling above.
>
>   (Imgalrea, in Woodbury 1984:30–31;
>   published layout of translation retained)

Kilbuck commented that "the difference between these huts [the smaller houses where women and children live] and the *Kashigi [qasgiq]* in the way of comfort—is great as night and day—and one wonders why the women never rebel" (in Fienup-Riordan 1988:14).

This idealized system of virtually complete gender separation was operational only in the permanent villages and camps. For much of the year, families lived together in small houses or tents at spring and fall camps and berry camps. Even here, though, a sense of spatial separation was preserved. Tents and houses were divided into de facto men's and women's areas. There was also the division associated with gender appropriate tasks:

> Separation of the sexes in Yup'ik society was not only residential, but characterized social life in general. Older women educated young girls, often by telling them storyknife tales, using a storyknife to illustrate stories on the snow or mud. Major figures were women. . . . [O]ne of the major themes of the stories was that males could be expected to exhibit nonrational behavior (Oswalt 1966:106)—a theme highlighting a sharp cultural distinction between the nature of men and women, from the point of view of women. (Shinkwin and Pete 1983:29)

The general conception was that gender roles were complementary and flexible. The adult couple was seen as the ideal productive unit, with most tasks clearly gender marked (Shinkwin and Pete 1983). Because of this complementarity, widowed or divorced spouses generally remarried. There was some flexibility in carrying out tasks. If there was a shortage of males, or females were needed for some activity, women could do men's work and vice versa. This meant that, in the past, boys without enough sisters might learn to sew and cut fish. Currently women check salmon nets when men are unavailable.

However, this sense of gender complementarity did not mean equal status: "It is true that man's position was higher than woman's. Baskets were not wealth, sealskins were. This sums up the difference" (Lantis 1946:246).

Some Yupiit, in addition to learning gender-appropriate tasks, also learned to perform the subsistence activities of the opposite gender. Traditionally, it was (and is) believed that essential aspects of a deceased person are passed on when someone (usually a newborn) is given that person's name. It was expected that such individuals would continue, in their new bodies, to enjoy and be successful at the tasks dear to them in their previous life. Since names are not marked for gender, it was not uncommon for children to be named after adults of the opposite sex. In these cases the child might sometimes be raised with the trappings and activities of the opposite sex. For a girl this could even include seal hunting on the ocean in her own kayak; for a boy it sometimes included having female-length hair and being dressed in girl's clothing, as well as performing female-appropriate subsistence tasks. [6]

There were no specialists in Yup'ik society. Even shamans hunted, fished, and gathered like anyone else, although a powerful shaman could "ask for things" with the expectation of not being refused. Many people had varying amounts of shamanic power.

As in most traditional cultures, children played at being adults. Young boys started playing with small bows and arrows at an early age, and girls cut pretend fish. A boy's first kill, usually a small bird or vole, was typically celebrated with a feast, as was the first bucket of berries or clutch of eggs a young girl gathered.

The Role of Men in Traditional Yup'ik Society

For males, the most prestigious goal was to become a *nukalpiaq* (great hunter). Even the word for man, *angun* (literally a thing or device for catching game), reveals this cultural preoccupation.[7] Kilbuck noted the prerequisites for becoming such a man among men:

> There is in every collection of [Yup'ik] Eskimos—one man in the prime of life who is the leader. Two qualities in particular are requisite for leadership—never failing success in the chase of deer [caribou], or bearded seal, in particular—and generosity in sharing with the unfortunate, the fruits of his prowess—and in giving liberally to all village causes. (Kilbuck, in Fienup-Riordan 1988:22)

Boys went from catching socially but not economically important game to contributing economically to the family in increasingly adult ways as they gained the complex skills necessary for successful hunting.

Viewed externally, this system was largely a meritocracy. Success and status could not be inherited, and the raw materials for necessary hunting equipment were locally available. Although hunting songs as well as equipment could be inherited, and training by one's relatives no doubt contributed to success, success was largely an individual accomplishment. Status was maintained through the continued success of a hunter or his sons. Decline in vigor and prosperity occurred with age. Men moved from being vigorous hunters to being elders, who advised more and participated less actively, but whose wisdom was revered. A Yup'ik man once told me that "the elders are our libraries," the storehouse of accumulated wisdom.

Men's preparation for subsistence activities generally took place in the village or camp, in the men's house if there was one. The activities themselves usually took place at some distance from the village or camp. Hunters usually went alone, or with a partner, except for activities such as bird or beluga drives, which required large groups to be effective.

Activities changed both daily and seasonally, depending on weather, re-source availability, personal and family needs, and the activities of oth-ers. In brief, traditional male activity occurred largely outside the village by solitary autonomous individuals or pairs. While a particular task—such as, for example, gathering wood in winter—might be repeated daily throughout a given season, men's tasks were generally quite varied.

The Role of Women in Traditional Yup'ik Society

Yup'ik women were rewarded for, and gained prestige from, their skills as seamstresses and for hardworking perseverance, fecundity, and beauty. Compared with men, their roles were much more home- and family-focused. Their roles were publicly marked in ceremonies through the foods, clothes, and other things they created.

Typical female subsistence activities included jigging, setting and checking nearby nets, snaring, and in some cases hunting small game such as rabbits and ptarmigan, and gathering large quantities of edible greens and berries. Women were also generally responsible for the pres-ervation, care, and distribution of game animals once they were brought home. This included cutting fish and game for drying, preparing food for meals, skinning and tanning hides, and making clothing, bedding, tents, baskets, and storage containers.

Girls gradually assumed adult roles as they matured, and were often partnered in arranged marriages soon after puberty. The traditional mar-riage pattern was arranged marriages between postpubescent girls and men in their mid-twenties to mid-thirties; thus a woman's first marriage might occur before she had fully mastered adult skills. Ideally, multiple pregnancies and births followed, with child rearing being a major re-sponsibility. Divorce, particularly before the birth of a child in a mar-riage, was common, and could be initiated by either sex. In the nine-teenth century, most women were married several times. Often, because husbands were older, women were widowed. Children and grandchil-dren were looked to for support in old age.

Although accidental death seems to have been more common for men, and the harshness of life for "man the hunter" has received more publicity, life was not easy for women either, as Imgalrea explains:

> In the autumn around this time,
> the women
> used to fish for arctic tomcod
> with dipnets.

Outside,
when it got cold, they used to wade,
    even when ice was forming,
and they wore only seal-gut rain parkas,
tied around their waist like so.

Otherwise, the women
wore nothing.
Oh, how they endured back then,
those women!

They closed off their rain parkas
by tying them around their waists,
to keep their bodies
from getting cold;
but from the waist down
their bare skin was exposed,
since they did not have their pants on
    in the water.

They fished,
and the mud sometimes froze.

That is how it was
when they tried to catch fish for storage
in the autumn.

(Tom Imgalrea, in Woodbury
1984:27–28; published layout
of translation retained)

TRADITIONAL YUP'IK BELIEFS

Traditional Yup'ik religious beliefs emphasized the connections and parallels between humans and the rest of the natural world. Animals, as
well as significant objects in the natural environment such as driftwood
and prominent rocks, were conceived as having a *yuk* (person). From this
the word *yua* (its person), a cognate with *inua*, is derived. Everything,
including the universe itself, was aware, sentient. In stories, animals
were conceived as living and behaving like people. A common theme
was of someone visiting a village, eating the food, sleeping there and
only later realizing that they have been staying with the blackfish, or
the seals, or indeed supernatural beings (Fienup-Riordan 1983a:177–81;
Morrow 1990).

Animals gave themselves to particular hunters out of choice. With proper treatment,[8] the animals could reclothe themselves with flesh and return to be killed again and again by the same hunter who could also be born over and over. Hunting was not conceptualized as a zero-sum game, in which the success of one hunter affected the success of other hunters. Rather, apparent animal populations and hunter success were both affected by how animals were treated. Improper behavior reduced populations; proper behavior maintained or increased them (Mather 1985; Morrow 1984; Morrow and Hensel 1992; Fienup-Riordan 1983a, 1990).

In summary, hunting was not a sport characterized by competition with the game but was rather the culmination of a relationship characterized by "respect" and proper use of game animals. This is similar to what Sharp notes for the Chipewyan:

> The necessity for the prey to consent to its death removes hunting solely from the realm of the natural and, more important, makes it a measure of the power/knowledge of the hunter. This turns subsistence activities into a system of measurement of men and provides both an explanation for the success of certain men (they have more power/ knowledge) and the causal basis for the success of certain men (they have more power/knowledge). (1981:226)

A parallel in Yup'ik beliefs was that success in hunting or fishing meant that the individual was in harmony with the world and had behaved correctly; lack of success meant that something was wrong, that the community's moral strictures had been broken (although Yupiit recognized that some people were luckier than others). Traditionally, lack of success in the chase required shamanic divination and/or confession by an individual to uncover the transgression(s) and effect a cure.

Subsistence products were used throughout the ceremonial cycle as gifts and the raw material for gifts. One celebration in particular, however, focused clearly on honoring the animals caught, as well as acknowledging the hunters chosen by those animals to be their captors. This was *Nakaciuq* (the Bladder Festival). The latter usually occurred in midwinter and lasted for four or five days. Yupiit believed that the souls of animals fled into their bladders at the instant of death. The bladders of large game, particularly seals, were cleaned, inflated, dried, and carefully saved for this festival. The bladders, marked with the identifying mark of the hunter who had caught them, were sung to and feasted, all the while attached to that hunter's harpoon (Nelson 1899:380, 383). At the conclusion of the festival the bladders were deflated and submerged through a hole in the ice so that they could return again (Mather 1985: 31–104; Morrow 1984:113–40).

EARLY TWENTIETH-CENTURY SEASONAL ROUNDS

The four ecological settings in the Y-K Delta are coastal, riverine, headwater-riverine, and tundra-marsh. Residents of coastal villages utilized marine resources and often wintered in a tundra-marsh area. Residents of riverine villages, situated on a river with major salmon runs, depended largely on migrating fish stocks in the river, and secondarily on tundra-marsh resources. Residents of headwater-riverine villages depended on both fish stocks and large and small mammals. Residents of tundra-marsh villages (particularly the large area between the Yukon and Kuskokwim Rivers) depended primarily on that environment, but often spent part of the year on the coast or a nearby river with salmon runs.

Residents of most villages utilized at least two of these settings in their seasonal round. Because of this multiple utilization, it is possible to describe general patterns of historic subsistence by contrasting a tundra/coastal village with a tundra/riverine village.

The historic tundra/coastal village is Kassiglurmiut, an abandoned village on the Kolivinarak River on Nelson Island. Most residents of this village moved first to Nightmute and later to Toksook Bay. The tundra/riverine village is Nanvarnarrlak, an abandoned village near Nunapitchuk, whose residents moved primarily to Nunapitchuk and then to Atmauthluk.

These villages provide an interesting comparison because they each used a different strategy in their subsistence approach. The Kassiglurmiut strategy was primarily to position themselves in two or three locations where different migrating species were concentrated, a kind of resource migration bottleneck. Each bottleneck worked for a series of different resources, so that they did not have to shift their residence as often. The tundra dwellers, living in an environment with much less species diversity, focused primarily on one resource (whitefish) and harvested it as long as possible. To do this, they followed the migrating whitefish stocks as these fish moved up into the lakes in the spring and summer, and back down past their winter village in the fall. Alternatively, the tundra dwellers migrated to the Kuskokwim River to intercept migrating salmon in the summer. They intercepted pike before the whitefish in the spring, and after them in the fall, and depended on blackfish stocks for the winter. Late spring and summer were generally seasons of plenty, though continued bad weather and low hunting/fishing success could cause spring famines. From December to February subsistence activity and success were low.[9]

Kassiglurmiut Seasonal Round

April   Move to coastal spring/summer camp
    hunting: ptarmigan, seals, later geese, sea ducks
    fishing: tomcod, sculpin
    gathering: cranberries, crowberries (from previous summer)

May   hunting: seals, walrus, beluga whale, ducks and geese, sea ducks
    fishing: herring
    gathering: cranberries, crowberries, clams, mussels, grass for braiding, herring, herring spawn on fucus

June   hunting: seals, sea lions, beluga whales
    fishing: capelin, king salmon, red salmon
    gathering: beach greens, fireweed shoots, wild celery, wild parsley, wild parsnip, willow leaves

July   hunting: seals, sea lions, beluga whales
    fishing: smelt, red salmon, chum salmon, halibut, sculpin, starry flounder
    gathering: as in June, plus sourdock, mountain sorrel, saxifrages, yarrow

Option 1: *August, September*

Aug.   Return to village, pick berries, then travel to inland whitefish netting sites
    hunting: moulting waterfowl
    fishing: whitefish
    gathering: salmonberries, blueberries, crowberries, sourdock, mountain sorrel, saxifrages, yarrow, grasses for the winter, mare's tail, tubers in vole caches

Sept.	hunting:	staging waterfowl
	fishing:	whitefish and pike
	gathering:	blueberries, bearberries, crow-
		berries, cranberries, greens listed
		for July, grasses for the winter,
		mare's tail, tubers in vole caches

Return to village by mid-October

Option 2: *August, September*

Aug.	Stay at summer camp	
	hunting:	seals, sea lions, beluga whales
	fishing:	halibut, sculpin, starry flounder
	gathering:	as in Option 1
Sept.	hunting:	seals and beluga whales
	fishing:	pink salmon, silver salmon, tom-
		cod, sculpin, starry flounder
	gathering:	as in Option 1
Oct.	hunting:	seal
	fishing:	tomcod, needlefish, blackfish,
		whitefish
	gathering:	cranberries, crowberries

Return to village by mid-October

Nov.	hunting:	mink, land otter, muskrat, bea-
		ver, ptarmigan, arctic hare, red
		and arctic fox
	fishing:	tomcod, needlefish, blackfish
	gathering:	cranberries, crowberries,
		driftwood
Dec. to March	hunting:	mink, land otter, beaver, ptarmi-
		gan, arctic hare, red and arctic
		fox
	fishing:	tomcod, needlefish, blackfish
	gathering:	driftwood

Nanvarnarrlak Seasonal Round

March	Move to spring camp in the tundra	
	hunting:	ptarmigan, arctic and snowshoe
		hare, mink, otter, muskrat, bea-
		ver, red fox

	fishing:	blackfish, pike
	gathering:	driftwood, spruce, alder
April	hunting:	as in March plus waterfowl
	fishing:	blackfish, pike
	gathering:	cranberries, crowberries, drift-wood, spruce, alder
May	hunting:	as in April
	fishing:	blackfish, pike, whitefish, sheefish
	gathering:	willow leaves

Return to village by late May

Option 1: *June and July*

June and July	Move up into large tundra lakes for whitefish	
	hunting:	beaver
	fishing:	whitefish, pike
	gathering:	wild celery, horsetails, poison water hemlock shoots, sourdock, saxifrages, coltsfoot, woolly lousewort, marsh marigold, fiddleheads, fireweed

Move to berry camp for a few days, then return to village

Option 2 (since at least 1920 and probably since 1900): *June and July*

June and July	Move to the Kuskokwim River and fish for salmon	
	hunting:	ducks and geese
	fishing:	king, red, and chum salmon
	gathering:	as in Option 1

Move to berry camp and then back to village

Aug. and Sept.	hunting:	moulting ducks, other waterfowl
	fishing:	whitefish, pike, loche
	gathering:	see berries' list in coastal round, grasses

Move to fall camp in the tundra by late September

Oct. and Nov.	hunting:	mink, land otter
	fishing:	blackfish, pike, whitefish
	gathering:	as in coastal list

Return to village by mid-November

Dec.	hunting:	ptarmigan, arctic and snowshoe hare, mink, otter, muskrat, beaver, red fox
	fishing:	blackfish, pike, loche
	gathering:	driftwood, spruce, alder
Jan. and Feb.	hunting:	ptarmigan, arctic and snowshoe hare, mink, otter, muskrat, beaver, red fox
	fishing:	blackfish
	gathering:	driftwood, spruce, alder

2

Contemporary Practices and Ideologies

DRIFT NETTING FOR KING SALMON

It's early June and a beautiful sunny day with temperatures of up to seventy degrees Fahrenheit forecast. The net is in the boat, and there is a full tank of gas. The gear includes a fish tub, oars, a fish club, rope, life jackets, rain gear, food, and two large buoys for the ends of the net, in addition to the fifty-fathom (one hundred-yard) net.

We motor slowly out through Brown's Slough, successfully avoiding submerged fuel drums, sunken logs, and derelict boats. After a brief discussion we decide to try what I've jokingly heard called the "Sears and Roebuck drift." It's an easy drift, like mail ordering fish, and is favored by non-Natives, though Yupiit drift net there also. It begins near the bottom of an island in the channel across from Bethel and extends downriver for more than a mile. The tide is still running out fairly hard, and this drift has the advantage of being relatively snag-free. With lesser used drifts, there is a greater chance of entangling the lead line around a sunken log or stump.

We unfold a tarp and put it over the side of the boat, so that the net will feed out without snagging. It feeds out fairly well, with one person tossing out the float line and the lead line running out free, but there are still places where the mesh is caught over a float, or wrapped up around a twig. The person running the engine backs the boat away from the net, setting it out diagonally upstream, and then, when all the net is in the water and the end tied to the boat, backs downstream so that the net makes a nice open curve facing downriver. While this is happening we are drifting downstream at about two to two and a half miles an hour.

A light wind has come up, but the day is still bright and pretty. We back slowly away from the net, keeping it taut, watching the floats for action—either the bobbing and thrashing of a fish, or the suddenly widening V-shaped disappearance of floats, which marks a snag. Once five or six floats disappear and we all have a momentary adrenaline rush, thinking we may be snagged, but then the floats pop back up. Seconds later a tail splashes, and at the same time the net jerks. It's a big one, or at least enthusiastic. We drift, the motor idling backward, watching the net and talking of fishing and friends. We get snagged briefly near the far end, but the net comes free before we have time to unhook and go around to pull it upriver and off the snag.

When we are even with a fish camp on a lower island I start pulling the net. The lead line is heavy, a steady pull on the back and upper body. When a fish is sighted, I try to make sure that it's properly "bagged," wrapped up in the mesh before I lift it from the water, so that it doesn't drop out. One of the fish is dead, but the other two are lively, smacking the side of the boat with their heads and tails. They're amazing fish, all the fight of a twelve-inch rainbow trout magnified to twenty or thirty or forty pounds. If you rap them sharply in the right spot on their heads they give a little wiggle, like a dog shaking off water, and become still, although they may thrash about reflexively (and unexpectedly) minutes later. I try to unhook the mesh from the mouth of one of the live ones before conking it with the club, and get one finger sliced up by a tooth as it clamps its jaw and slams its head around. I should have known better. Two of the fish are around twenty pounds, the other a nice female around thirty-five pounds. They are strikingly beautiful, deep-bellied and thick, dark with black spots above the midline, and silver below. Someone wets a clean gunnysack and covers them as we head back to the top of the drift.

The net goes out easier this time. It always does when it's wet. The tide has slowed and we drift about halfway down, then come to a virtual stop. A couple of fish hit when the tide turns, then the net just sits there. After about an hour we pick the net, curious to see what we've gotten. We have four kings and one chum this time. The chum is about eight pounds, and only slightly watermarked. Later this Christmas-tree-shaped pattern of bruiselike discolorations will be brown-black against the chum's reddening sides.

We make two more drifts, catching two kings one time and five the other. Since this is about as many as we want to process, and it's getting late, we wash out the tarp and clean up the boat a little, then head home.

INTRODUCTION

In the past 150 years there have been significant changes in the Y-K Delta. First Russian and then U.S. explorers and traders penetrated the area. Initially this contact was intermittent and peripheral, but with the arrival of large numbers of missionaries in the 1880s and 1890s this contact gradually became continuous and encompassing. Schools were established in many villages between 1920 and 1940, and trading posts were established throughout the region. Both attracted Yupiit, either to new village sites or to established sites, for longer periods of the year. There were several catastrophic epidemics as well, of which the post–World War II tuberculosis epidemic is the most recent.

If one compares nineteenth-century accounts of Yup'ik life with contemporary village life, two conflicting views emerge. Sometimes it appears that nothing has changed; sometimes it seems as though everything has changed. The mainstays of traditional transportation, the kayak and dog team, are only incidental to modern life. Sod houses are found only occasionally at camps. The larger *qasgiq* (men's house), where it exists at all, is now used primarily for taking firebaths. Beyond that, it is only an item in stories.

The startling masks and ornate ivory hunting tools reside in museums (see Ray 1967, Fitzhugh and Kaplan 1982), and the descendants of their carvers are deacons, priests, doctors, and teachers, as well as commercial mask and ivory carvers. The changes have been tremendous. And yet, even sitting in a contemporary oil-heated, electrically lighted wood-frame house, with the TV going and children playing video games in the back room, there is a feeling of continuity as well. The focus is on this village, its resources, and the people here and in nearby villages. There is interest and concern with larger issues—of legislation in Washington, D.C.; of ANCSA stock being alienated; of school funding and Yup'ik language use—but there is usually a clear and shared sense of viewpoint, not necessarily in terms of agreement but in terms of situatedness, of a perspective from "here."

It is this sense of looking from, of having, knowing, and caring about, a place, and of examining issues in terms of their effect on that place, that so intensely connects the past with the present and future. The speakers may be more or less cosmopolitan, but they share their connection with a particular local area. The Yupiit of today are the descendants of and—through naming—are the same people who harvested these same resources, in the same places, with many of the same techniques used before either written or oral history.

The Y-K Delta is very unusual in this continuity. Unlike the Yupiit, most other Native Americans have been separated from the resources they depended upon at contact. Most Native American groups have been moved, often long distances to a different, usually less productive eco-zone, and then restricted to an area too small to maintain their traditional subsistence regime. Many groups were forced into new subsistence patterns of mixed agriculture and herding.

· It may be useful to imagine for a moment what might have happened if the Sioux could have maintained control of a reservation large enough to encompass sufficient buffalo to feed them, and the buffalo had not been virtually exterminated. It seems likely that buffalo would have remained a broadly contemporary focus or interest, rather than, as appears to be the case, a historic one, with primarily mythic and religious connections. The distinction is between something which is *historically* important (symbolically and economically), and whose importance still resonates with *that* meaning, and something which is both *historically and contemporarily* important, and resonates with *both* meanings. What makes the Y-K Delta, and much of Alaska, unique within the American context is that Native peoples have not lost access to the resources upon which they traditionally depended. This is not to deny the evils that have befallen some groups: genocide in the Aleutians, displacement in Southeastern Alaska, and depletion or diminution of some resources. In the Y-K Delta, however, continued and uninterrupted access to historic resources has been largely unaffected by outside intervention.[1]

As someone who did not grow up in the delta, I have occasionally run headlong into the difference that my own lack of this connectedness makes in my outlook. I was once talking to a Yup'ik man about a portage route to a large lake system. I pointed to an old camp on the U.S. Geological Survey topographical map, fantasizing about visiting there, maybe looking for ducks, and he said, "I have a brother who is buried there." I had not realized that that place was his family's traditional spring and fall camp. When he said, in effect, "Oh yeah, we used to live there, that's our home, or one of our homes," and told the story of his brother's death, I had a moment of self-awareness that almost took my breath away. I had been seeing the land in my mind as "wilderness." Suddenly I saw that my vision was part of Manifest Destiny, that in another sense my fantasized "expedition" to that spot made no more sense than mounting an expedition to explore the living room. That wilderness, "terra incognita," is unconnected land—a place that either lacks "knowers," or those whose knowledge is officially recognized. That is why Lewis and Clark could still "explore," even though they depended upon Native American guides, and why colonial powers could "claim" land already owned and occupied. I realized anew that wilderness is both destroyed and created by Euro-American culture. Destruction is the process that makes headlines—strip mines, oil pipelines, roads (see, for example, Brody 1986)—but the process of creation is every bit as real and violent. Destroying the knowledge and ties that the aboriginal inhabitants have with the land creates wilderness. Only then can wilderness be explored; those who know it intimately must first be removed from the scene. Generally, geographic features are renamed to mark this change. For example, the mountain that Tanaina Athapaskans called Denaali was (re)named McKinley (for other examples of this process, see Basso 1979; Cruikshank 1979, 1981).

This process is largely complete in most of the United States, and has occurred in some parts of Alaska as well.[2] It is worth noting that except for the most inhospitable environments, such as permanent ice fields and glaciers or extreme deserts, the "Age of Exploration" took place when there were no empty places in the world to explore. Someone lived and used every place, at least seasonally. This fact is at odds with current (Western) ideology about land use, which comes from our pastoral and agricultural past. Lands are either productive, inhabited, and controlled, that is, used for urban, agricultural, grazing, or timbering purposes; or they are wilderness: unproductive, uninhabited, and uncontrolled. Such a dichotomy does not work well with hunter-gatherers. Their lands were and are, to various degrees, inhabited, productive, and controlled, although often at low enough levels to pass unnoticed to the untrained eye. One reason has to do with sheer population density. Outside the tropics, virtually all contemporary hunter-gatherers are restricted to marginal land that is too cold, dry, or unproductive to have been worth usurping for some other purpose. Such lands usually support a population of limited density, and at such densities most hunter-gatherer subsistence strategies, with the exception of fire, leave few marks on the land. Usually these marks are rapidly erased by natural processes.

Therefore, flying over the delta, or examining it on a map, Euro-Americans often assume that the land is "wilderness," that is, unoccupied, unproductive, and uncontrolled. In actuality, though largely uncontrolled, it is hardly wilderness. It has been occupied for thousands of years, its resources are known intimately, and there are travel routes appropriate to each season. Straight lines through brush or grass and wear marks on the tundra give evidence of snow-machine routes, and clumps of taller grasses and greens mark sites of old villages and middens, as do graves.

CHANGES IN MIGRATION PATTERNS AND RESOURCE USE

Historical resource-use patterns for the villages were given in the previous chapter. Current subsistence activities target largely the same resources, although some of the techniques and harvest locations have changed. Kassiglurmiut and Nanvarnarrlak were abandoned because bureaucrats with the Bureau of Indian Affairs felt that those sites were unsuitable for schools, and built schools at the nearby sites of Nightmute and Nunapitchuk. The later movement by residents of Nightmute to one of their historical spring camps, Toksook Bay, occurred so that they would no longer have to move to their spring camp to dry herring. This exemplifies a general trend toward lower reliance on seasonal camps in most areas. The 1950s and 1960s brought compulsory schooling, and, as a result, men began to move to the seasonal camps alone, leaving the women and children in the village.

Currently, for most families, seasonal moves are reduced to moving to fish camps and/or berry camps. The use of large outboard-powered skiffs and snow machines has allowed harvesters to continue to rely on resources in traditional areas and yet return home at night. Many men also spend some time at trapping camps, and from Nunapitchuk they leave for a period of time for moose hunting. This innovation relates both to their increased mobility and to the relatively recent occurrence of moose in the area.

A final innovation is that it has become more common for men in Nunapitchuk to go seal hunting. They either go down to the coast to hunt seals with friends or relatives, or make trips to the Kuskokwim Bay in August.

Overall, the following changes have occurred in resource use in the delta since the turn of the century. There has been a net per capita reduction in total harvests, as more store food has come into the diet, although consumption of wild foods in Y-K Delta villages is among the highest in the state. There has been a shift in the availability and importance of particular foods. The use of freezers and salt has made it easier to preserve some foods. Shifts in village locations have changed the accessibility of other foods. There is much less dependence on wild greens. It is unclear whether berry consumption has decreased or increased.

Clearly, the ubiquitous use of freezers has increased the harvest of some species. Blueberries, which were previously of minor importance, are now gathered in quantity and frozen (the above information taken in part from Wolfe et al. 1984).

There is also less dependence on certain staples, such as needlefish and blackfish. These winter-caught fish were important for dog food. Now that dogs have largely been replaced by snow machines, these fish are somewhat less important.

CHANGING TECHNOLOGIES AND TECHNIQUES OF SUBSISTENCE

Sea-mammal hunting was the most highly developed system of capture at contact. There were a variety of harpoons and floats of different weights and sizes; most were beautifully and elaborately decorated as well. There was a whole range of equipment for use with kayaks and large skin boats, including paddles, sleds, floats and line holders, and boat, meat, and retrieval hooks. These have been almost completely replaced. The minimum gear necessary for hunting sea mammals currently consists of an outboard-powered skiff, binoculars, rifle and shells, and a harpoon for retrieval. Small-caliber, high-velocity rifles with or without scopes are preferred for seals, with larger calibers used for walrus. For coastal communities, seal hunters also need a snow machine and sled to transport their boat to the ice edge in spring, the most important and productive season.

At contact, caribou were hunted from kayaks on lakes and at river crossings. They were also taken in surrounds. Large land mammals are now hunted with rifles instead. Travel to the hunting grounds is by outboard-powered skiff, snow machine, all-terrain vehicle, or plane.

Fishing used to be based on several systems. Of these, jigging through the ice using a short stick with a line and a lure attached is still extremely common and productive. While families often jig together, this is a particularly common activity for women, including older women. People still make lures, although most lures are store-bought, and twine has replaced sinew. To my knowledge, fish spears (leisters) are no longer used.

Funnel-mouthed basketlike fish traps were once made in a variety of sizes for different species and settings. They were crafted from split wooden strips bound with spruce root. Such traps are now largely restricted to two sizes. The smaller size is constructed from half-inch-mesh galvanized steel screen and is used to catch blackfish and mink, with slightly larger traps occasionally used for taking otter. In some cases the funnel is still made of wood splints. A larger version is used on the lower Yukon River and middle Kuskokwim River to take loche.

Dip nets, which look like oversized butterfly nets, are still used at winter weirs for whitefish and sheefish. They are also used for smaller species that run in a compact mass or in huge numbers, such as smelt and needlefish. At contact, king salmon were caught with dip nets. Drift and set gill nets are now used.

Setnets and drift nets used to be made in mesh sizes from herring to beluga, and consist of three basic parts. The float line, or top line, has the floats attached to it. The mesh or webbing is tied to the float line at the top and to the lead line at the bottom. The lead line holds the bottom of the net down, so that it hangs like a curtain in the water. The mesh is sized so that when fish try to go through it they get caught on or behind the gills, hence the name "gill nets." For seals and beluga, the mesh is larger and the material used is much heavier. Proper mesh size for beluga, for example, is one's hat size, that is, the circumference of one's head at brow level. For seals the mesh is somewhat smaller. With these nets, sea mammals become entangled and drown. Gill nets are used in two ways. As "setnets" they are attached to the shore at one end and to an anchored float at the other. As drift nets, they are used while drifting down the river, or on the ocean, with the boat attached to one end and a large float attached to the other end.

Gillnetting is now much more common than it was at contact, although people certainly made and used small gill nets at that time, with the webbing or mesh made from seal skin, sinew, or willow bast. The introduction of linen, cotton, and, later, nylon for net mesh has made fishing much easier and more productive. Now people use mesh sizes from two to eight inches to target various fish species, from herring to king salmon. As far as I know, nets are no longer used for sea mammals, except in school cultural heritage projects, having been replaced by guns.[3] Often nets are purchased as components (lead line, float line, floats, mesh, and twine) and assembled (hung) by the user. Gillnetting is so efficient that during peak periods of some salmon runs, it is not uncommon to set only a part of the net to avoid catching more fish than can be processed. Catching three hundred silver salmon in a short drift (at six to seven pounds each) is all too easy if one is not cautious. Setnets can be even more efficient, since they catch continuously, as long as they are in place. Typical setnet sites include: eddies along rivers, where the fish encounter the nets while trying to rest; at the ends of peninsulas; and at narrow spots in lakes, where the nets obstruct the passage of the fish. Nets are almost invariably worked from outboard-powered skiffs.

In the past, flightless moulting ducks and geese were rounded up, either on foot or by kayak, and driven into nets. This is still occasionally done for ducks. Now the process involves outboard-powered boats, gill nets and shotguns (see Morrow 1991). Otherwise, birds are taken with shotguns and occasionally twenty-two-caliber rifles. Bird spears, bird arrows and bolas are no longer used.

Snares, which were set for large and small game as well as for birds, are now generally used for snaring rabbits, beavers, and perhaps ptarmigan. Metal traps have replaced earlier bone-and-sinew braining traps for taking furbearers, particularly foxes.

Berries continue to be gathered by hand, although the use of small one-hand berry rakes is common for cranberry and blackberry picking. Outboard-powered skiffs have made access to distant berrying grounds much easier.

Much of the specialized skin and fur clothing that was associated with various seasons and activities has been replaced by manufactured cloth and clothing. Locally made items still in everyday use in subsistence activities include fur mittens, hats, and ruffs. Fur parkas and fur mukluks are often used in extremely cold weather, particularly by women who are jigging, when their relative inaction compounds the cold.[4] Furs used in clothing include those of locally caught animals such as seal, beaver, mink, muskrat, otter, ground squirrel, wolf, wolverine, and caribou, either home tawed or commercially tanned, as well as purchased skins. The latter skins include Canadian wolf, Siberian raccoon, shearling lamb, calf, and domestic rabbit. Seal intestine rain gear is rarely made for use any longer, though it shows up in doll costumes, as does fish skin.

CHANGES IN PRESERVATION TECHNIQUES AND UTILIZATION

Yupiit have readily adapted new preservation techniques into their repertoire. There is a strong ethic against waste, and people generally work very hard at using all parts of the animals taken. In general, changes in techniques and practices have speeded food processing and made preservation more predictable and controllable. Probably the first introduced change to have a major impact on processing was the replacement of slate ulu blades and knives by steel and iron. This process was widespread by the 1880s.

The first major change in preservation came with the importation of inexpensive salt. Salt is important in two kinds of preservation techniques. The more salt-intensive method is called hard salting, where sufficient salt is packed between pieces of fish or meat to preserve them without refrigeration. Most of this salt is leached out prior to consumption. The name for hard salted fish, *sulunaq*, is a Russian loan word, indicating that the process is likely to have been introduced during or not long after the Russian period, which officially ended in 1867.

In addition, the ready availability of salt has made it easier to dry fish in inclement conditions. Dried, smoked king salmon "flats," or "blankets"—where the fillets are not separated at the backbone—appear to have become a major staple only after the introduction of salt, as the very oiliness that makes the fish so flavorful and nutritious renders them difficult to dry successfully.[5]

There was initial resistance to increasing dietary salt. Yupiit in the Bethel area, for example, were initially unwilling to send their children to the Moravian school because of the amount of salt that was consumed there. They believed that the consumption of such quantities of salt would make it impossible for shamans to cure the children if they became ill. Sugar has played a lesser role as a preservative.[6]

Probably the most important new preservation technique available today is year-round freezing. Yupiit had no doubt always frozen foods to preserve them, but now large electric chest freezers are ubiquitous in villages and in Bethel. Most families own one or two, and many larger families own several, one of which may be dedicated primarily to berries. Foods are not only frozen fresh but are also dried, smoked, or aged and then frozen to preserve quality. Many foods that were available only seasonally, or that were difficult to hold at the peak of flavor, can now be frozen to be enjoyed throughout the year. Arvin Dull talked about his delight in eating subsistence-caught foods: "I grew up eating subsistence-caught game, and I prefer it. I can go to the store and buy just about anything I want to buy, but every single day we eat subsistence-caught food, and in some cases it's like eating delicacies every day" (transcript of an interview, June 24, 1991). Balancing this trend toward freezing for preservation, there has been a trend toward lesser reliance on fermentation as a storage and preservation process.

TRADE, CONTACT, AND CHANGING LOCAL DIETS

Tea and tobacco were being traded into the delta from neighboring areas in advance of Russian contact, and after contact they were eagerly sought, as was sugar (Zagoskin 1967). However, because of the continued isolation of much of the delta, the process of culinary acculturation proceeded more slowly than in much of the rest of Alaska. This isolation was due to the difficulties of travel in the region and the lack of surplus extractable resources such as gold, whales, timber, or salmon. The one exception was furs, particularly mink, beaver, and fox.

The northern part of the Y-K Delta has, since initial contact, always had a stronger non-Native presence. This presence began with the Russian trading post at St. Michael, and later expanded enormously as the Yukon became the major trade route to the interior gold fields. The upper and middle Kuskokwim have had a similar history of an early Russian trading post followed by mining activity.

Tea, coffee, sugar, salt, and flour had became staples in the local diet by the 1930s, as had rice and noodles (Lenz 1985:83; Nash, in Woodbury 1984:38–9). At present, many dishes that are considered traditional contain some nonlocal components. *Akutaq*, which used to be made with indigenous fats such as caribou tallow, bear fat, or seal oil, is now often made with hydrogenated vegetable oil, although seal oil is often added for flavor. Sugar is generally added. Early fry breads were fried in seal oil, but this is now less common. The replacement is again hydrogenated vegetable oil. The use of onions, rice, noodles, and/or potatoes in soups made with fish or meat is standard practice. However, subsistence foods continue to play a central role in the Yup'ik diet, especially as a source of protein. Introduced food items have generally been adapted into local epicurean traditions rather than replacing those traditions.

CONTEMPORARY SEASONAL ROUNDS IN LOWER KUSKOKWIM VILLAGES

Contemporary seasonal rounds are similar to the historic ones given in chapter 1. The seasonal round of a family in a given village is likely to be some combination of possibilities from the four idealized settings: coastal, riverine, tundra-marsh, and headwater-riverine. One might expect that the nearby resources would be heavily exploited, and more distant ones less so. However, the number of exceptions to this generalization render it relatively useless. For example, the Nelson Island villages are very dependent on herring, with annual catches of one to two tons per family (Pete 1991a:11). The villages of Platinum and Goodnews Bay also have a herring run available, and there appears to be no a priori reason why herring are not more heavily exploited in those villages. Nonetheless, dried herring is not a staple there; instead, dried salmon is the mainstay. In addition, many hunters travel long distances to the coast to harvest seals, and inland to harvest moose.

Even within a given village there are significant variations between extended families.[7] This is due to personal preference, knowledge, and skill, and available equipment and family connections with other areas and resources. If, for example, members of a particular family have moved to their present village site from an area down on the coast, or from far up one of the clear-water rivers, then their psychological, social, and practical linkages with that area are likely to be ongoing. Furthermore, various circumstances may shift the focus of a family or village in a particular year. Under conditions of scarcity, people may focus their harvesting efforts on other species. This happened in 1991 on Nelson Island, after a poor herring run, possibly caused by overharvesting of stocks by a commercial bait fishery based in Dutch Harbor. Normally, a family's yearly herring supply can be caught in one or two good tides, but in 1991 it took two or more weeks, and some families were unable to catch as much as they needed even by extending their harvesting period. These shortages were exacerbated by the high fat content of the herring that were taken, which made them very difficult to dry without spoilage. (Usually only the first run of herring contains that much fat, and Nelson Islanders wait until the second run to catch the bulk of their herring.)[8] Fish caught later in the herring season are also more prone to spoilage, as the weather is often less conducive to successful drying. The combination of the fat content of the herring and trying to dry them later in the year resulted in spoilage losses of up to ninety per cent for some families. Many Nelson Island families were forced to shift their subsistence efforts to smelt, halibut, pacific cod, salmon, pike and cisco. However:

> Local residents do not consider halibut or Pacific cod adequate or even improved, substitutes for herring, as non-local people may, but these species are certainly preferred by Nelson Island families to non-local, imported foods. Herring is *the* traditional winter food for Nelson Island families. Changing subsistence fishing strategies often means purchasing new gear and more gasoline, adjusting processing and drying facilities, investing more time fishing for other species and altering subsistence production roles in the family. (Pete 1991b:9–10; emphasis in original)

SUBSISTENCE CALENDAR

It is perhaps easiest to include subsistence activities for the lower Kuskokwim River and Bay and Nelson Island in this list, since many resources occur broadly across the area, and people travel widely to participate in various harvests. This description is an approximation, based on an abstracted ideal year. Actual years vary considerably.

Month	Resources	Techniques	Quantity and Importance
January	blackfish	fish trap	low to moderate
	pike	jigging	low to moderate
	ptarmigan	hunting	low to moderate
	furbearers	trapping, hunting	low to moderate
	tundra hare	hunting	low
February	blackfish	fish trap	low to moderate
	beaver	trapping	low to moderate
	tundra hare	hunting	low to moderate
	ptarmigan	hunting	low
	pike	jigging	low
March	seal	hunting	moderate to high
	tomcod	jigging	moderate to high
	ptarmigan	hunting	low to moderate
	blackfish	fish trap	low to moderate
	pike	jigging	low
April	seals	hunting	high
	bear	hunting	high
	walrus	hunting	moderate to high
	waterfowl	hunting	moderate to high
	pike	jigging	moderate
	trout	jigging	low to moderate
	berries	gathering[9]	low
May	seal	hunting	high
	herring	netting	high
	muskrat	hunting	moderate to high
	waterfowl	hunting	moderate to high
	bird eggs	gathering	low to moderate
	bear	hunting	moderate
	greens	gathering	low
	berries	gathering	low
	Breakup usually occurs in May		
June	herring	netting	high
	king salmon	netting	high
	seal	hunting	moderate
	pink salmon	netting	moderate
	red salmon	netting	moderate
	halibut	jigging	moderate
	beluga whales	hunting	low
	greens	gathering	low

Month	Resources	Techniques	Quantity and Importance
July	chum salmon	netting	high
	red salmon	netting	moderate to high
	pink salmon	netting	moderate
	beluga whales	hunting	moderate
	greens	gathering	moderate
	berries	gathering	moderate
	waterfowl	hunting	moderate
	halibut	jigging	moderate
	seals	hunting	low
August	berries	gathering	high
	silver salmon	netting	moderate to high
	waterfowl	hunting, driving, netting	moderate
	whitefish	netting	moderate
	greens	gathering	moderate
	beluga whales	hunting	low
September	moose	hunting	high
	caribou	hunting	high
	berries	gathering	high
	pike	netting	moderate to high
	seals	hunting	moderate to high
	bears	hunting	moderate
	salmon	netting (coastal)	moderate
	whitefish	netting	moderate to low
	waterfowl	hunting	moderate
	halibut	jigging	moderate to low
	beluga whales	hunting	low
October	pike	netting	high
	loche	netting, fish traps	moderate to high
	whitefish	netting	low
	blackfish	fish traps	low
	berries	gathering	low
November	furbearers	trapping, hunting	high
	needlefish	dipnetting	high
	whitefish	netting, dipnetting	high
	pike	jigging, netting	moderate
	tundra hare	hunting	low
	blackfish	fish traps	low
	ptarmigan	hunting	low
	Freeze-up usually occurs in November		
December	blackfish	fish traps	moderate
	furbearers	trapping, hunting	moderate
	pike	jigging	low
	ptarmigan	hunting	low

CONTEMPORARY YUP'IK GENDER AND FAMILY ROLES AND SUBSISTENCE

There are still clear differences in gender roles in subsistence, with men focusing on procurement and women on processing. One aspect stressed in several interviews was that the most critical segments of fish cutting are performed only by older women. Many women discussed not beginning to cut king salmon "blankets" or "flats" until their mothers were infirm or dead, as the following interview emphasizes. (The first excerpt contextualizes the following two). Janet Shantz (= J) is a member of an old Bethel family and possesses a bicultural background; Ron Kaiser (= R), her husband, is a non-Native.

J: Like I don't consider myself, even though when I was growing up here I had a full Yup'ik grandmother, and so I've had all this exposure to all this very traditional activity. But the way I was raised was, I was not raised like that. I was exposed to it, but I was not expected to, you know,

C: To do it

J: Right. The up-and-coming thing of the '50s and '60s was transition, and let's get with it, you know, let's get jobs and get with the program here.

C: Yeah, get with the program.

J: And that's how I was raised, but now that I have chosen to live here myself and raise my family here, these things are important to me again. And I'm only coming to see how important. I think it helps me identify. I don't know if it's exact, Ron identifies with some of this stuff too, but from a different perspective. I feel like it kind of puts me in touch with the Yup'ik part of who I am, that feels real good. And it's also, it puts me in touch with a big activity that's going on here, that's around here. (transcript of an interview, July 22, 1991)

J: My mom when she started doing her fish, she started when she was pretty old, like I wasn't even living at home any more when she started her cutting and smoking, she did it after her mom died. She learned how to do it. Our grandma had provided all of our smoked fish for us. And you probably know from your talking to people, that the younger people, if you can be considered young when we're forty, are not really allowed, as long as there's somebody older

R: OLDER

J: in the family. The older people are the ones who are in a position to cut the fish. Somebody else can fish and get them, but the actual cutting and drying and processing is only done by certain people in the family. My mom said she tried to help my grandma as my grandma grew older, but my grandma always said, "You're gonna butcher the fish, you're gonna butcher them, you're gonna mess them up."

R: They're too precious to people.

J: Yeah, they are. And she wouldn't let my mom help. And my mom said when, after her mom died, it was a year or two, it wasn't immediately when she started smoking, but, soon after my grandma died, within a couple of years I'd say, when she went to make her first flat fish, which is the more elaborate bunch of cutting that you have to do, she stood there at her table, with no help, and made the cuts. And she said it was as if my grandma's hand was on her hand, as she made her cuts.

      And she said she just [was able to], from watching all those years, and she made a blanket for the first time. And she said it was as if her mom's hand was on her hand, like with all the cuts. And it wasn't perfect, but it was all there.

      I myself have memories of watching my grandma and my mom both cut fish, and I don't know. I don't think I would have that same [experience] as she did, because I didn't spend that many years watching those blankets being cut, but that was her feeling. And I have, I'm thirty-eight, and I have friends who have just taken up the knife, and had the same thing happen that happened to my mom.

      My friend Anna Thompson, she went to help my sister Stacy last summer, Stacy thought Anna knew all about making blankets, and she said, "Anna, could you come over and help me?" and Anna [said], "Oh, sure, I'll come over and help you," and it was like, a few days later, Anna couldn't wait to tell me, she said, "Would you believe that was my first?" She said, "Did you like the way those blankets turned out, didn't the fish turn out nice," like setting me up. "Oh, they turned out really good, you guys did such a nice job, they're beautifully done, I'm so glad you helped Stacy." And she smiled and she said, "Would you believe that was my first time cutting, my sister Carrie never lets me cut fish." She takes care of all that they need for their family, a big family, and she takes care of all of it.

      And Anna was so proud, and I told her the story of how my mom experienced making her first blanket, and Anna said, "Yeah, I could do it." (transcript of July 22, 1991, continued)

This theme of "growing into" subsistence activities as one's parents died or retired from active roles and one's own children began to grow up was repeated several times in different interviews.

J: When I grew up here, we always had salmon, and we had all the bounty of the land, provided by my grandmother and then my mother. Now that we don't have them around, and I have kids, I feel that I'm in a position to provide for my kids. And so what Ron was saying about our use of the resource is [it] seems to be growing. Our interest is there, and I think our interest is there because we have kids. If my kids grow up here, I want them to partake of what's special and particular about the place we live in, and I have to start doing it.

And we both were just talking this summer how things have become important to us. Ron and I have been together as a couple for like twelve years now, and we could have done this at any point during the last twelve years. But it just seems like things are focusing for us towards this particular [time], learning how to cut fish and smoke fish, and have it for our families to enjoy.

R: [I] Think as you get older, and you're providing for your family this stuff means more. (transcript of July 22, 1991, continued)

The generational recycling of personnel at the fish-cutting tables was a major theme in interviews with women. They also spoke of the importance of ensuring that meat and fish not be wasted throughout various types of processing. Bev Hoffman (B), a member of an old Bethel family who herself has a bicultural background, noted the importance of these activities in her family in a conversation with John McDonald (J), her non-Native husband, and myself (C).

B: One thing I really enjoy about putting up our fish, [is that] over the years it's become a gathering of friends and family, my brothers and sisters. It's a family thing that we do together, and that, I think, means a lot to all of us, that we're doing something together. And we're putting up our fish together, and we crank [complain] at each other about the way it's done, but everybody gets to do their thing their way.

And then there's also the product, which of course is greatly appreciated all year long. . . .

My family getting back together, doing things together, and that's all a part of it, the hunt together, and gardening together.[10] My brothers go out and hunt, there's five brothers that hunt, and then we split it amongst the nine families. We split

J: The moose

B: the moose and caribou,
and we all get together and we butcher, just like we do the fish. And
there's a lot of good feeling of accomplishment there, working together to provide not only for your immediate family but your extended family too. And you know, I think that happens a lot here,
the sharing between families, the sharing of fish, the sharing of moose
and I think that's a good thing. . . .

You know, growing up here was real interesting, we ate fish all
summer. I have a brother who doesn't even eat fish, he hates fish,
'cause we ate it all summer. Except for Sundays, we had fish, and all
winter we had moose, supplemented can goods, but we didn't subsistence garden. But all my family, they all enjoy that part of our life
here, you know, not only just us but my brothers and sisters and
their families, the fishing and the hunting together.

I think most families here, you'll see fish camp families, and families that go up moose hunting together, and that's all a part of it too,
you know, you're surviving together, and helping out. And you see
less and less of it, compared to early years in Alaska, I suppose, but
it's still there and it still feels good.

John and I've been putting up fish since we first got here, sixteen
years ago. That first summer we started. And it's been over the last,
I'd say, five years my brothers and sisters have all joined our operation.

J: Yeah, they used to not even fish, at all,

B: No, not even fish.

J: I mean we'd get all, if they wanted some they'd
call us up and we'd get them some fish, you know, they never even
fished . . .

C: So they used to, used to still do the moose hunting?

J: Yeah, they were really into the hunting part, you know, but not so
much fishing and cutting fish. (transcript of an interview July 15,
1991)

SUBSISTENCE AS AN INTEGRATED ACTIVITY

Part of the power of subsistence practices as a system is that they combine many areas of life that are quite separate for most contemporary
Americans. Subsistence is also broadly integrated through links with traditional beliefs and practices. It receives some validation in religious con-

texts, though there is considerable variation among Christian denominations. In addition, subsistence is the conversational staple for men, and
one of the two most important topics for women, children being the
other.

Subsistence activities are a major focus of time and energy for most
people in villages, even for those who have full-time jobs. This includes
not only the time spent shooting or checking nets but also the usually
greater number of hours spent making and repairing equipment, scouting
locations, and so on. This also applies to processing, where preparation
and cleanup, drying, smoking, and storage may take more time than the
actual "cutting." As Bev Hoffman stressed earlier, the productive unit is
usually kin-based. The use of kinship to define and shape the groups
that prepare for, harvest, preserve, distribute, and consume subsistence
products both actuates and reinforces kinship ties (see Fienup-Riordan
1983a).

Subsistence activities form a year-round calendar of activities that
link Yupiit with the land. In the past this link was reflected in the common use of the Yup'ik names for the thirteen lunar months. Most of
these names mark either natural phenomena, such as frost or the moulting of birds, or subsistence activities, such as the clubbing of fish or the
corralling of caribou (Jacobson 1984:670). There was considerable variation in month names between areas because such names denoted particular local events and resources, and activities varied between areas. It is
also difficult to correlate the contemporary twelve-month calendar with
this more accurate version that has thirteen lunar months. Contemporarily this is usually reconciled by dropping the name of one of the winter
months.

Many of the activities memorialized in the month names reflect ongoing activities or concerns. *Kaugun* is not June in the abstract, but (king
salmon) clubbing time—a time when everyone is hitting king salmon
close behind the eyes as they take them out of their nets. My sense is
that those month names used most commonly are linked either with natural phenomena such as the hatching of bird eggs, or contemporary subsistence activities such as the clubbing of fish. Names that denote obsolete practices such as the cutting of a summer entrance in one's sod house
are used less frequently.

This calendrical link between people and their surroundings is unusual in contemporary America. Thanksgiving, a harvest festival, is celebrated at the same time in Alaska—where (for much of the state) the
harvest ended months earlier—as in Florida and Hawaii, where the harvest never ends. Unless one lives in New England, Thanksgiving is an

arbitrary date for a harvest festival. And while Christmas is associated with the winter solstice, and Easter and Passover with older festivals marking the vernal equinox, the symbolism of snow-covered trees or spring herbs is often unsynchronized with local climatic reality.

In comparison, "breakup," the movement of the river ice in the spring, marks an intensely local, as well as vital, event. Now one can travel by boat; before, one could not. Summer has started. Snow machines, sleds, skis, and skates are put away. Boats, nets, and outboard motors are the order of the day. When someone catches the first king salmon, it is announced on the local public radio station, and everyone knows the rest are not far behind.

"Freeze-up," when the river is capped with ice, has the same power. Now one can jig and set nets through the ice, and be partly freed from the tyranny of travel along the tortuous meanders of river and slough.

Another way in which the subsistence system is omnipresent in peoples' lives is that it is the source of food, particularly special or specially marked foods: foods from the land and the waters—not restaurant food or pastries from a special shop—that form the talked-about and remembered meals. In the same way that turkey is obligatory for Euro-American Thanksgiving, *akutaq* (Eskimo ice cream) is required for feasts.

Subsistence foods are also the day-to-day, meal-to-meal foods that appear on the table. This includes not only what non-Natives see as the desirable parts of fish and game but other parts as well: salmon stomachs, moose nose, the half-dried salmon backbones. The traditional system of drying salmon includes techniques for preserving almost the entire fish. For example, a king salmon is disassembled into the blanket (that is, the two fillets joined at the ventral side), the head, the collar (throat piece), two thin pieces skived off the fillets (to reduce their thickness), and the backbone. All of these can be dried. Optionally, most of them may be salted, and the head fermented. The eggs can also be dried or fermented.

These foods may appear as traditional Yup'ik items, such as a lunch of dried fish and seal oil, or may be incorporated into non-Native systems of cuisine. In many households they appear in both ways. According to Arvin Dull:

> [There are] many different ways that we prepare our salmon. Of course we make our salmon strips, dry fish, *egamaarrluk*, that's the half-dried [salmon] and then we freeze it. And then we could eat them at any time, just boil them, and have them with seal oil and onions. We even make kippered salmon. We pressure-cook salmon, so we could make like tuna salads and tuna salad sandwiches, and things like that, and we

put a lot of that away, we even salt salmon in slabs *(sulunaq)* and so during the winter we could have pickled salmon. . . .

And another way we prepare that is to just take a slab out and soak a lot of the salt out, to where it's just a little salty, and then you could bake it or fry it, or do what you want with it. (transcript of an interview, June 24, 1991)

This same trend of gastronomic adaptation is apparent to varying degrees in non-Native households as well.

Hosting requires feeding guests, and commonly they will be fed with whatever is locally in season (not strawberries but loche liver and cranberry *akutaq*) and sent home with a gift of food as well. This is true even if the guest is harvesting the identical resource. To perceive this as sending "coals to Newcastle" is to confuse the actual gift with the function of the gift. My wife and I recognized early in our village stay that we were unable either to host or gift people properly, since we lacked the proper foods. While a Yup'ik-style beef soup was always graciously appreciated, it was still ersatz, like instant coffee compared to the real thing. The same Yup'ik guest who was very pleased to take home some leftover cake was thrilled to take home some frozen whitefish. The cake is nice, but the whitefish is redolent with memory, of home and child-hood meals, of *Slaaviq* (Russian Orthodox Christmas) feasts and first-catch parties. It has the potential to bridge the past and present.

Subsistence practices also connect areas of peoples' lives that are often separate in Euro-American culture. This is particularly true in what might be called "recreation." Few adult Yupiit have hobbies as such,[11] any more than they take vacations or exercise. All these categories seem to have arisen after the industrial revolution and are most strongly marked in their comparison with work: they are what work is not. While practicing a hobby or sport, one is usually in control, unpaid, and doing the activity for inherent pleasure. Vacations are periods away from work; exercise is a kind of self-propelled unpaid physical labor. For older Yup'ik men, at least, the questions "What do you do for fun?" and "What do you do for work?" generally receive the same answer: "Hunting and fishing." For many younger men, basketball is also a major interest, in which participants replay the intervillage rivalries of traditional ceremonies in a new arena. Dog mushing, now primarily dog-team racing, has sportslike aspects for some people. There is some evidence that at least a few Yupiit recognize this distinction and classify these dog teams as sport teams. For example, I have been told that some Yup'ik women on the lower Yukon River are making their husbands and sons responsible for the processing of fish to be used as dog food. These women justify this departure from traditional roles because the dogs are not used (primarily) for subsistence but for fun.

As mentioned in chapter 1, much of the ceremonial cycle of feasts and celebrations was directly linked with various subsistence activities. These traditional ceremonies have been almost totally suppressed. Mather (1985, summarized in Morrow 1984) has explored the incorporation of traditional beliefs into Christianity: for example, the Christian concept of saying grace, of thanking God for one's food, parallels the Yup'ik concept of being grateful to the animals and to *ella* (variously translated as world, outdoors, weather, universe, awareness, sense) (Jacobson 1984:140). Non-conflicting beliefs were and are added to the Yup'ik belief system: For example, fast days or meatless days do not contradict traditional beliefs and are somewhat analogous to traditional food restrictions. Conflicting beliefs have been and are suppressed, although sometimes this process has been a slow one, for example the ban on hunting on Sunday. This conflicts directly with the Yup'ik belief that if an animal appears, it is giving itself to you and you risk bringing bad luck upon yourself and the community by not taking it (see also Fienup-Riordan 1991).

There are a number of ways in which the power of subsistence as a system is strengthened through its connection with tradition. First, there are the Yup'ik names for geographical features. Often these names are both descriptive and transparent to speakers, for example, *Nanvarpak* (big lake). However, names are often descriptive of the subsistence focus of that place, as in *Cuukvagtelek*[12] (place where pike are plentiful), *Tuntutuliaq*, "Tuntutuliak" (place of many reindeer) and *Curarpalek*, "Chuathbaluk" (place with huckleberries, literally, place with big blueberries). Naming both codifies the landscape and links particular places with activities and accumulated knowledge.

The omnipresence of subsistence activities in traditional stories provides another connection between past and contemporary subsistence.[13] It is useful to compare the themes in traditional Yup'ik stories with commonly known Euro-American stories deriving from a combination of written and oral traditions. The most obvious conclusion is that there is a much more confusing variety of stories from the different cultures and time periods that make up a typical Euro-American corpus. Aesop's *Fables* and the *Labors of Hercules* rub shoulders with Paul Bunyan and Pippi Longstocking. Yup'ik stories, on the other hand, both reflect a more uniform cultural setting and support that setting with less ambiguity. In the same way that the Grimms' collection of German märchen lauds obtaining wealth as the goal for males, and is the point at which a story can end, one class of Yup'ik stories, about orphans, often concludes with the orphan becoming a *nukalpiaq* (great hunter). As with the younger son who becomes rich, the rest of the story is predictable. Barring ill fortune, the hero will be well respected and happy, and live the good life.

However, for Euro-American children, even the nonmagic elements in such stories are removed from their tangible experience: woodcutters and shepherds, sword fighting and castles. For Yup'ik children, though there have been changes in techniques, many of the practices occurring in the tales, particularly the fundamental practices and ideology of subsistence, remain extant.

A final connection with tradition is the link between success in subsistence activities and rightness and health. One Yup'ik woman interviewed said that there had been a period when her family was eating a large percentage of store-bought food. This was a period when her parents were drinking heavily. Now her parents are doing much more subsistence and drinking much less. She explicitly connected doing subsistence and not drinking, and drinking and not doing subsistence: "With drinking you just don't have the energy to do subsistence. And when you are doing a lot of subsistence, you feel really special. They have even been going away on overnight trips to other areas with another couple their age" (notes from an interview, July 1991).

SUBSISTENCE PRACTICES IN BETHEL

The range of subsistence practices in Bethel is complicated indeed, particularly if one tries to make generalizations in order to correlate practices with particular categories of people. It may be useful to begin with a general outline of the situation, examining high-, moderate- and low-subsistence users.

At the high-use end, subsistence is a major commitment in terms of time, money, and energy, and it is also a major food source. There are actually two types of usage in this category. The first type includes those whose use parallels that of Yupiit in surrounding villages, both in terms of varieties of resources used and in terms of processing techniques used (half-drying, drying, salting, freezing, aging, preserving in oil). This might be called the "Village" model. The second type includes those whose subsistence activities focus heavily on big game (particularly moose and caribou), who harvest a somewhat reduced variety of resources, and who rely heavily on freezing for preservation and storage. This might be called the "Big Game" model. The problem arises when one tries to categorize either users or households ethnically based on their practices (see Fall 1990, for a discussion of ethnic differences in subsistence usage patterns in Dillingham, Alaska). At the crudest level of generalization, most Yupiit in Bethel tend toward the "Village" end of the continuum, and some of the non-Natives toward the "Big Game" end.[14] However, there are some non-Natives who follow the "Village" model, as well as many whose use falls somewhere between these two poles. There are also Yupiit whose focus is more toward upriver villages, where the traditional diet is based considerably more on large-mammal hunting. In addition, there are many long-term Bethel residents of mixed Native and non-Native ancestry, and their use seems to cover the entire continuum, as well as the situation mentioned by Janet Shantz and Bev Hoffman above, where use changes through time.

At the low-use end, the situation is just the reverse of the high-use end. Users either focus on a very limited number of resources or are sporadic in their usage. Even for people who focus on only a few or a single resource(s), harvesting techniques are usually the standard ones: techniques are limited by law and practicality. Processing and storage techniques are likely to be simplified, or more capital intensive, such as freezing or canning/jarring versus drying or aging. Most such users would identify themselves as non-Native. However, there are some people of mixed background whose use is rather limited as well.

Moderate users are even more difficult to categorize. This group includes many newcomers to Bethel—both Yup'ik and non-Native—whose use is increasing, and longer-term residents whose use is more stable.

There appear to be three different ideological systems by which subsistence users in Bethel classify their actions. These are the contemporary manifestations of traditional Yup'ik beliefs, traditional Euro-American rural subsistence ("pothunting"), and aristocratic hunting as a status marker ("status hunting").

CONTEMPORARY YUP'IK IDEOLOGIES ABOUT HUNTING AND FISHING

The traditional conceptual system—where humans are thought to be part of a sentient world that includes animals and fish—still guides the behavior of most Yupiit. People behave with an awareness that human thoughts, words, and actions powerfully affect interactions with animals and the natural world. Because of these beliefs, it is important to speak and act respectfully toward animals. This includes not bragging about past success or foretelling future success, in addition to killing quickly wherever possible. Subsistence foods should be protected from spoilage, shared, and never wasted. Inedible parts should be disposed of properly.

Hunting and fishing gear should be kept clean [15] and in good condition, if possible. Many people may not state that animals and fish will "choose" the hunter or his gear for this reason, but the underlying belief is widely reflected in traditional stories and elders' narratives. John Active, a Yup'ik man who works at KYUK, the Public Broadcasting radio and television station in Bethel, summarized contemporary beliefs in response to possible restrictive subsistence regulations.

> Even though my ancestors were much more attuned to nature than we modern Yup'iks, we still have an inner sanctum of understanding, albeit subconscious, of nature's laws. Her laws are our laws, and because of this we practice conservation, taking only what we need.
>
> Our closeness to nature is religious. We call it spirituality. We believe everything has a spirit. The animals, birds and plants have an awareness, and we treat them with the same respect we have for ourselves.
>
> The non-Natives refer to these animals as "game." Hunting for them is a game. We do not play games with animals.
>
> When we bring animals into our homes, we treat them as guests. We give them a little drink of water because we think their spirits might be thirsty.
>
> We pray to our fish and animals. We tell them we caught them because we need them to survive and we will eat them with care.
>
> We thank them for having been caught and believe their spirits will return to their gods and report about how they are cared for. If the animals have been treated well, then these same gods will provide more of the same.
>
> If the animals are not treated well, then these gods will tell them to be scarce for the hunter, and the family of the hunter suffers. . . .
>
> Our ancestors didn't learn this from your book [the Bible]; they learned it from real life, because it is true.
>
> I write this with joy in my heart. I am doing my small part for Alaska's Yup'ik humanity.
>
> As long as I remember this truth, my people's spirituality shall not die, my people will not die, I shall not die. (1992:B9)

NON-NATIVE IDEOLOGIES ABOUT
HUNTING AND FISHING

There are two separate but partially overlapping strands of non-Native ideology about hunting and fishing: pothunting and status hunting.[16] From the time of early colonization onward, rural dwellers have sought to subdue and control nature, and they looked upon wild fish and game as important resources for consumption or for sale on the market. Such resources have often been vital in times of crop failure or other disaster. Hunting for consumption—what I have called "pothunting"— has continued, at least until recently. Several people who lived in eastern Washington and Idaho have told me that they lived mostly on deer and jackrabbits during the Great Depression. Market hunting and trapping for meat, hides, pelts, and plumes was and is a continuation of this prac- tice. One important image for white Alaskans is that of the self-sufficient woodsman, the Daniel Boone or Davy Crockett of the North, living off the land.

A later trend, appearing after the Civil War, is modeled on British aristocratic practice. Prior to this period, hunting and fishing were either strictly utilitarian ways of putting meat on the table or, if pursued too avidly, likely to be seen as a character flaw similar to an addiction to horse racing or public drunkenness (Reiger 1986:25). However, the post– Civil War period was a time when there was tremendous social mobility, and it was very difficult to tell "new money" from "old money." In this climate, " 'correct' hunting and fishing increasingly became a chief means of distinguishing the 'gentlemen' in a post–Civil War America best known for its Philistinism and commercialism" (26). This new meaning was avowedly at odds with older utilitarian uses of wild resources. Speaking of Henry William Herbert, a British aristocrat who immigrated to America in 1831, a friend once said, "Like all true sportsmen, while fond of following the game in season with gun, dog and rod, he was a bitter and unrelenting enemy of all poachers and pot-hunters" (26).

Here the dichotomy between sportsmen—for whom hunting and fishing are avowedly noneconomic status markers—and all others, for whom its economic aspects are paramount, is clearly enunciated. In America, this originally British aristocratic view was increasingly prom- ulgated in a variety of new magazines, such as *American Sportsmen*, founded in 1871, *Forest and Stream* (1873), *Field and Stream* (1874), and the *American Angler* (1881). For approximately 120 years, there has been such an effort to convince Americans to reconceptualize hunting and fishing that knowledge, approach, and presentation have become more important than actually catching something and taking it home to eat.

> It is not the mere killing of numbers, much less in the mere killing at all; it is not in the value of the things killed . . . it is not the inevitable certainty of success—for certainty destroys the excitement, which is the soul of sport, but it is the vigor, science [correct technique], and manhood displayed—in the difficulties to be overcome, in the pleasurable anxiety for success, and the uncertainty of it, and lastly in the true spirit, the style, the dash, the handsome way of doing what is to be done, and above all, in the unalterable *love of fair play*, that first thought of a genuine sportsman, that true sportsmanship consists. (William F. Parker, *American Sportsmen*, November 1872; quoted in Reiger 1986:28–29)

Contemporary "catch-and-release" fishing (where fish are first caught, and then let go) and "fair chase" hunting, where hunters forswear many efficient techniques, are direct outgrowths of this movement, as are many, if not most, contemporary game regulations. Hence the "unsporting" use of traps, snares, nets, bait, live decoys, and airplanes is lumped together and outlawed.

In Alaska, such regulations set aside specific areas where only moose with antlers having a thirty-six-inch (or greater) spread may be taken, as well as some "dual use" areas. In these areas only relatively small or trophy moose can be taken, accommodating pothunters who will presumably shoot either type but are statistically more likely to kill the more numerous and less experienced small moose. It also accommodates status hunters, those who are after a mountable trophy, by assuring that some moose reach their maximum potential size (Alaska State Hunting Regulations July 1, 1991 to June 30, 1992). State and federal game regulations also clearly favor sports hunters, who hunt one or a few species, over subsistence hunters, who harvest a large variety of fish and game.

It was estimated that subsistence hunters in the Kotzebue area would need up to thirty different licenses and permits to carry out their traditional subsistence activities legally. Many of these forms are available only by mail and may take weeks to acquire. Not only are they issued by several different agencies but they also expire at different times. Further, regulations are couched in highly implicit jargon, with terms such as "bag limits" (of the household, the extended family, or the hunter?), "possession" (who is the possessor of game shared in the field?), and "processing location" (some parts may be eaten in the field, others not processed until after they have been shared in the village). Such usages reflect non-Native, rather than Native, realities (Shaeffer et al. 1986). One non-Native sportsman in Bethel gave clear statements supporting these state-promulgated values of fair chase:

> To me, it [catch-and-release rainbow trout fishing] is much more important than any of the other uses except moose hunting. Of importance, I'd have to say that moose hunting would be first, rainbow- and basic freshwater-trout fishing would be second, and fox [trapping] would have to go third. . . .
>
> Yeah, I do catch some chum salmon, once I did catch a king salmon. I used to go down to Quinhagak and catch king salmon, strictly catch and release on all the salmon. (transcript of an interview, July 1991)

Two other significant aspects of status hunting are the focus on trophies and the disposal of game. To some extent, the importance of game as trophy is widespread throughout Euro-American culture, though now somewhat muted by the environmental movement. Since hunting is a "contest" with nature, trophies show that the hunter "won" the "game" (in both senses): the trophy validates the victory.[17] At a meeting of the Alaska Board of Game in Anchorage, March 1, 1992, board member Don Hanks, a non-Native, described his perception of taking a trophy as securing "bragging rights" to that animal. He attempted to generalize this to all cultures in Alaska, citing potlatches and "first catch" celebrations, but he received no support from Native board and audience members (Mary Pete, personal communication, April 5, 1992).

It seems clear—based on convictions for not salvaging all usable portions of an animal as defined under "Wanton Waste" laws—that many trophy hunters are relatively uninterested in the meat. Viewed symbolically, this makes perfect sense. How better to show that one is status hunting, rather than pothunting, than by not eating the game? It is a kind of conspicuous nonconsumption, akin to breaking coppers at a potlatch. One non-Native fisherman in Bethel gave the following description of his fishing:

> Then, once June rolls around, and the river's dropped, then I start using them [the rivers] for recreational purposes, mainly camping and fishing. My fishing is mostly catch and release. Last year I probably caught three or four hundred rainbows [trout], and I think I brought five or six of them home. I probably ate a couple of dozen while I was up there. Most of what I catch goes back into the river, unless it's going to die anyway. Quite often by the end of the trip I've got, you know,

a dozen or so fish that are dead, and so I'll stop in Kwethluk or whatever and drop them off, [SOFTER] to the old folks. And that goes all through summer. (transcript continued)

FISH AND GAME STOCKS TO SUPPORT FUTURE SUBSISTENCE IN BETHEL

Subsistence will continue to be of vital importance in Bethel for the foreseeable future, barring either massive resource depletion/destruction or regulatory exclusion. I would hope that local anadromous fish stocks remain strong, although they are at risk from several possible sources. There has been a history of high-seas piracy of salmon by Japanese, Taiwanese, and Korean longline and gill-net fleets, but this appears to be coming to an end. Almost equally out of local control, and as potentially damaging, is an intercept fishery in the False Pass region of Alaska, which catches large numbers of Kuskokwim-bound chum salmon while targeting Bristol Bay red salmon. In terms of other threats to salmon stocks, habitat loss has been minimal so far. Rising levels of high-seas pollution pose a significant long-term threat, as do spills from possible offshore drilling in Bristol Bay and elsewhere in the Bering Sea. Currently, however, with the exception of chum salmon, salmon stocks are generally healthy.

As far as small-game stocks go, snowshoe hare populations vary cyclically, as does the beaver population, according to local Yupiit. Muskrats are also subject to abrupt population changes. All three are in no danger of being hunted or trapped out, particularly with the current low fur prices, and the same is true for other small game. Goose and duck populations have been in decline but seem to be rebounding. Sea-mammal populations are generally good, with the exception of Stellar's sea lion, whose population has declined precipitously in the early 1990s.

Large land-game populations seem to be holding steady over the long term, with caribou populations in the Kilbuck Mountains on the increase. Conflict between user groups over large land mammals is likely to increase over time.

Future Subsistence in Bethel

The major variable, in terms of subsistence usages, is whether people will choose to continue to hunt, fish, and gather. My sense is that people will continue to do so. In twenty years the population of Bethel is likely to be made up of three groups: current residents, descendants of current residents, and new immigrants from inside and outside the region. Assuming that the fish, game, and flora are still available and harvestable, I would predict that the current residents will be harvesting at roughly current levels, subject to changes in personal health. As I mentioned in chapter 1, there is at least one trend toward a lower reliance on subsistence-caught foods. This is particularly visible in the diets of younger people. On the other hand, the countertrend, noted earlier by Janet Shantz, is that some people want their children to have the experiences they themselves had; their harvesting increases as a result. It is possible that for at least some people, a decreased reliance on subsistence foods may be a stage that they undergo as adolescents in order to distance themselves from their home culture. This home culture, either Yup'ik or pothunting non-Native, is often devalued in other important settings, such as school and the media.

I assume that new migrants from villages will bring their subsistence practices and food preferences with them and will continue to be subsistence focused. Further, I assume that new migrants from the continental United States will continue to be drawn to Alaska and to Bethel at least in part because of opportunities to hunt and fish. Consequently they will continue to adopt local subsistence practices, both because of their suitability to the local ecosystem and because of the symbolic allegiances portrayed through these practices. Bethel and the region seem to attract considerably more pothunters than status hunters. Some possible reasons for this are that there are few other aristocrats to impress; some aspects of status hunting are antithetical to local practice and ideology; and there is a strong egalitarian ethic in both the Yup'ik and non-Native community.

REGULATING SUBSISTENCE

As far as regulatory exclusion is concerned, the future of subsistence law in Alaska is unclear. Proposals and counterproposals are aired in the media, and the outcome is uncertain, except that whatever happens will almost certainly be challenged in court. It seems probable, however, that any attempt to disenfranchise a large segment of the population, or to curtail current subsistence activities, will result in widespread civil disobedience. As mentioned above, one older Yup'ik man I interviewed felt that something equivalent to the Barrow "Duck-in"[18] was almost inevitable if subsistence rights were curtailed.

Such regulatory exclusion is more likely to happen in regards to waterfowl and large game, than to small game, fish, or marine mammals.

Kuskokwim River salmon stocks are currently managed for subsistence needs first, followed by commercial uses, and finally for sportfishing. In the ten-year period between 1983 and 1994, there were an average of 67,000 king salmon caught for subsistence and 63,000 for commercial purposes; 35,000 red salmon for subsistence and 151,000 for commercial purposes; 95,000 chum salmon for subsistence and 547,000 for commercial purposes; and 33,000 silver salmon taken for subsistence and 607,000 for commercial purposes. Since subsistence fish are subtracted first, before fish are allocated for the commercial fishery, it is clear that considerable increases in subsistence harvests could be made in all species except king salmon with relatively little impact on the commercial fishery. Over this ten-year period, the subsistence salmon fishery on the Kuskokwim River harvested 14 percent of the cumulative harvest (Anderson et al. 1994:22).

Subsistence, the Law, and Disciplinary Technologies

One recent trend in the delta has been a continuing increase in the regulation and enforcement of laws pertaining to human/animal interactions. Such enforcement is not new. There have been sporadic attempts to enforce the ban on spring waterfowl hunting since at least the 1950s. Several men have told me of personal or family incidents where guns and game were confiscated by U.S. Fish and Wildlife Service enforcement agents. Such attempts have, in the past, been met with a combination of resigned acceptance and civil disobedience. Stories are legion of shooting holes in the floats of U.S. Fish and Wildlife Service floatplanes so that they could not land and issue citations.[19] These stories are told in the vein of Robin Hood against the sheriff's men (with risks to all participants downplayed). Setting aside such sporadic resistance, the larger question is whether Yup'ik people are, in the long term, winning the battle but losing the war. At issue is whether, at the very time that cooperative management agreements such as the Hooper Bay Agreement are being made, such agreements provide a larger space for Yup'ik hunting and fishing practices or whether they bring such practices under regulatory control for the first time by the very agreement that allows them. Mere participation in this process brings Yupiit into tighter enmeshment with the system of regulation. Until recently, regulations regarding what is legally defined as subsistence have been largely ignored by most Yupiit. To some extent these laws are still ignored: Anchorage and Washington, D.C., seem very distant when one is out hunting or fishing. Away from Bethel, Yupiit have been able to treat such laws and regulations largely as if they pertained to some other system unrelated to them. One neither needed to know about such regulations nor cared about them.

Now, however, this very ability to be oblivious to the law is increasingly at stake. Control—that is, a system of disciplinary technologies—is being extended (Foucault 1979). The significance of this extension is that this system of control is designed to become internalized. This generally occurs at the point when the rules are recognized as rules by those involved, even if they are broken. A comparison may be made with the children's game played by the residents of Macondo, in Gabriel Garcia Marquez's novel *One Hundred Years of Solitude*, when they were suffering from insomnia and hoped to be bored to sleep. In the course of the game, the narrator would ask the audience members if they "wanted to hear the story about the capon" (1970:51). Once the narrator was chosen, the universe of the game was closed. Any answer—or, indeed, no answer—furthered the course of the game. If the members of the audience answered yes (or no), the narrator would reply that he had not asked them to say yes (or no) but simply whether they wanted to hear him tell the story about the capon. If they remained silent or started to leave, the narrator would say that he had not asked them to remain silent or to leave but simply "whether they wanted him to tell them the story about the capon, and so on and on in a vicious circle that lasted entire nights" (1970:52).

The connection of this game with systems of disciplinary control is that such systems do not require one's assent: laws and regulations apply equally to all and are not subject to individual ratification. After the narrator (or game manager) *announces* the rules of the game, all present are, by definition, playing the game regardless of whether specific individuals ignore, deny, or abide by the rules. Once the game exists, it is difficult either to initiate a different discourse or to disengage oneself from the game. Any answer, or even no answer, still serves as an opportunity to further this dialogue of control. This includes resistance: "Foucault holds that power needs resistance as one of its fundamental conditions of operation. It is through the articulation of points of resistance that power spreads through the social field" (Drefus and Rabinow 1982:147). Certainly resistance, often couched as civil disobedience, is frequently discussed when the future of subsistence is raised. Direct resistance (either covert or overt) to regulation is also common and is becoming increasingly politicized.

Yup'ik perceptions about this extension of control can be inferred from the referential terms and categories that people employ when referring to state or federal actions. In common conversation, almost all such distinctions are collapsed, and the bureaucratic "actor" is merely "the government," "the hospital," or "Fish and Game." It is often difficult, except on the basis of jurisdiction, to know whether, for example, the incidents of armed resistance previously mentioned involved U.S. Fish and Wildlife Service agents or Alaska Department of Fish and Game agents (potentially of several different divisions). The more politically interested and involved Yupiit are quite knowledgeable about differing state and federal agencies and subagencies, including the personalities involved. However, in general conversations, these distinctions are often ignored. Although bureaucrats typically see their particular job and agency as having a discrete, bounded, and specific identity, such that the Commercial Fish Division differs greatly from the Game Division, lo-cally they tend to be all lumped together. I would argue that this lump-ing together is at least partly a recognition of the inseparability of these systems of control, as well as a very complex type of strategic practice.

The larger question is whether Yupiit will continue to judge their actions by their own standards or whether (even if they continue illegal practices) they will come to accept Euro-American definitions, and thereby be defined by them. In Morrow and Hensel 1992 we noted the statement of one young Yup'ik man, who said that whenever endangered or out-of-season birds were within range, "I feel guilty if I shoot and I feel guilty if I don't shoot." The first action would violate Western law, the second Yup'ik morality.

I am uncertain as to the long-term outcome, even if the legal status of rural subsistence remains basically unchanged. As I will discuss in the following chapter, other aspects of a positive Yup'ik identity have been problematized for many younger people. I am unsure whether this lack of concern for Western regulation can be nurtured in the face of so many forces.

A parallel situation occurred almost one hundred years ago, in rural Maine, when status hunting by urban sportsmen on vacation became an economic force, and as part of the same process, market hunting was legislated out of existence. Even though there was widespread disobedi-ence of the law, with significant local support, eventually the law won. Older market hunters retired due to ill health and were not replaced. Even if these older market hunters wore the label "poacher" half in hu-mor, half in pride, their sons found some other way to make a living (Ives 1988).

John Active (of KYUK radio) described his worries about the spread of government control into the lives of Yupiit:

Yup'iks are spiritual by being aware and conscious of everything around us: animals, plants, and the environment. We are part of them and they are part of us. Laws which interfere with that fragile relationship are like cancers. They start by eating just a little of us but end by consuming us completely. (1992:B9)

3

Subsistence, Identity, and Meaning

CUTTING SALMON FOR DRYING AND SMOKING

My wife (Phyllis Morrow) and I have been asked by some friends to help them get started cutting king salmon strips. They have a one-half interest in a boat, and are going to give us a call when they have some fish. We've talked to them about the process, and they have made a small drying rack to which sides can be added when it's time to smoke the fish.

We arrive with ulus and a boning steel, bowls, some white plastic buckets, and extra twine. Our friends are actually quite well set up, except that they've forgotten to get salt. They have six kings to process. Phyllis starts cutting and demonstrating filleting while I return home for some salt and a washtub. When I get back she has filleted the first two and its cutting them into strips about an inch wide while one of our friends tries filleting a small king. She does an OK job, and the strips will probably dry without spoilage if the weather holds clear.

I make up some brine, then start tying the strips in pairs of about equal size. Getting the knots right is important so that the strips don't slip out and fall to the ground. The sun is shining, and it's hot and still. The mosquitos have certainly found us. We start brining the first bucketful, then go back to tying. We talk about the frustrations of working at the hospital, various friends we have in common, and how the fishing is. I hang up the strips and start brining the second batch, then cut out the cheeks (a scalloplike delicacy), and trim off the narrow piece of meat and skin left along the spine for hanging also.

In a little while Phyllis has filleted a couple more, and the husband tries the final one while the wife cuts strips. He does OK too, though he leaves some meat on the backbone, which he skives off afterwards to cook up. She does a better job cutting up a good-sized sockeye, which she proposes would make a great dinner. We accept.

After a brief wait it's time to hang up the second bucket and start brining the third. While we are waiting for them to brine, we clean up the table and fold up the cardboard cutting surfaces. The cheekless heads and virtually meatless backbones go to feed the team of a dog-mushing neighbor, as do the guts and milt sacks. Two of the fish were females, and we talk about recipes for red caviar. No portion of the fish is wasted, though a Yup'ik family would probably have prepared more for human consumption, and less as dog food. We hang up the third bucketful, then dump out the brine and close up the drying rack/ smokehouse.

INTRODUCTION

A cursory examination of what subsistence means to people in Bethel would conclude that not only does subsistence mean different things to different people but it also means different things to the same people at different times. To explain why this is so one must look at subsistence from a number of perspectives, and on a number of levels.

There are always multiple meanings attached to any action or utterance. A father and son checking their fishnet together may be validating their Native identity and maintaining age-old ties with the land. They may be procuring traditional food, as well as simply fetching dinner. The father may also be serving as a gender role model for the son, and strengthening family ties. They are getting fresh air and exercise, and maintaining their mental health in the process of exercising their legal rights to fish. They may be engaged in an act of saving money or one in which money is converted into goods not available for purchase. All these meanings (and still others) occur repeatedly in discussions about subsistence, particularly in the present political climate. The meanings are inherent in any subsistence act.

Against this background of a multiplicity of overlapping meanings, two main factors determine which meanings are emphasized or validated in an interaction or event: context and strategy. Like any other pervasive form of practice, the meaning of subsistence is highly context-dependent. This is most obvious in conversation, where meaning is always subject to ongoing negotiation. By this I mean that in any negotiated and ongoing conversational setting, the entire summation of subsistence meanings is too great to be brought into the interchange, or perhaps even to discursive consciousness (Giddens 1979:5). Instead, most or almost all of the meanings are assumed to be understood between conversational partners, and attention is focused on some (usually small) aspect or activity that is being disputed, clarified, or examined. In a sense, it is like a variation of the story of the blind men and the elephant, with, in this case, the interlocutors being merely nearsighted. Each person can see much of the elephant, albeit dimly and myopically, but is choosing to focus on the leg, trunk, or tail, defending this pillarlike, snakelike or ropelike feature as seminal, diagnostic, or primary about the elephant. Although with subsistence the metaphoric elephant may actually be too large for even the clear-sighted to see in its entirety, conversations and debates still often have this character.

This dependence on context is not limited to conversation; it applies to practice as well. This is true spatially, where a subsistence technique, say the use of fish wheels, may be legal in one drainage but not another. It is also true temporally, where gillnetting changes in definition from "subsistence fishing" to "fishing in closed waters" a certain number of hours prior to a commercial fishing period. At a set number of hours before the commercial fishing period begins, all subsistence nets must be removed from the water. Any nets remaining in the water are no longer subsistence nets; they are now illegal commercial nets, and will be until a certain number of hours after the commercial fishing period, when they will become subsistence nets again (if they have not been removed by Fish and Wildlife Protection). What changes is the legal meaning of the practice, not the practice itself.

Another factor that makes it more difficult to analyze what subsistence means in any given act or conversation is the fact that there is usually a simultaneous subtext of one or more metalevel meanings included as well. As a source of symbolic as well as metaphoric power, subsistence is eminently amenable to strategization; it can be used for saying things; for example, to make statements not only about ethnicity but also about my Yup'ik-ness as opposed to yours. Thus an additional challenge is to determine in what way a given subsistence practice or conversation is used strategically, and to what end. Because these two levels occur simultaneously (and the meta-level can always be denied if queried), it is very difficult to separate them, or tease out what one is without the other. This strategic component is even more difficult to apprehend cross-culturally, since in Euro-American society these meta-messages are usually stated much more explicitly than in Yup'ik society (see Morrow 1990).

CREATING AND MAINTAINING IDENTITY

A major contemporary issue in anthropology is how people create and maintain a sense of personal and cultural identity. Whereas in the past anthropology often sought out and privileged situations of stability in isolated settings, contemporary anthropology seeks to unravel and understand the currents and countercurrents of change in multicultural settings. In such settings individuals are faced with a range of choices as to how and who to be. Each choice, however, closes some opportunities as surely as it opens others. None are free of costs.

Euro-American notions of ethnicity generally accept ethnicity as biologically determined at birth. There is a homology between ancestry and culture. Ethnicity is not an achieved category. However, at least in Bethel, and I would argue elsewhere as well, ethnicity is neither that simple nor clear-cut. The dichotomies (white/other, Native/non-Native) are unsatisfactory on two levels.

First, there is considerable leakage between categories, both permanent and temporary. In certain settings, individuals may "pass" as either real or fictive members of the other group.[1] Successful "passing" carries its own risks as well as rewards. The reward is the ability to appropriate unequally distributed cultural capital, such as knowledge, status, wealth, opportunity, but also kinship ties and gender roles. The costs are possible rejection by members of one's own group, as well as (possibly) increased stress inherent in such a bicultural balancing act (Goffman 1963).[2]

Second, and more importantly, this dichotomous notion of ethnicity overlooks an issue that is of intense local interest: how a person fits into his/her category.[3] The question is not "Is she white?" but "How white is she?" In other words, where is she along an overlapping continuum of possibilities?

This sense of ethnicity as achieved rather than ascribed is an old one in Bethel. There has been a long history of intermarriage. Until the 1950s, there were separate school systems for Native and non-Native children. However, any child with a non-Native parent was classified as non-Native (for this purpose) and attended the state-supported school; Yup'ik children attended the Bureau of Indian Affairs school. There seems to have been a great degree of freedom for people of bicultural background to choose their ethnicity, particularly if there had been intermarriage in previous generations as well. Ethnicity was not and is not judged on the basis of genetic heritage but on the basis of practice. It was and is validated through practices and interactions that symbolically situate one as a certain kind of person on a continuum, recognizing that such placement is always context-dependent. That is, people are likely to show themselves differently in different situations, for strategic purposes.

Traditional Yup'ik views of categorization are likely to have contributed to this flexibility. Traditionally, Yupiit have seen categories as inherently flexible and indeterminate. There has been more focus on the content and less on the definitional character of a category. Previous ethnographers of Yupiit have often struggled to define a category, when the items categorized seem contradictory (to the ethnographers). For example, some narrators describe members of a particular category of supernatural beings as small, others as large. Some narrators describe them as humanlike, others as animallike. Yupiit do not seem to be bothered by this, although the ethnographers are. Yupiit accept that this is the way that a person heard the story or experienced the incident. Others may have heard or experienced something else. What is important is giving a true telling, rather than trying to tailor reality to fit neatly into a particular taxonomy (argument from Morrow 1990). I suggest that this approach to understanding the world has reinforced local attention on enactment rather than on categorization.

The significance of this question to ethnicity theory is that "fitting in" is based on performance, and that subsistence activities and subsistence discourse are primary stages upon which such identities are enacted.

This focus differs from previous ones. In an important early work, Barth (1969a) argues that identity is the ability to make a successful claim to be judged by certain agreed-upon standards and criteria, "since belonging to an ethnic category implies being a certain kind of person, having that basic identity, it also implies a claim to be judged, and to judge oneself, by those standards that are relevant to that identity" (14). However, such a definition is useful only in an idealized, dichotomized world. In actuality, as Barth himself portrays in his Pathan/Baluch data (1969b), identities are always situated in some social field. The criteria upon which such claims rest are extremely vague and difficult to specify, except in past and present practice. In a counterview, Anthony Cohen holds that the criteria most often used are in fact the ongoing performances of everyday life that occur "most frequently in the context of rather mundane circumstances: how to evaluate your neighbor's work in making a wheelbarrow; where, and in which tidal conditions, to fish for particular species; when to cut hay; how to tell a yarn" (1982:5). Furthermore, Cohen perceives the symbolic construction and portrayal of identity as occurring not, or at least not exclusively, in vast symbol-laden events—betrothal and marriages, funerals and religious rites—but in the management of everyday life. I would add that locally situated language is an important part of that management, specifically the knowledge needed for the correct application of contextualization cues and co-occurrence. There is an American slang aphorism that highlights practice over discourse: "If you're gonna talk that talk, you gotta walk that walk." The reverse is also true: it does no good to be able to "walk that walk" if one cannot "talk that talk."

One feature of this approach is that it highlights participation. One learns one's culture's/subgroup's habitus interactively through having been "confronted with the situations most frequent for members of that class" (Bourdieu 1977:89). Future practice is guided by previous interaction. Drawing on the work of Bateson and others (Bateson et al. 1956, Auerswald 1968, Hoffman 1981), but restricting the focus to issues of cultural identity, it seems plausible to think of such identities as both validated by early experience and changeable through later interaction and participation. It is through interaction that individuals become bicultural as well as bilingual. Goffman (1959, 1974), Garfinkel (1967), and Heritage (1984) have shown the tremendous work involved in maintaining interactions, as well as the kind of continuous feedback involved. One requirement of maintaining successful interactions is that participants share sufficient discourse-level knowledge of linguistic and contextualization conventions. When these conventions are shared, participants constantly make use of such locally embedded and understood references to mark local knowledge implicitly and explicitly.

These references to local knowledge are also important in the maintenance of image or "face" (in Goffman's terms), that is, of portraying what kind of person one is. Interactions offer an opportunity, at least partially, to "see ourselves as others see us," by how they react to and interact with us. If the image we hold of ourselves is vastly different from that held by others, the interaction will be subject to breakdown.[4] In this sense, interactions are at least grossly self-correcting for most people. Within a cultural group, successful and unsuccessful interactions guide future practice and future interactions. I will argue that the same occurs cross-culturally as well, with more possibilities for misinterpretation. Furthermore, it is in such interactions that we learn how we ourselves are stereotyped. One's image of one's self is at risk in cross-cultural interactions, where the potential exists for learning to see ourselves in the limited and possibly negative ways that others may see us. This process of internalizing an image of one's group held by others has been, and continues to be, very damaging to the mental health and concepts of self of Native Americans and other minority groups.

Ogbu has used a tri-part schema to classify minority groups: autonomous, caste (pariah), and immigrant minorities (1978:22). This schema has significant explanatory power in elucidating issues of race, occupation, and class in America. It locates the ultimate causes of school "success" or "failure" for members of various minority groups not in the individual but in the larger system: that is, it avoids victim blaming. However, Ogbu's level of generalization makes this schema less useful for many Native Americans and especially for Yupiit. Ogbu contends that the crucial factor is whether an individual derives his or her self-image from the minority- or majority-culture viewpoint. However, in the Yup'ik case, there is an appreciable difference between younger and older people in terms of where they derive this image. Under Ogbu's terms, Yup'ik elders appear to be members of an immigrant minority, while many young Yupiit appear more like a caste minority. The elders reference the world and their role in it against their Yup'ik view of things, and are relatively less affected by the majority culture's view of them and their world. On the other hand, the younger people have, to various degrees, internalized the majority culture view of themselves. For these middle-aged and younger people the self-definitional issues of how and who to be are the most intense and problematic, precisely because the whole area is open to constant reinterpretation and negotiation. At issue is what it means to be Yup'ik, who is included in that definition, and who is able to decide (see Morrow and Hensel 1992). These issues must be understood not only in terms of culture but also in terms of hegemonic power and political economy.

BOUNDARIES AND BOUNDARY MARKING

Anthony Cohen describes the complex interplay of boundary and stereotype, "inside" and "outside":

> The boundary represents the mask presented by the community to the outside world; it is the community's public face. But the conceptualization and symbolism of the boundary from within is much more complex. To put this another way, the boundary as the community's public face is symbolically simple; but, as the object of internal discourse, it is symbolically complex. . . . In its "public" face, internal variety dis-

appears or coalesces into a simple symbolic statement. In its "private" mode, differentiation and variety proliferate, and generate a complex symbolic statement. (1986:13)

Prior to grappling with the complexities Cohen so eloquently describes, some background may be useful. Much of the contemporary anthropological theorizing is descended from the work of Fredrik Barth 1969a. In this work, Barth closely examines what ethnicity consists of and how it is maintained and/or changed. He states "Categorical ethnic distinctions do not depend on an absence of mobility, contact and information, but do entail social processes of exclusion and incorporation whereby discrete categories are maintained *despite* changing participation and membership in the course of individual life histories" (9, emphasis in the original). Elsewhere he notes:

> I have heard members of the Baluch tribal sections explain that they are "really Pathan." What is left of the boundary maintenance and the categorical dichotomy, when the actual distinctions are blurred in this way? Rather than despair at the failure of typological schematism, one can legitimately note that people *do* employ ethnic labels. . . . (29, emphasis in the original)

He goes on to suggest that, in the general case, membership is (at least) somewhat fluid, and as such subject to change for strategic purposes. The Pathans who became Baluchs did so for strategic (economic and political) reasons, because it represented the best option for them within that context. What is interesting is that although the categories (Pathan/Baluch) are invoked as dichotomous, they are not enacted as dichotomous. The Pathans who became Baluchs remained free to claim (to Barth) that they were actually still Pathans when that was strategically useful. Though ethnic labels allow inclusion and exclusion, what label is used, by whom, and to whom, is a matter of strategy, limited but not determined by ascription.

The issue of how to talk simultaneously about boundaries as indeterminate, and yet still talk of discrete groups, troubled Barth as well. At one point he says that a boundary occurs where there is "a recognition of limitations on shared understandings, differences in criteria for judgment of value and performance, and a restriction of interaction to sectors of assumed common understanding and mutual interest" (1969a:15). I suggest that there are actually two different boundaries here. One is the situation where those interacting share many or most interactional conventions, but "agree" in the co-constructing of the interaction to see each other as "different," as, for example, Pathans who became Baluchs interacting with Pathans. The "former" Pathans would theoretically have no problems in communciating with Pathans, but are making a claim to be judged by other (Baluch) standards. The other type of boundary situation occurs where there is a change in the Schutzian typification that sustain interactions, the point where coparticipants are unable to communicate fully.

Broadly speaking, this boundary occurs where there is a shift in contextualization conventions (Gumperz 1992; discussed further in chapter 7). These may include differences in foregrounding and backgrounding (Scollon and Scollon 1982), preferences for explicitness versus implicitness (Morrow 1990), ideology and worldview (Morrow and Hensel 1992), as well as the more obvious mismatches of language, dialect, and register (Gumperz 1982a). Some or all of these factors contributing to communicative breakdown may be occurring simultaneously.

In conversations within interactional communities (which by definition share communicative conventions), breakdowns and repairs of communication occur constantly. At an interactional boundary, however, breakdowns become increasingly less repairable. Often, attempts at repair only worsen the miscommunication. Frequently, the most intransigent situations of miscommunication are those in which participants share a language but use differing contextualization conventions (Gumperz 1982a, 1992). In such situations participants often appear to be oblivious to the fact that they "mean" different things, and that later noncompliance is not the result of treachery or ill will (Gumperz 1982a, Morrow and Hensel 1992).

If we think of all of the above as conversational conventions, the boundary marks not the line of noninteraction but the (generally broad) area where such conventions change. In many situations, the boundary also marks a change in identity, where one ceases to have one's identity as an individual acknowledged by those on the other side. The individual begins to be seen as a member of a group and as exemplifying the traits associated with that group. Beyond the boundary, it is more difficult to interact as a full human being, rather than as some sort of caricature or stereotype judged by others.

There are a number of social practices that serve to keep such communicative boundaries broad, diffuse, and permeable. Even if extremely constrained, there is always interaction and often transfer of personnel across categories (Barth 1969a). Further, many individuals have at least partially internalized more than one set of contextualization conventions, although Gumperz and others have argued that nonsemantic conventions such as intonation and presentation styles are less amenable to change than semantic ones (Gumperz 1982a, Jupp et al. 1982). They argue that this is at least in part a matter of insufficient interactional exposure to new patterns. For example, they suggest that proper conventions for peer interactions can be learned only through peer interaction. If peer interactions with native English speakers are rare, such conventions are difficult to learn.

This is, in fact, the most common situation for foreign immigrants. Most foreign immigrants are drawn to immigrant communities and buffer themselves from their host culture. Their interactions with members of that host culture are often restricted to brief interchanges in instrumental and interactionally limited situations, such as placing orders in shops or receiving orders from a supervisor. Many immigrants are only infrequently exposed to extended peer interactions with members of the host culture. This can have important ramifications, both for individual immigrants and for society at large. For example, in Euro-American culture, some hierarchical situations such as job interviews may be treated as fictive peer interactions. An insufficient command of such conventions often handicaps immigrants, leading to communicative breakdowns in gate-keeping situations. Such breakdowns often play an invisible but decisive role in decision making, determining who, for example, is seen as collegial and thus is hired; that is, who becomes a colleague.

These conventions often persist even when the languages spoken change. There are some situations, such as those in which English has replaced Native languages in rural Alaska, where the same speech communities have continued to exist, albeit relexified. People interact in a new language primarily with the same people or the children of the same people with whom they interacted in the old language. Typically, there have been gradual changes, but fundamentally there is continuity in social and economic interactions, and in ideology and worldview. Preexisting relationships have continued. Generally, there is very little effective modeling of different conventions. In these contexts, people have changed their language and changed English in the process by adapting and tailoring English to serve (most of) the functions of the Native language, but without changing many other contextualization conventions (Kwachka 1990, Gumperz and Cook-Gumperz 1982:3). In such situations, sharing grammatical structures and lexical items often turns out to be insufficient for effective communication.

BOUNDARIES, STEREOTYPES, AND PRACTICE

Another aspect of the interactional constitution of boundaries is the issue of how and why certain traits become constituted as boundary markers. In a larger sense, researchers (Hewitt 1986, Nadel 1984, Schneider and Weiner 1989, Hobsbawm and Ranger 1983) have demonstrated that almost anything *can* be used as a group boundary marker, including age, language, dialect, accent, pigmentation, religion, ethnicity, class, clothing, music preference, drinking style, political affiliation, occupation, residence, and length of residence. Any of these features is capable of being made to stand for something larger, more inclusive, and more important, the difference between "us" and "them." Almost the only absolute requirement is that some aspects of a feature be minimally contrastive. Dichotomies are almost always carved from a continuum:

> Since boundaries are inherently oppositional, almost any matter of perceived difference between a community and the outside world can be rendered symbolically as a resource of its boundary. Members of a community can make virtually anything grist to the symbolic mill of cultural distance, whether it be the effects upon it of some centrally formulated government policy, or matters of dialect, dress, drinking, marrying or dying (see Needham, 1979:14). The symbolic nature of opposition means that people can *think themselves into difference.* The boundaries consist essentially in the contrivance of distinctive meanings within the communities' social discourse. People construct their community symbolically, making it a resource and a repository of meaning. (Cohen 1986:17, emphasis in original)

Cohen is writing of the variety of matters that *can* be the raw material from which boundaries are constructed. I suggest that there is a clear link between the features that become highlighted as markers and the kinds of stereotypes to which members of a given group are subject (see later discussion).

Stereotyping plays a vital role in justifying the oppression that subordinate groups receive: "Now these representations are not arbitrary: since they apprehend and rationalize the unequal distribution of material, political and social power by virtue of group membership, they must, by definition, ascribe such inequalities to the intrinsic nature of the groups concerned" (Comaroff 1987:308).

The central social fact of stereotypes is that they naturalize oppression. Bourdieu calls this process "learned misrecognition," where oppressors learn to misrecognize oppression as arising from some natural characteristic of the subordinate group, rather than resulting from the concerted action of the benefiting group. Such "victim blaming" is a common underpinning of most situations where power, wealth, and status are differentially distributed. McIntosh (1988) describes how a focus on mechanisms through which sexism, racism, and homophobia disadvantage those so categorized hides a more important issue: the superordinate groups that benefit from this process are in fact "advantaged" by it.

> As a white person, I realized that I had been taught about racism as something which puts others at a disadvantage, but had been taught not to see one of its corollary aspects, white privilege, which puts me at an advantage (1)

> In proportion as my racial group was being made confident, comfortable, and oblivious, other groups were likely being made unconfident, uncomfortable and alienated. Whiteness protected me from many kinds of hostility, distress and violence, which I was subtly trained to visit in turn on people of color. (12)

Markers as Signs

Markers are effective only if they are understood by the intended audience, though their impact may be either conscious or unconscious. The interpretation of signs is itself situated knowledge. Americans, for example, are notoriously poor at interpreting the class marking accents that the British themselves find transparent.

There are some markers that primarily (though never exclusively) intergroup markers, and advertise one's membership to fellow members, or convey special information to fellow members. This is particularly true for groups who could largely pass in the local cultural milieu, or whose "special" status was not immediately apparent. For example, when attending Alaskan bilingual/multicultural conferences, Athapaskan high-school students often wear marten fur hats indoors to mark their ethnicity to other Native Alaskan participants. In the same context, Yup'ik students often wear skin mukluks (boots), and students from Southeastern Alaska wear vests—sometimes striking beaded felt ones, sometimes store-bought, down-filled ones. My sense is that students recognize both their own and other groups through this clothing, although except for the mukluks and fancy vests, such meanings would be opaque to the general public. The fact that the conference hotel was always quite warmly heated emphasized the point that wearers were making symbolic statements with their indoor use of this ethnically marked outdoor clothing.

There are also signs that are both inter- and intragroup markers. In mainstream America in the late 1960s and early 1970s, long hair on males was such a marker. Such signs can be either positively or negatively sanctioned by the other group. Pink hair in spikes and safety pins through cheeks were, one assumes, at least in part oppositional markers. For disenfranchised groups, oppositional markers can be very powerful delineators.

Markers as Practice

There are usually a variety of subsidiary stereotypes that occur along with the primary ones. A group may be stereotyped as "primitive and childlike," and therefore needing to be "taken care of" in a paternalistic, colonial sense: that is, they may be exploited "for their own good."

In addition, they might be thought "clever with their hands," or "musical," or "hardworking," or "loyal." There will almost certainly be some positive subsidiary stereotypes.[5] These subsidiary stereotypes are open to strategic manipulation. They represent a kind of cross-cultural capital, ideological images that individuals may successfully claim to embody. If manual dexterity is a subsidiary stereotype for one's group, it will (potentially) be easier to obtain a job as a mechanic or shop assistant. A stereotype of loyalty, too, can be exploited. It is rather like cultural aikido, where an opponent's strength is used against him or her. So much effort is required to erect and maintain stereotypes, against all evidence to the contrary, that this very force makes it difficult to refute claims made on the basis of that stereotype. Subsidiary stereotypes represent points where ideology may potentially be converted into cash. For members of a group subject to the effects of negative stereotypes, these subsidiary stereotypes represent much of what little systemic flexibility exists.

Members of subordinate groups commonly recast or rework some facet(s) of the mainstream culture's stereotypes of them, and, in the process, often reify the character of those stereotypes in intergroup relations as well.

Members of subordinated groups cannot easily invent attributes for the supraordinate group to hold about them. They are (largely) restricted to working with supraordinate imagery, a store of potential symbolic capital upon which they may draw. The most effective imagery for members of subordinated groups to use is that shared by both the subordinate and supraordinate groups. And, typically, the emphasis is on those aspects of the subordinated culture valued by both cultures. For example, there are ancient Asian traditions of scholarship and learning, though many ethnic groups in Asia have historically been at the periphery of large state systems and have only been indirectly affected by these scholarly traditions. However, in the United States, the contemporary racist stereotype of Asian students as "super students" is potentially available for exploitation. For example, some educated, Euro-American friends recently acted as "host" parents for a Southeast Asian refugee child. They were able to trigger selectively the image of Asian students as hardworking, high achievers (particularly in science and math) in the minds of the child's teachers, anticipating that the teachers' default image was that of "pitiful unschooled refugee." They felt that such a change was vital to the child's chances of school success.

Of course, the situation is rarely as straightforward as this last example. The more typical situation is of a variety of traits and actions that are differentially valued by each group. The same behavior will be interpreted differently from different vantage points. This issue of cross-cultural miscommunication will be discussed more fully in chapter 7.

STEREOTYPES OF INUIT: HISTORICAL AND CONTEMPORARY VIEWS

Most Euro-Americans seem to have a general stereotype of Inuit[6] that dates from contacts between explorers and Canadian Inuit in the high Arctic in the sixteenth to eighteenth centuries. This stereotype includes igloos, breathing hole hunting, blubber eating, nose rubbing and wife swapping. Even for most non-Native Alaskans, the distinctions between various Inuit groups are generally hazy if known at all, although most seem to think that Inuit hunt bowhead whales. In general, the historical stereotypes oscillate between Inuit as animal-like savages that eat "like brute beasts" and Inuit as primative children of nature, as the following quotations illustrate:

> There is no flesh or fish which they find dead (smell it ever so filthily) but they will eat it, as they finde it, without any other dressing. (Hakluyt 1589:224, 227, in Fienup-Riordan 1990:12)

> They are intelligent beyond what might be expected of them, and have good natural abilities. They are quick in providing ways and means in cases of emergency. . . . They know no other motive than that of

selfishness. . . . Everything is right if it coincides with their wishes, and everything wrong if it is contrary. Any man may have their friendship if he can pay for it; otherwise he must take the consequences, good or bad. (Wells and Kelly 1890:17)

[They are] a community of children in their simplicity, honesty and happy lack of care. (Peary 1898:483, in Fienup-Riordan 1990:150)

The moral status of the Eskimos is very low, not above that of the brutes. (Wells and Kelly 1890:21)

Variations of these historical images, plus new ones, seem to be current in Alaska, judging from interviews, conversations, radio, television and newspaper accounts, graffiti, and jokes. The central image still wavers between the "noble savage" of yore and some sort of rural lumpenproletariat with severe social problems and with "all of our vices and none of our virtues," to recast Freuchen's aphorism. There is also a small dash of northern oil sheikh image thrown in. The most persistent media image overall is of a dysfunctionality of individuals, families, and communities, generalized to the entire Native population.

It is true that many Native villages and individuals suffer from alcohol and drug abuse, violence, accidental death, and suicide. The problem with this media image, however, is that it constantly recreates and reifies a particular image of "Natives" in a way in which the actions by individual members of majority culture don't. A Euro-American mass murderer, serial killer, or suicide victim seems to be generalized in a different fashion. It is seen as saying something about society as a whole. It rarely reflects on all members of the group and is not seen to stand for general group proclivities. As a result, it does not contribute to stereotypes.[7]

Many of these images of Alaska Natives are clearly structured so as to provide justification for continued stewardship, that is, a continuation of the present colonial enterprise in Alaska.[8]

It may be germane to speak here about image expropriation. If imitation is the sincerest form of flattery, than expropriation provides clear evidence of envy, at least of the item or trait expropriated. Hewitt (1986) talks about white teenagers in London adopting aspects of Afro-Caribbean-British culture, including music, speech, and gesture. Such teenagers are making a statement about having shifted their referents in those areas from their home culture to another. Given British notions of race, they are restricted to a kind of pseudo-Afro-Caribbean-ness; that is, they could never truly pass. Their allegiance to Afro-Caribbean norms is at least in some cases negatively sanctioned by their white peers, but it can never be a real identity in the sense that, in their British context, they can never become Afro-Caribbean. They will be marked by their Afro-Caribbean identification as long as they choose, but the choice to assert their allegiance to some other subculture is always there. They are not permanently or even temporarily changing from one group to another, though they are acting as if they were. What they have done is create an additional category, Afro-Caribbean–identified whites, the reverse of Fanon's "black white men" (1968).

Hewitt describes a mixed reaction to such youth by Afro-Caribbean youth. Some Afro-Caribbean-British youth are apparently quite accepting of the pseudo-Black youth, as friendship carries them across the line from "other" to "us." The more common reaction is one of intermittently expressed hostility, and this, Hewitt suggests, may relate to perceptions that they are playacting at being Afro-Caribbean. They never have to *be* Afro-Caribbean: they are merely asserting their hegemonic position of control to appropriate selected aspects of Afro-Caribbean culture, the equivalent of "slumming," in terms of ethnicity. They appropriate those aspects of Afro-Caribbean identity that typify society values, such as music, dress, and dialect, without having to live with the negative aspects of that identity.

NON-NATIVE ENVY OF SUBSISTENCE SKILLS AND SUBSISTENCE AS AN IDENTITY MARKER

Alaska Natives, and particularly Yupiit and Inupiat, have a limited number of positive stereotypes with which to formulate strategies. Their historic reputation as mechanically adept is useful in some lines of work, although so many jobs now require certificates and licenses that this image has somewhat limited contemporary usefulness. There is also an older image of rugged self-sufficiency, now being challenged by images of massive transfer payments, such as Aid to Dependent Families and Children, Food Stamps, WIC (Women, Infants, Children), Social Security, and old-age pensions, including the Alaska Longevity Bonus.

There remains, however, one complex of Native practices that many white Alaskans envy and would like to master. This is the complex of hunting, fishing, wilderness travel, and camping skills, as well as systemic ecological knowledge now reified in the image of Natives as the "original conservationists." Many Alaskans who immigrate from elsewhere, particularly males, as well as many native born, non-Native Alaskans have, or would like to acquire, an image as skilled big-game hunters and fishers. This applies to both pothunters and status hunters. For members of both groups, their existence as office workers and suburban dwellers may in fact enhance the hunger they feel to expropriate this image of wilderness knowledge.

This envy is one of the reasons why subsistence is being reified as an identity marker: subsistence is one of the few aspects of Alaska Native life that is also valued by mainstream culture in Alaska. In the preceding chapters I outlined a number of reasons for its importance to the Native community as a system and as a practice. I am convinced that subsistence has become politicized as an external marker of identity because it offers the opportunity to say symbolically to members of Euro-American culture, "We have something you want, and [this time] you can't have it."[9] The opportunity to make this statement is particularly important because so much has already been appropriated from Native peoples. In the face of persistent negative images about being Native, having something that non-Native Alaskans want is food for the soul. It proves that the media images and the hidden curricula in textbooks are wrong and that being Native is a positive attribute. In the contemporary political battle over subsistence hunting and fishing rights, the side opposing preferential Native/rural use is funded largely by urban white sport hunters, who strongly desire what Native people have (in much of Alaska)—the right to a priority use of fish and game stocks.[10]

YUP'IK PRACTICE AS IT AFFECTS NON-NATIVE PRACTICE

For those non-Native Alaskans whose ideology of hunting and fishing has as a referent primarily prearistocratic subsistence hunting, most Yup'ik practices are interesting and imitable. Yupiit have managed to harvest the riches of what seems to outsiders to be a difficult, even hostile, environment. Some of the techniques used are phenomenally successful, particularly the netting of migrating salmon and whitefish. In most of the United States, and in fact in much of the rest of Alaska, such techniques are limited to commercial fishermen, and even then are both strictly regulated and (often) less effective because of low fish stocks. For this group the Y-K Delta offers almost undreamed-of opportunities.

One non-Native I interviewed who expressed this clearly was Brian Sanders, a long-term Bethel resident. He talked about how privileged he felt to be in Bethel, to be able to do subsistence, particularly subsistence fishing for king salmon. He noted the depleted king runs in the lower forty-eight states, and talked at length about the last of the "June hogs" (seventy-pound June-run king salmon on the Columbia River), made extinct by Grand Coulee Dam, which blocked off their spawning grounds.

He went on to say that there just aren't very many places where one can fish with nets for king salmon for one's own use. This is true not only in Alaska but in the whole world as well. In his opinion, this region may continue to be one of the last places in the state (and in the world) where such fishing is possible, and that the opportunity to participate in such fishing is an exquisite privilege. At the same time that people are lining up on the banks of the Kenai River, hip to hip, three deep to fish for king salmon, Bethel residents can go out and catch as many fish as they can use.

Another longtime non-Native Y-K Delta resident described the effects of Yup'ik subsistence knowledge and skills on his own activities:

> Little did we know about the way of life out here when we first got here. And I really believe if we had stuck to being just the traditional White people, coming in from the United States, then we probably would never have succeeded out here.
>
> But we had people who saw us, and who wanted to teach us things, and we were open to learning, and I think that really helped us. . . .
>
> The people today, who just stick to being just strictly White and American, are going to have problems out here. (transcript of an interview with Paul Longpre, June 24, 1991)

Almost the only techniques that such non-Natives are less interested in emulating are those for catching species such as needlefish (sticklebacks), a spiny minnow, which they may not wish to eat.

Based on my interviews with non-Native subsisters, this group of non-Natives is most likely to adopt Yup'ik ideology as well. Of this group, some are indeed changed by life in the Y-K Delta.

Although this was never directly stated, I sensed that it is relatively easy for non-Natives to maintain a competitive attitude toward game when, for example, they are fly-fishing for an elusive trout in some small Western stream. The equivalent Y-K Delta fishing expedition, however, is to go out with a hundred-yard-long net and catch hundreds of pounds of salmon—as much as can be processed and used without waste. It is harder to see this as a competitive venture when one is astride a vast stream of fish, straining them out with a huge net and stopping not when the fish are gone, or when some legal limit is reached, but when one has enough.

In the face of this abundance, when catching the fish is the easy part (compared to cutting them for drying and then hanging and smoking them), it is difficult to maintain the general Euro-American image that one is acting out the competitive mastery of Man over Nature. Once it can no longer be seen as a contest, the usual Euro-American metaphors collapse. Winning and losing each provide a kind of closure. The experience of this abundance, however, has no obvious closure, except perhaps a prayer of thankfulness, which for many, at least at first, is inadequate.[11] A major attraction of Yup'ik beliefs about human/animal interaction may be that they provide a way of closing and balancing this equation. In the Yup'ik system, one has obligations to share, to be respectful and thankful, and not to waste. If one meets these obligations, then things are in balance and will continue to be so. This difference is highlighted by a T-shirt commonly sold in Alaska (Ray Troll Associates), which shows an angler having a nightmare about all of the fish he has caught in his life. In his dream they are coming back to revenge themselves on him. The equivalent Yup'ik dream would be that the fisherman goes to the village of the fish where he is feasted and instructed. This juxtaposition of viewpoints was also clear in the description of a non-Native woman in Bethel who had worked on a salmon seiner in Prince William Sound. She said, in reference to the quantities of salmon caught, "I began to feel like a mass murderer." In comparison, Yupiit with whom I have fished in Bristol Bay (home of the largest sockeye [red] salmon fishery in the world), were thrilled by large catches.

The larger issue of whether, and to what extent, Yup'ik ideology is internalized varies. At least in some cases, though, where Yup'ik culture is already positively valued and there is sufficient interaction and participation in activities with Yupiit, aspects of Yup'ik ideology may be transferred. My interviews would suggest that such transfers are more likely to happen with non-Natives who are catching a full range of subsistence fish and game than with those who focus their attention on big game. With moose, caribou, and bear it is easier to continue to envision hunting in terms of a contest rather than an exchange. Still, one non-Native described his own surprise at suddenly recognizing that he had internalized such beliefs:

Paul said that they had killed a moose, and had the pieces of the moose in the boat, including the head. He looked over from shore, and this guest who was visiting from the lower forty-eight states had taken two carrots (which they had raised) and stuck them up the moose's nostrils, so that it looked a little like a walrus. Paul was almost surprised by how upset he was by this show of disrespect to the moose. He was also upset that the guest had used carrots they had raised. Whether this was because it made them more complicitous, or because those carrots were food too, and should also be respected, is unclear. (Notes from an interview with Paul Longpre, June 24, 1991)

Another non-Native told how his attitudes about hunting were changed by the example of Yupiit:

My dad never hunted, and actually I didn't think much of a lot of the hunters back there [in the eastern United States]. I remember even in high school, the guys commenced bragging, saying, "Oh yeah, we heard a whole bunch of little birds, and boy I just aimed that shotgun there and blasted them, boy, and it was great, blood and feathers all over the place," and you know I didn't think very highly of that.

And then coming up here and being exposed to the kind of hunting and fishing that a lot of people do, although there are some around here who do the same kind of things, and it really changed my attitude, like even now, I hunt. I still don't enjoy seeing the animals die. I always try to make sure that I can kill them as quickly as possible, so they don't suffer.

It's something that we enjoy doing. I mean, we enjoy having that food. It gives us a lot of good food to eat that we really enjoy, and there's a real sense of satisfaction in providing for yourself, and having that. And I don't know, you always at the end, at freeze-up, you always have a sense of accomplishment, when your larders are full . . . [LAUGHS]

And I guess that was a pretty striking change in me. And I guess I would attribute that to being around the people here. (transcript of an interview, July 1991)

Grant Fairbanks (=G), a third non-Native, talked with me (=[C] about his annual moose hunt, but again in completely non-competitive terms.

G: I spend February first to February tenth up the Holitna, moose hunting. I usually go up there with myself and one or two other people. We usually get two or three moose.

C: Do you fly into your homestead or fly to Sleetmute?

G: Mail plane from here to Sleetmute. I keep a snow machine in Sleetmute, [and] snow-machine up to my homestead.

C: Then hunt out from there?

G: Then hunt by snow machine, and we usually kill a moose within a half mile of my cabin, maybe two miles.

C: Wow.

G: There's usually twenty, thirty, forty of them within a mile.

C: Is that an either sex hunt?

G: Uh-hum, either sex.

C: You can pick out a nice fat cow, and . . .

G: Yeah, so we usually go around and wait until we find a moose that's close to a snow-machine trail, shoot it, gut it, quarter it, put it on the sled, take it back to my house, cut it up, package it right then, freezer wrap it, put it in cardboard

C: Wow

G: boxes, freeze it outside. Then, when we come back to Sleetmute by snow machine, we ship it down by mail plane with us. Pretty efficient. (transcript of an interview, July 15, 1991)

The situation is very different for status hunters. Here there are still emulated aspects of Yup'ik knowledge and practice, but it primarily involves big game—moose and, to a lesser extent, caribou and bear—and secondarily travel and camping techniques. There is a general sense that this knowledge is wanted so that it can be put to different ends. For example, a status fisherman may be interested in learning to navigate the small, fast, clear-water rivers that flow into the Kuskokwim River and Bay not to hunt beaver or net and dry trout or Dolly Varden but in order to practice catch and release fly-fishing. In general, my sense is that Yup'ik knowledge of travel, habitat, weather signs, and animal behavior is respected.

To the status hunter, however, Yup'ik activities look too much like those of the poacher and pothunter. Given that this orientation was originally—and probably still is—linked with upper-class and upper-middle-class values (witness President George Bush on his annual deer-hunting trips to Texas and fishing trips to Maine) or with attempts to enter those social classes, non-Natives holding these views may be less likely to accept Yup'ik values. There are two reasons for this. First, accommodating Yup'ik values would seem to require greater changes in this group's ideology. They would have to value animals and fish both for themselves and as food, rather than as status markers.

Second, as they are less interested in emulating Yup'ik activities, they are less likely to spend time with Yupiit as interested quasi-apprentices. Effective learning usually takes time and interest. The effective transfer of ideologies probably requires respect as well (Luhrman 1989).[12] Finally, as mentioned in chapter 2, it seems that relatively few status hunters settle permanently in Bethel, and stays of short duration provide little time for this transfer of ideology. Many Yupiit also avoid such individuals, especially when hunting and fishing, since from a Yup'ik perspective, the practices of status hunters and fishers are morally compromised as well as repugnant.

4

Subsistence as an Identity Marker

PICKING BLUEBERRIES

We drive out along the road to the old Bureau of Indian Affairs site, then park in a sandy area along the road where it looks like we probably won't get stuck again. We've seen various other cars parked along the road also. The weather is scattered sunshine, with rain clouds brushing the tundra off to the north and west, and a fairly dark mass towards the southwest, where the wind is blowing from. I'm wearing hip-waders and keeping my raincoat handy.

The party consists of my wife and children, and a visiting friend. We hike off across the tundra, heading for some lower ground where we hope there will be more moisture and more blueberries. It has been a relatively dry year. Walking on tundra tussocks can seem like walking on hairy basketballs; but fortunately the ground is mostly drier and flatter than that, though you still sink in several inches with each step.

We get to a place where the berries seem thick enough to start picking. It seems to take a long time for the bottom of the container to be covered enough that it doesn't ring with each new handful of berries, but it eventually happens. This kind of picking is different from picking domesticated berries, where the goal is to efficiently pick all the berries in a given area. Here the goal is to graze around and maximize the amount of berries picked. It doesn't matter if you pick haphazardly, as long as it's done efficiently.

We spread out as each person follows their own notion of where to pick. A couple of people scout further, I stop at what seems like a reasonable patch. I pick for a while along the shore of a small lake, where the tundra drops down fairly sharply. It's actually quite nice, I can lean or kneel into the hill and pick without stooping over. The kids pick along nearby, and only have to be separated occasionally. After a while it begins to mist and then drizzle lightly and we all put on our rain jackets. We talk sporadically as we pick, whenever someone happens to be within earshot. After a while the rain lets up, and we shed our jackets and feed the kids a snack. We keep following the berries slowly north. After another hour we quit as the rain begins again in seeming earnest. We hike back to the car in the rain and wind, then drive home. We've picked around a gallon total. The berries are smaller than commercial blueberries, but much more intensely flavored. In midwinter their tart intensity will take us back to summer for a moment.

SUBSISTENCE AS A MARKER FOR A YUP'IK IDENTITY

With the background sketched in, it is now possible to examine why and how subsistence practices might be used as an identity marker by Yupiit and by other Alaskan Natives as well. First, they are among the few aspects of Yup'ik life that non-Natives want to emulate or appropriate. Second, subsistence was the traditional ideological focus of Yup'ik life, and continues to be of major importance socially, economically, and gastronomically, as well as symbolically. Since subsistence crosscuts so many of mass culture's usual dichotomies of public/private, work/play, production/consumption, it provides an arena in which membership, allegiance, and role-appropriate competence are portrayed.

Two aspects of this portrayal can, with difficulty, be separated. The first are the *actual* activities of preparation, hunting, fishing, gathering, processing, and the repairing and storing of equipment. Of these tasks, however, most of the actual hunting, fishing, and gathering occurs offstage, alone or in very small groups. People's entrances and exits are noticed (and commented on), but (at least for men), the critical scenes occur elsewhere. The second aspect of subsistence is the talk of subsistence as a conversational staple, as information, and as a critical form of practice (to be covered in chapter 7).

Giving Private Ventures Public Meaning

The visible elements, other than the preparations and comings and goings, are the catch, the processing (most clearly, hanging up to dry) and distribution. An important part of the cultural salience of distribution is that it recreates on center stage symbolic proxies for actions that have happened offstage.

Such distributions were a focus of the traditional Yup'ik ceremony of *Kevgiq* (the Messenger Feast), as well as a subsidiary theme in *Kelek* (the Inviting-In Feast). In addition, every ceremony involved some gift giving (Mather 1985, Morrow 1984, Nelson 1899, Hawkes 1913, Kilbuck in Fienup-Riordan 1991). Morrow (1984) has described the elaborate ceremonial cycle as highlighting the tension between the need for successful individuals and the quest for equality among people. In *Kevgiq*, for example, successful hunters were honored and mocked in the same festival. I would add that an additional strand of meaning here was the symbolic public reenactment of private male success.

The extent of a man's catch was most clearly enunciated in *Nakaciuq* (the Bladder Festival), where the bladders of the animals that each man had slain were publicly honored in the men's house. Here again, the focus was on honoring the animals, particularly seals that had been caught, and only indirectly those who caught them.

This pattern has been most obviously preserved in coastal villages that still celebrate *Uqiquq* (the Seal Party) (Fienup-Riordan 1983a). Here the mothers and wives of hunters publicly mark their husbands' and sons' hunting success by distributing strips of seal blubber and a variety of store-bought goods to other women in the village. Fienup-Riordan describes the Seal Party celebrating a boy or young man's first catch of a bearded seal as being particularly elaborate, and argues that the women to whom gifts are distributed are those who are sufficiently unrelated to the young man to be potential marriage partners (although they may already be married or too old). She sees the Seal Party as marking the distribution and socialization (that is, social production) by women of natural goods produced, but not socialized, by men.

I see an additional strand of males' private production re-created publicly through women's distribution. Significantly, at the men's house, the distribution of "shares" of meat was done by men, to men. At the family houses, which were historically "owned" by women, women distributed to women. This was, and is, an example of parallel frames for signification in a society with pronounced gender divisions. To a large extent, women stage events for women, men for men. I suggest that while Seal Parties may publicly mark marriageable males to an audience of potential spouses, this "function" never arose in numerous conversations with Yupiit (including Nelson Islanders) about Seal Parties. (It also begs the question of why so many Seal Parties are given by women for their husbands.) An alternative view might be that for Yup'ik women, other women, not men, are their reference group, and the Seal Party is an example of an activity by women for women. In this sense, then, women in Toksook Bay told Fienup-Riordan that she had "come at the best time of year, that the seal parties were about to begin" (1983a:39). I have often heard men from coastal villages, including Nelson Island, talk with joy about spring being the best time of the year. For men, however, spring is the best season because of the seal hunting, not the Seal Partying.

SUBSISTENCE AS A MARKER FOR A NON-NATIVE RURAL ALASKAN IDENTITY

Hunting, fishing, and gathering figure prominently in the lives of many non-Native residents of Bethel and the Y-K Delta. Non-Natives also cite this as a reason why they stay in Bethel. Non-Natives tend to be more display-oriented than Yupiit, in terms of equipment and trophies: for instance, it is common to see guns leaning in a corner somewhere in a Yup'ik household, but protected and displayed in a gun cabinet or rack in a non-Native household.[1] While there may be Yupiit who collect guns or knives, I have never met any. For Yupiit guns and knives are tools, useful but not fetishized, expendable and, in time, expended. Collecting them would make no more sense than collecting shovels or hammers.

For non-Natives, the motive may partially be general consumerism, but guns and hunting knives have symbolic import as well. They are the symbolic props of American heroes (and some heroines as well). Setting aside military heroes, one still has the Pilgrims with their blunderbusses, Daniel Boone, Davy Crockett and Jim Bowie, the cowboys, gunfighters and sheriffs, and gangsters and G-men. All are portrayed as being heavily armed. For non-Natives, owning guns is being able to take part in, being part of, that history. I have, for example, known various non-Native men in the Y-K Delta who owned some very impractical guns, that is, ones that were poorly suited for actual hunting in the Y-K Delta because of their age, frailty, high value, or lack of efficiency. Such hunting is almost unavoidably hard on firearms. Having a gun immediately at hand often makes the difference between success and failure, but it means that guns spend their useful life bouncing around in boats in the rain and being carried on sleds and snow machines, both of which frequently overturn. Local preference is for simple, reliable, sturdy, reasonably priced, multishot weapons—durable tools for efficient killing. Because firearms are used up in the course of usage, I suggest that old, fragile and/or valuable weapons are kept for their symbolic rather than practical value. In this light, then, there is a clear connection between one man's "falling block" Sharps black powder buffalo rifle (from the 1870s) and his collection of Westerns (including a complete set of Zane Grey's writings). For another, it was a connection between the West German helical bore assault rifle (which I was assured was the same kind Patty Hearst had used with the Symbionese Liberation Army) and his sociopolitical identification. These are not guns as tools.

This same basic cultural difference also seems to apply to the keeping of trophies. The symbolic counting of coup through the enshrining of the secondary sex characteristics of moose and musk oxen is more common in non-Native houses. Visually, this is the difference between mounting a set of moose antlers on a wall and tossing them on the roof of the steambath, where the dogs won't get them. For non-Natives, these mounted antlers commemorate a victory over nature; for Yupiit they are more often raw material for some possible future project. Their storage for possible future use is part of respecting the animal as well. It may be in this light that conspicuous display of trophies is seen by many Yupiit as inappropriate bragging. At least some Yupiit also wonder what has happened or will happen to the animal's person (*yua*) when an animal has been mounted as a trophy. Even items that non-Natives might interpret as trophies, such as ptarmigan tail feathers or snowy owl feathers, are typically saved either for raw materials for future projects, such as dance fans, or as toys for children.

It is possible that the importance of trophies is also related to the relatively impoverished redistribution networks of many non-Natives. Since for most non-Natives sharing doesn't serve to make the private and off stage public and onstage, trophies serve in their stead.

TALK OF PRACTICE FOR YUPIIT AND NON-NATIVES

The third and most important way (at least for Bethel) in which the private activities of subsistence are made publicly visible is through talk. As mentioned earlier, subsistence talk is *the* conversational staple for Yup'ik men, and a major topic for Yup'ik women as well as for many non-Natives. In Bethel, its conversational importance is such that, like sports in Euro-American culture, even those (non-Natives) uninterested are constrained to feign interest. The very ubiquitousness of this discourse assumes that everyone has something to contribute, and that everyone either participates or at least follows the action. Where elsewhere people might talk about movies, sports, or work, in the Y-K Delta they are more likely to talk about subsistence.

Very often, conversations about subsistence are an immediate follow-up to formal greetings. In the search for a shared topic of interest, it is the one most often seized upon. According to Arvin Dull,

> Yeah, with my friends, when I talk to them, we always, almost right after we say hello, we say, "Did you go hunting, ptarmigan hunting?" If it's in winter, "Ptarmigan hunting?"
>
> They say, "Oh, no, I haven't gone yet, but I'm going out this weekend." [Then] they say, "Well how 'bout you?" [I say] "Oh, yeah, I'd like to go."
>
> He says, "Well, I'll call you, we'll go."
>
> Or if it's in the spring, "Have you gone out smelt fishing?" right after the river went down. Or "Have you gone fishing yet? How many fish did you get? How many fish you got cut up so far?"
>
> Or later on in the winter, jackrabbit hunting season. It's like a fever, you know. You have to go out, you know, during the season for jackrabbits or especially moose hunting.
>
> Now that's the big one, moose hunting. Everybody that we talk to, all the men, or even the women, [we say] "Hey, has your husband gone out yet?" "Oh, no, but he's going out Thursday." They know exactly when they're going because the husbands are talking about it, getting ready, sighting in their guns, cleaning the guns, oiling them, getting all their food ready, gas and oil, and everything that they need to go hunting. (transcript of an interview, June 24, 1991)

This is only one kind of subsistence conversation, of the form "What are you up to? What's happening?" It is subsistence discourse at its most public, occurring at the airport, the post office, on the streets or the riverfront. Implicit in the public nature of these questions is an assumption of neutrality; it is akin to talking about the weather. Talk about the weather can reveal one's attitudes toward the weather and climate in general, and as such be used strategically—to claim local allegiance, for example—but it need not be used that way. The same appears to be at least somewhat true of this most public talk about subsistence.

Subsistence discourse is also the stock-in-trade of private discourse, between small groups of men or women resting sweaty and exhausted in the outer rooms of steambaths, of evening stories and intermittent comments over routine tasks, such as filing papers or mending nets. It is the staple of coffee breaks as well as trips to the riverfront to check for the start of breakup. Subsistence discourse, then, is not simply a basis for casual sociability; it also forms part of the foundation of continuing, long-term interaction between people. In the following quotation, Arvin

Dull talks about the importance of subsistence discourse in his day-to-day business as manager of the Kuskokwim Branch of the First National Bank of Anchorage: "You know this is three-fourths of my business, talking about hunting and fishing. I mean, we do talk about [financial statements, profit and loss], but an awful lot of it is talking about hunting and fishing" (transcript of an interview, June 24, 1991).

SPECIFIC SUBSISTENCE PRACTICES AS MARKERS OF IDENTITY

My data suggest that people use the activities they engage in, and the way in which they situate those activities, to make statements about their ethnicity. While it is possible to categorize activities in some general sense, this is of limited use. Practices are usually simultaneously evaluated on a number of different bases, so that one aspect of a practice may be seen as more Yup'ik, while another is seen as more non-Native. This shared system of categorization can, for example, be explicated by looking at the meanings attached to the ways in which a freshly caught king salmon can be preserved. Each of these techniques has a situated local meaning. Together they produce a virtual continuum of signification.

The typically Yup'ik way of processing would be to make blankets out of the fillets (that is, dry the two fillets attached together along the dorsal line), dry the collars (pectoral fins) and extra slices from the fillets, and bury the heads to age. These techniques presuppose skilled cutting ability, as well as knowledge, significant equipment including a drying rack, aging pit, and smokehouse, and the time required for drying and smoking.[2] Slightly less strongly marked would be to hard salt the body and/or head. This is a relatively quick and easy technique, requiring only barrels or buckets and salt, but it is an uncommon one for non-Natives to use.

Making strips by brining, drying, and smoking long strips of fillet is an activity that is still marked as Yup'ik, but less so than making blankets. Many non-Natives in Bethel successfully make strips. Producing strips still requires knowledge and skill, as well as racks and a smokehouse, but it is a faster and easier process, as strips dry more rapidly than flats and are less prone to spoilage.

Next on a continuum from Yup'ik marked (and marking) to non-Native marked practices are kippering (brining and hot smoking), canning, and freezing. To keep more than a few days, fish that has been kippered must be frozen or canned. My sense is that it is the volume of fish processed that identifies the category to which these activities belong. There are situations in which non-Natives and Yupiit freeze or can equivalent (per capita) amounts of salmon. The difference is that the freezing and canning done by Yupiit make up only a small amount of their total harvest. Canning several cases of kings in jars in addition to the blankets and strips one has prepared is a very Yup'ik statement. Relying exclusively on freezing or canning to preserve one or two hundred pounds of salmon is a typically non-Native approach. The final way of preserving salmon is either to take a picture of it and give it away or have it mounted. This is the epitome of a non-Native approach.

A similar continuum can be constructed for almost any category of activity (see Fall 1990 for a more ascriptionally based statistical approach). A second example would be fishing for king salmon. This example, however, is structured as a mirror image of the first example. In the first example, practice was ascribed to ethnicity. Now, ethnicity is ascribed to practice. Such ascriptions (whether or not they are confirmed) will be used to judge the actor's fit into a category, when and if that category can be determined.

The scene is a June day on the Kuskokwim River across from Bethel. In the distance is a boat. It is too distant to recognize anything except the type and size of the boat, number of crew and their actions, and the length of the net. Diagnostically, two men (or a man and a boy) drifting with a full shackle of gear (one hundred fathoms of net) in a large wooden or welded aluminum boat, who fish steadily until they have several hundred pounds of salmon, are likely to be Yupiit. Three men and two women taking turns picking a small net from a smaller riveted aluminum boat, who stop after they catch one or two hundred pounds, are more likely to be non-Native. And while I have theories about why, for example, non-Natives usually fish in larger groups than are physically required and Yupiit will occasionally fish alone, these are post-hoc theories cut to fit the practice. And again, these practices are only possible indicators, not hard-and-fast diagnostic traits. I have occasionally seen several young Yup'ik men out fishing together, and I have commonly seen non-Native pairs fishing; many non-Natives use full shackles of gear, and sometimes Yupiit use short nets and so on. If the location was different and the distant boat was engaged in rod-and-reel fishing, one would still need to read other signs to situate the practice. Sometimes Yupiit fish with rods and reels, though seeing someone release a fish would be strongly suggestive of non-Native practice. Still, most signs signify possibilities, not certainties. None are incontrovertible; all are read together with a variety of other signs.

Each time a story is told, or an action is observed, or food is eaten or given away, certain signs are (potentially) read, and their significance noted. Culture is continually acted out in this fashion. Someone can act more or less Yup'ik or non-Native not only in the way in which they preserve and serve their fish but also how (and whether) they share it, what interactional patterns they use, how they dress, and so on. Subsistence activities are only part of an almost infinite number of signs that are locally understood to be statements about ethnicity.

Most individuals interviewed seemed quite aware of this signaling power. The sending and receiving of meta-messages is an inherent part of communication. Analogously, one person interviewed stressed repeatedly throughout the interview that he rarely (and certainly had not recently) fished for salmon to use as dog food. Since there was a proposal at that time before the Alaska State Board of Fisheries to eliminate such usage, this continued refrain of denial seemed marked. The interviewee was reassuring me (as well as going on record) that he was not that kind of subsistence user. This issue of signaling and intent will be covered further in chapter 7.

5

Development and the Marking of Gender and Ethnicity

MY FIRST MEMORABLE STEAMBATH

I was visiting a village and had been invited to take a steambath by a Yup'ik man I knew somewhat, but had never steamed with. When we arrived the porch was full of men, so we undressed outside in a light drizzle. We laid our clothes on the roof of the porch, then bundled them up in our jackets and laid them on a board with a piece of cardboard over them.

We ducked into the porch, my host handed me a hand towel, and we crawled into the inner room. It was already the hottest place I had ever been in my life. It was like crawling into an inferno. The stove barrel glowed red between the rocks, and the water boiled furiously. There were already four or five men in there, and two or three came in after us, nine of us total. We ranged in age from the late twenties to mid-sixties. We were leg to leg and knee to knee. I was sitting on the toes of the man behind, with the man in front of me sitting on mine. My host folded his hand towel in half diagonally, and tied it around his head to protect his ears. I did the same. I wondered if I was nuts to be doing this.

The last guy in pretty much blocked the door. He looked huge. Furthermore he was blind. How was I going to get out when I wanted to, which I already sort of did? There was no room for people to move. They hadn't even started pouring, and I was ready to leave. What if I really needed to bail out, and I didn't have time to get the attention of the guy in front of the door? I didn't

113

*know him—I didn't know how much English he spoke, and in my slightly
panicky state, my Yup'ik wasn't up to extricating me. Then it hit me: sweating
like we were, I could just slide right out across his naked lap if I had to, no
problem.*

*The man on the right front poured a cup of water on the stove. There was
a brief delay, then the steam started biting our shoulders and backs. The steam
let up. He poured again. It was hotter, burning my knees as well. It let up. He
poured again. There was a rhythm here. If Finnish saunas are like ovens, this
was like being under the broiler. I later learned that the goal is to raise the heat
in such a fashion that you get satisfactorily "cooked" before you become exhausted
by the overall heat and have to go out, but at the time this distinction was lost
on me.*

*There were occasional comments I didn't fully understand. The others were
obviously enjoying themselves, while for me it had degenerated into an endurance
contest. Could I make it until the first contingent went out? The heat dissipated
a little: the man on the right poured, on and on. A couple of times I told myself
I would just count to twenty slowly, then go out, but each time the heat eased.
Everyone else seemed to be having a great time. They may very well not have
realized how hot it was for me, because I wasn't making the right kind of
noises, the kind of deep* HUH *or* AHH *that you make when the steam is really
good, but you are heading toward the limit of your tolerance. On the other
hand, there's a long tradition of testing the mettle of strangers, particularly non-
Natives, in the steam. Mostly I think it was like being invited to a dinner
where the food is highly spiced and you're the only one not used to the peppers.*

More pours. Finally there were some exchanges like Anlua! Anlua! *(I
should go out! I should go out!) until a consensus was reached that it was time
to go out. Five of us lighter-weights went out, while the remaining four stayed
in to reach satiety. We crawled out on the porch, then right on outside and sat
on some cardboard.*

*Coming out of a hot steam, it's all you can do for a few minutes to just lie
there. It's like when you've had too much to drink, and imagine you could talk,
but would prefer not to try.*

*After several more pours the serious steamers came crawling out, looking
dazed and light-struck. After a really good steam older Yup'ik men often look
like they need, or may soon need, medical attention. They pant and gasp, barely
able to breathe, and collapse in heaps until they cool off. All were covered in
blotchy red and white patterns of vasodilation, as was I.*

*Unlike in the inner room, where there was little conversation, men were
talking about their subsistence activities, telling stories and teasing each other (or
rather some pairs were teasing each other). When we cooled off, we went back in
again. This time everyone heated up more easily, and I bailed out early. I*

figured I'd already proven myself. My host suggested later that I should try rolling over on my side, to expose fresh cooler flesh to the heat, and to indirectly let people know that I was reaching my limit, rather than abruptly going out. I gathered that it was preferable to reach some consensus before exiting, although I didn't know how much that had to do with maintaining face versus not spoiling the experience for others by suddenly letting the accumulated heat out, just when it got really good.

After a third series of pours, men started washing up. They passed out basins to be filled with fresh water, then soaped and shampooed. Somebody was shaving. They seemed relaxed and satisfied, like when something you've looked forward to turns out to be every bit as good as you'd hoped. More talk, more teasing, more stories. I caught bits and pieces of the Yup'ik; some things were told in English, or occasionally translated to include me in the conversation. The stove and hot water container were refilled so that later the women could steam. Thank-yous were offered in departing, and men went off home. Another night, another steam. As for me, I didn't just feel clean, I felt purged. Even my bones seemed rubbery.

INTRODUCTION

There have been some clear differences in the effects that one hundred and fifty years of Western contact have had upon Yup'ik women and men.[1] One effect of these changes for some individuals has been to provoke questions about one's gender and ethnic identity. Subsistence activities and discourse provide one way of addressing these questions publicly.

Culture change has included changes in ideology, activity, and opportunity, as well as changes in gender space and power in both home and community. I suggest that such changes are a major causal factor in disproportionate female outmarriage and emigration, and may be linked to high rates of young male suicide and social dysfunction. Finally, I will suggest a link between these factors and the importance of subsistence practices and discourse for marking a positive valuation on a Yup'ik identity.

NONDIFFERENTIAL EFFECTS
OF CULTURAL CHANGE

Some changes have made life easier for both men and women. Many traditional tasks have become less taxing, through the use of introduced labor-saving devices such as oil stoves, washing machines, snow machines, and chainsaws. Also, tasks such as catching and preparing dog food for dog teams, or sewing skin parkas and boots for the entire family, have become primarily a thing of the past. Except for hats and mittens, skin clothing now consists primarily of fancy clothing for special occasions, rather than for everyday wear. Store-bought food, much of it already prepared, has somewhat reduced food production and preparation. On the other hand, living in a sod house and owning a single suit of clothes limited how clean one could be, as well as how much effort was expended upon cleaning as an activity. There is some indication that rising opportunities for (and community standards of) cleanliness have increased this burden, which falls largely upon women.

One substantial change has been demographic. In the past, infant mortality was high, keeping families small. Infant mortality rates have plummeted in recent decades, though they remain higher than in the United States as a whole. Women are now able to rear many more children to adulthood, and currently large families are the norm. I have been told numerous times that "six children was not a large family." Some older women have commented that this change has markedly increased the amount of time women devote to child rearing (Mary Pete, personal communication, July 4, 1991). It has also increased the amount of subsistence hunting and processing that must be done to feed these large numbers of children, effectively increasing the ratio of nonproducers to (potential) producers. Overall, however, given the complexity and variability of these changes, it is impossible to say whether women's or men's lives have, on average, been made easier.

HISTORY OF WAGE LABOR

Yup'ik men and women seem to have been recruited into the wage economy on the basis of extant Yup'ik and Euro-American gender roles, which largely coincided. In the postcontact period, Yup'ik men were recruited for outdoor work such as placer mining, reindeer herding, and freight hauling, and women were recruited as seamstresses. Such work was often abandoned when it conflicted with subsistence priorities.

The real penetration of new kinds of labor into villages began with the siting of Bureau of Indian Affairs schools in villages in the 1920s to 1940s, with Yupiit working as cooks, cleaning and maintenance personnel, domestic helpers, and as the occasional teacher. Here again work roles seem to have followed Euro-American gender roles. During and after World War II, Yup'ik men were also recruited for commercial fishing and cannery work in the Bristol Bay area. Many new opportunities were available after the 1971 Alaska Native Claims Settlement Act created a variety of village-level positions. As the oil revenue increased, the state of Alaska began an ambitious building program of clinics, schools, safe water projects, washeterias, housing projects, boardwalks, and airports. Some of these projects also involved federal monies. From the mid-1970s to mid-1980s there was usually a large construction project occurring in most villages each summer. Such a project might provide one relatively high-paying seasonal job for every few interested men (and they were limited primarily to men). However, by 1985 State of Alaska project monies (both federal and capital) began to decline, and construction decreased markedly.

Occupational Changes for Men

Currently, many Yup'ik men, particularly those in villages, are caught in a sort of double bind. They are faced simultaneously with two conflicting models of male behavior: the traditional Yup'ik model of "man the hunter," who provides for himself and his family through his hunting, fishing, trapping, and gathering; and the introduced Western model of "man the worker," who holds a job and buys what he and his family need.

The problem is that these ideals are largely unattainable: male subsistence activities are too expensive to be self-supporting, and work alone will not provide the kind of food necessary to feed a family properly. Hunters' cash requirements are high: it takes thousands of dollars a year to hunt, fish, and gather. In addition, there are bills for fuel oil, electricity, telephone, housing, store-bought food, clothing, etc. The only subsistence products that can be legally sold without being incorporated into handicrafts are furs, and few trappers make more than a fraction of what their family needs through trapping (see also Jorgenson 1990).

For wage earners, the foods that are almost irreplaceable for day-to-day eating, as well as properly hosting and feasting others, are solely the product of subsistence activity. Most are not for sale in any quantity.

To acquire the money to do subsistence, one either has to work, although little work is available, or (in some cases) depend on transfer payments. Furthermore, the current employment situation in most Yup'ik villages is bleak. There are few year-round jobs, and only a slightly higher number of seasonal jobs (which often pay higher wages). Further, the pool for many of the seasonal jobs is restricted. To fish for salmon commercially one needs a Limited Entry Permit, which is akin to the taxi-medallion system used in many cities. That is, the number of permits in circulation is regulated: they can be purchased on the open market, but are most often inherited. (Indeed, if they come on the market they are almost invariably purchased by non-Natives.) The few construction jobs available typically go to middle-aged or older men with families, and are generally distributed by the City or Indian Reorganization Act (IRA) Council. Seasonal jobs such as commercial fishing or construction are intense but of short duration. Such jobs often occur simultaneously with the peak of subsistence harvesting in the summer, but people are usually able to work their subsistence activities around these schedules. This is in part because there are never enough jobs or fishing permits for everyone, so the burden of subsistence harvesting is shifted to the underemployed.

Most of the available work is either clerical or maintenance—checking groceries at stores, pumping gas, maintaining the village generator, plowing the airport, maintaining the school—and is largely low-paying and often part-time. Exceptions such as teaching or being a principal all require either advanced schooling or a commitment to continue one's education (teacher's aide, health aide).

Teaching might seem an ideal occupation, combining relatively high pay through the winter with summers off. In reality, however, there is much less time off than this. During the summer, teachers are often occupied with summer school or school district summer training sessions. During the school year there are constant weekend trips as chaperons to other villages and Bethel, for sports, band, debate team, and so on, as well as after-school activities to be coached or supervised. Furthermore, acquiring credentials requires either years of education away from the village or an incredible dedication to graduate via an off-campus program. For most people this program requires simultaneously working, fulfilling all of one's village roles, and going to school full-time, via distance delivery. It also requires giving up one's summers to attend summer school for the foreseeable future.

Individual men seem to be faced with the choice of having either the time for subsistence but no money, or the money but no time. Some families find a balance in which the wife works for money and the husband hunts. Other families are able to work this out by sharing capital expenses and subsistence foods as a larger unit (Wolfe 1987), transferring money and store-bought equipment from a family member with a full-time job to one or more others who hunt and fish for the family. Still, elders often refer to the old days as more satisfying, if more difficult; it seems that now neither the worker nor the hunter is as satisfied as Yup'ik men were in the past. At that time, there was only one symbolic male standard of success through hunting. Now there are two competing ones, neither of which is readily attainable.

It may be useful to think of this situation in comparison with other situations in which one group of people is working two different shifts. An example of this phenomenon, of "double-shifting," occurs when contemporary middle-class Euro-American women perform one shift of wage-work, and a second shift of domestic work at home. This is seen as a change from a generation earlier, when relatively few of the mothers of such women engaged in wage-work (the period of World War II being an obvious exception). It has been suggested (Phyllis Morrow, personal communication, November 9, 1994) that double-shifting may be a more general pattern in situations where labor roles are changing. Presumably, those most likely to be put in the position of double-shifting are those already in subordinated positions, or those who are caught trying to meet older ideological goals while simultaneously being pressured to meet new ones.

Occupational Changes for Women

For women, it appears that the new possibility of woman as worker has been grafted on to the old role of processor/mother. In the past, women's contributions were acknowledged to be vital, but not equal, to men's contributions. Now women have the potential of competing equally with men in the work world. Furthermore, because of the generally greater flexibility involved in subsistence processing, wage-work and subsistence are less mutually exclusive for women than they are for men. Men's mobility places men at a much greater disadvantage than women's sedentism places women in terms of pursuing subsistence and long-term employment simultaneously. For example, a woman may stay up late cutting moose, often with the help of other female relatives, but she can do that in the community. On the other hand, the (generally male) hunter may have spent one to three weeks traveling and hunting to catch that moose. As a generalization, her subsistence obligations do not interfere with her wage labor to anywhere near the same extent that his do. They are also somewhat less site-specific in that fish can be dried in an urban backyard but cannot be caught there.[2]

THE GENDERED CONSTRUCTION OF WORK

Although there are a number of other factors involved in the differential rates of male and female employment and educational success, I would argue that traditional and contemporary gender roles make the transition to Western work easier for Yup'ik women than for Yup'ik men.

Historically, the work of Yup'ik women has been spatially restricted, repetitive, and multifocused. Women simultaneously sewed, cooked, and cared for children. This work has often been both social in nature (childcare), and externally controlled—observed, if not directed, by someone else (usually a mother, aunt, or mother-in-law). Men's work, on the other hand, has typically been spatially unrestricted, of limited repetitiveness, and focused on a single task. Not only has it been self-directed but much of it has also been asocial, since men often hunt alone. Office work, schoolwork, and health aid work is much more like women's work was (and is) than men's work was (and is). It is as if the female domestic sphere has expanded and now includes this kind of work as well.

With the partial exception of teaching, such jobs may not be considered gender appropriate for men, and, in fact, "village high school students of both sexes told us that education was 'a girl type thing,' meaning that females tend to do better and have higher aspirations in this sphere" (Hamilton and Seyfrit 1994:17). The social construction of Western work as similar to women's work may be one reason why many more Yup'ik women than Yup'ik men are successful in college. It is unfortunate that there are no statewide statistics providing graduation rates for Alaska Natives by Native group. However, Yupiit appear to represent a proportionate share, 40 percent of Alaska Natives entering as freshmen. For the entire University of Alaska system (nine campuses), from 1986 to 1990, Alaska Native/American Indian women received almost three times as many baccalaureate degrees as men (200 versus 71). Alaska Native males and females enter the system in nearly equal numbers (females outnumber males four to three as first-time freshmen), but the disparity increases year by year until graduation (Yarie et al. 1991).[3]

The number of Yup'ik men and women employed in the Yup'ik area is even more difficult to establish. Yupiit are employed full and part time by a variety of state and federal agencies, and many Yupiit are also employed by village governments, corporations, and cooperative and private stores. Obtaining an accurate count would require conducting a village-by-village census. Government statistics generally include only those "actively looking for work," so that the underemployed as well as those no longer looking for work are excluded. What does seem likely is that Yup'ik women and men tend to obtain different types of jobs. Yup'ik women are more likely to take jobs where education is either mandatory (such as teaching), or required eventually but not initially (such as being a health aide). In the Lower Kuskokwim School District, which includes Bethel and eighteen nearby villages, for example, Yup'ik female certificated teachers outnumber Yup'ik male certificated teachers at a ratio of two to one (twenty versus eleven) (Gary Baldwin, Lower Kuskokwim School District, personal communication, March 26, 1992). If this included teacher and classroom aides, the ratio would probably be higher. For full-time health aides in the Y-K Delta, Yup'ik women outnumber Yup'ik men at a ratio of more than nine to one (128 versus 14) (Linda Curda, Health Aide Training, Kuskokwim Campus, University of Alaska Fairbanks, personal communication, March 27, 1992). This latter figure may also reflect the attitudes of Yup'ik men that being a health aide is not role-appropriate for men. Although men do teach and hold clerical jobs, they have generally preferred construction, maintenance, mechanics, and heavy equipment operation, which tend to be high-paying and seasonal. The year-round clerical/teaching/health aide jobs are typically filled by women, who remain in these jobs for years.

There is some evidence of more successful adaptation by women to year-round wage-work in other Alaska Native groups as well. Although there are major differences between Alaska Native cultures, particularly between Inuit and Northwest Coast Indians (see later discussion of Tlingit), as well as very different contact histories, there are also noticeable similarities. For the Inupiat of the North Slope, another Alaskan Inuit culture, the pattern in the early 1970s was "for women to work full-time 'pink-collar' jobs while men preferred seasonal construction with flexible time which allowed them to hunt" (Bodenhorn 1994:183; see also Kruse et al. 1982; Kleinfeld et al. 1983). While Inupiaq women have, according to Bodenhorn (1994) broken out of the "pink-collar" ghetto, Inupiaq men still feel the force of the double bind of wage work and subsistence. Bodenhorn suggests that

> women's control over their labour has perhaps allowed them to move more easily into waged labour than has often been women's experience elsewhere. In fact, it is sometimes thought by Inupiat to have been an easier move for women than for men. . . . Men must go out on the tundra or the ice to hunt. Earning money is needed for survival, but it conflicts with what men have to do to fulfill their ritual responsibilities to the animals and to their fellow humans. Women, whose ritual work (sewing and butchering) is not restricted spatially, can more easily accommodate "real work" and jobs. (1994:200)

Elsewhere she quotes a North Slope Inupiaq woman who says that "men have a harder time of it, maybe: their minds are somewhere else" (Alice

Solomon, in Bodenhorn 1990:61). In this light it is noteworthy that the North Slope Borough (the Inupiat-controlled regional governing body)

> established employment policies allowing men time off for hunting, but did not reinforce women's role in subsistence by creating similar opportunities for them. Female employees were apparently expected to take part in activities such as butchering and processing of meat for storage, preparation of skins, etc. during after-work hours—the equivalent of working an additional shift. (Fogel-Chance 1993:96)

For the Tlingit Indians of Southeast Alaska, Klein notes that

> the women in the area hold most of the year-round jobs which are Euro-American by nature. Office workers, postal workers, store employees, school employees, bank workers, and the like are usually women. One commonly reported reason for this is that women are steadier than men as they will not quit when the fishing is good in order to cash in on that industry. . . . (1980:103)

It would be interesting to have follow-up data from this area.

An additional issue in terms of trying to combine wage work-and subsistence is that of who controls the family finances. This was not a major topic of my research, and my data is provisional. However, my sense of the finances of Yup'ik married couples is that if both wife and husband are working, the wife's income is generally hers to spend as she sees fit, with the proviso that she will probably be financially responsible for clothing and buying presents for their children. If the wife is working and the husband is not, there will be considerable pressure on her to spend the money as her husband dictates, acquiescing to his priorities, particularly those involving major subsistence-related expenditures.

If the husband is working and the wife is not, the wife's position, as female and non-income producing, is weak. She may have some difficulty securing money to fund her priorities, which may include clothing and store-bought food.

The general case (acording to Moore 1988), is that "women are differentially affected by capitalist development, and that their overall position is one of extreme vulnerability" (70). In terms of work and education, the situation of Yup'ik women and Alaska Native women in general is one where "development" seems to have had more positive economic effects upon women than upon men, although double-shifting undoubtedly creates personal stress. While it seems likely that a major thrust of colonialism is "the encouragement of male exploitation of female labor and forced economic dependency of women" (Buenaventura-Posso and

Brown 1980:127; see also Boserup 1970; Tinker et al. 1976), the effects of these forces are by no means universal, even after articulation with wider market systems.

CHANGES IN YUP'IK GENDER SPACES

There is a general sense in Yup'ik culture that men should be with men and women with women, with children quietly around either, or often, with other children. As in many cultures, possible sexual attraction and interest as well as conflict between men and women is minimized by separating the sexes. People are generally careful to avoid situations in which they would be alone with someone of the opposite sex, in order to avoid the appearance of impropriety (see also Bogojavlensky 1969:134–35).[4] In general, "[Yup'ik] men and women did not spend time socializing with one another" (Shinkwin and Pete 1983:29). This division was clearest in the traditional system of separate residences. In the 1970s, Bogojavlensky wrote about the then extant men's-house system in the Bering Strait region, the adjacent Inupiaq area to the north of the Y-K Delta. "If a man is not either asleep at home or out hunting, he will be in his men's house" (1969:174). In the Yup'ik area this sex segregation was even more complete, because men slept in the men's house as well. However, with missionization came strong sentiment and pressure against this system. One Moravian minister expressed his church's attitudes: "The *Kashigi [qasgiq]* has robbed the family of homelife—for the father and son virtually live in the *Kashigi [qasgiq]*—not even being regular boarders at what should be their home—for their meals are sent to them" (Kilbuck, in Fienup-Riordan 1988:19). Over time, the missionaries were successful in changing the Yup'ik residence system. In most villages the shift to mixed-sex family residences occurred shortly prior to or following World War II. In many villages, however, until the 1960s or 1970s, the men's houses remained important as sites for firebaths, as well as a workshop space for large projects and meetings (Shinkwin and Pete 1983:28–29).

THE STEAMBATH AS AN INSTITUTION

Paralleling the decline of the men's house has been a proliferation of smaller steambath houses. Few villages still have structures for taking the older-style firebaths, and the men who firebathe are mostly older. As an institution it is currently on the wane. The steambath, having replaced the firebath, is thriving. Most extended families have one or more such structures, and in many villages these are fired up every evening. These small, low, plywood buildings, often in two visible parts, are ubiquitous.

When pressed, people will give practical reasons for steambathing. It does get one very clean using a minimal amount of water, no small feat in villages without running water. One can begin the process with mostly ice and still clean a number of people. Still, the main reason people steam is that they like it. It's a very social time, and quite relaxing. There is time for jokes and stories, teasing and competition. Further, men and women both become habituated to regular steambathing, and miss the "high" that a steambath gives.[5] It is common for Yupiit who are visiting in Bethel or a larger city to try to figure out how they can take a steambath.

The taking of Yup'ik-style steambaths has also become a marker of local identity in its own right, where to be "really" Yup'ik is to take very hot steams, nightly if possible. Guests from out of town, Native and non-Native, are often invited to steam, an invitation that is a combination of offering hospitality and tossing down the gauntlet. And sometimes what was an offer of inclusive hospitality becomes an endurance test anyway, as one is caught in the cross fire of competing cross-cousins "hunting" each other with the intense heat (see later discussion). It is one of the few contexts in which people are overtly comparative as well as evaluative. Men will talk about how much "steam" (heat) other men tolerate and enjoy. At least in my (non-Native) presence, such narratives often include both descriptive and evaluative comments, denoting some general Yup'ik ideal of quiet endurance. Given the deep local resonances of this activity, knowledgeable non-Native participants are generally positively evaluated and often asked who (presumably a Yup'ik) "taught" them to steam. Steambathing is also a favored topic of discourse (at least for men), particularly when preparing or taking a steambath. It serves a similar function to that of Native foods in this regard. Yup'ik men will frequently note that simply talking about steambathing has been enough to cause them to bead out in sweat on their foreheads or upper lips.

The Steambath as a Replacement for the Men's House

The steambath seems to fulfill some of the roles of the men's house. It is one of the few spheres where competition is legitimated. Whereas in the men's house men sometimes competed in gift giving, strength, and agility (and I imagine in endurance to the heat of the firebath as well), in the steambath men compete in endurance. The object is to (appear to) enjoy the heat while one's cousin is driven out by its intensity. Analogously with traditional ceremonies in the men's house, the fiercest competitions are usually between cross-cousins, the so-called joking cousins with whom one is not supposed to lose one's temper, no matter what the provocation.

The steambath also provides, at least temporarily, a defined male space. I say temporarily because in many villages women steambathe together. Husband and wife pairs, usually with their younger children, may also do so. Still, men have clear priority. They steambathe whenever they want, and if there is insufficient wood for both men and women to steambathe, the men typically get the wood. Women may have to make do with burning oil-soaked household trash and used disposable diapers, or old (spoiled) sea mammal oil and fat. While this is a change from having virtually sole use and occupancy in the men's house, the steambath remains an important place for men. I've been told by groups of men that they have been steambathing together for twenty or more years, since they were teenagers. Steambathing can provide a strong sense of continuity, of being in a male space with the same men, night after night and year after year.

I've also felt that many men were most comfortable and relaxed in the steam or out of doors. The houses, summer tents, and particularly the kitchen areas are in some way women's territory, or at least not the proper place for healthy men. The following field notes are from the summer of 1991:

> The men were just returning from fishing when we arrived. After helping carry the fish up to the waiting wheelbarrow, I wound my way back through the tents, sheds, and smokehouses to the kitchen tent. It was a very female scene, with a senior woman in charge of things (a friend of my wife's and mine) and two of her sisters-in-law finishing eating, along with a gaggle of young daughters and cousins. Someone who was finished (or claimed to be finished) vacated a place for me at the table, where her husband and brother-in-law (I think) soon joined me at other newly vacated places. We had a leisurely and delicious meal. The three women sat with us, or nearby, and various girls stood around, played with the baby, or changed diapers. But the gender shift at the table was pretty obvious. Just as obviously, when the meal was over, the men got up and went out. It really wasn't our place, except to eat, and when done, we vacated it for the women. I followed the husband out to the fish racks, where he watched his mother and sister cut fish for a while, seemingly very relaxed, like he was between tasks and could rest a while, even if others were working, then he started getting ready to go fishing again.

In retrospect, I was reminded of staying at another fish camp in 1977, where I felt comfortable only when working, steambathing, eating, or in our tent at night. I didn't feel that there was any place for me just to "be," except the steambath. This feeling was reinforced when I once tried to confront what seemed to me to be gender-role inequities by getting up and starting to wash the lunch dishes. One of the women walked out, saying within my hearing (and no doubt for my edification), "Men! They think they can do everything!" After this I fixed up an old steambath in need of some repairs.

It is not that men are rushed or hurried at the table, even at feasts, where there are others waiting to eat. In inclement weather, too, men may spend long periods at the table drinking tea and talking. However, my general sense has been that men remain in that space for a task or purpose, after which they move to another part of the room, to another room, or outside.

There are, of course, functions of the men's house that the steambath does not serve. It is neither a ceremonial center nor a place of residence, although it is still a place where out-of-town guests are entertained. It does not provide a work space for large projects, but contemporary houses are larger in any case; and other public spaces, such as the school and armory, are sometimes available for projects. Such spaces are readily appropriated for both work and conversational space, as Fienup-Riordan details (1991:39).

CHANGES IN GENDER RELATIONS AND POWER

Changes such as the availability of wage-work and the breakdown of the traditional residence system have been reflected in, and paralleled by, changes in interpersonal relationships as well.

In the nineteenth century, male power and abuse in marriage were mitigated by the ease of divorce. Most first marriages were arranged by the relatives, and "arrangements usually reflected political decisions on the part of parents (especially fathers)" (Shinkwin and Pete 1983:23). Subsequent marriages seem to have been arranged by the participants themselves. Judging from elders' narratives about the pre- and early missionary period, divorce was both easy and common. Lantis states that on Nunivak, "Both men and women had a succession of marriages, three or four for most people, five or six for a few men. Although in practice, men were able to take the initiative in separation more often, women were supposed to have equal freedom" (1946:159).

Apparently Yup'ik women were, on the whole, sufficiently empowered to be safe from physical abuse. Yup'ik elders report that "wife beating was extremely uncommon" in the early decades of this century (Shinkwin and Pete 1983:22). The elders interviewed clearly linked physical abuse with the rise of alcohol abuse; almost all contemporary battering is alcohol related. Such violence endangers not only women but also children, elders, and other men.[6]

Shinkwin and Pete see clear links between the destruction of the traditional system of marriage and residence, the loss of female autonomy, and current high rates of domestic violence. The shift from separate residences, easily dissolvable marriages, and relative equality to the current male-dominated nuclear families founded upon church-sanctioned permanent marriages has clearly placed women at a disadvantage. In the past, "freedom to separate and remarry . . . also functioned to manage conflict between married couples" (Shinkwin and Pete 1983:24). Now women find strong public and private sanctions to remain in marriages, including potentially fatal ones. (Alaska Native women are four and a half times more likely to be homicide victims than women nationwide [Berman and Leask 1994:1].) This intervention may include public lectures in church by religious functionaries (usually male) and scolding by village council members (also usually male), and male and female relatives. Shinkwin and Pete suggest that the strong patriarchal biases of Christianity have worsened the situation for women by shifting power from women to men. They further speculate that this shift has been exacerbated by the destruction of the former system of separate residences, since the sexes now spend so much more time in proximity, and the control over male violence exerted by other men has been lost.

Generally, the system of arranging marriages has broken down, and there seems to have been a concurrent shift in marriage ages. The older pattern paired a man in his late twenties to late thirties with a girl immediately past menarche (some older women describe themselves as still playing with dolls when they were married). The current pattern for first marriages has women in their late teens to early twenties marrying men in their early to mid-twenties. Probably more significant than the relative age difference in marriages is a change from the older pattern, in which most adults were married, to a situation in which there are many more single adults living alone or with their families.

Young Male Suicide, Accidental Death, and Social Dysfunction

For the period from 1985 to 1990, in the Y-K Delta, rates of suicide averaged 68/100,000 per year, with men accounting for 86 percent of these suicides. Accidental deaths averaged another 167/100,000 per year, again with men heavily overrepresented. Many of the accidental deaths occurred after heavy drinking or showed fundamental disregard by the victim for his own life (Marshall 1992). To put this into more comprehensible terms, consider the following: (1) between 1985 and 1992 the author of a 1992 study on suicide and accidental death lost eight Yup'ik friends to suicide; (2) for the village of Alakanuk (population five hundred) cumulative losses were fourteen suicides and nineteen accidental deaths in the twelve years from 1979 to 1990, or one person in fifteen (op cit.); and (3) "a Native man who never married has a 25% chance of dying violently before age 60" (Berman and Leask 1994:1). Men in these communities are also lost to long-term incarceration.

It is important to note that there is tremendous variation between villages in terms of social integration. There are villages that seem to function well. These are places that are sober, responsible, and autonomous in the sense that most social problems are handled locally, rather than involving the legal system.[7] The same is true of individuals: there are many Yup'ik men of all ages who are sober, responsible, and caring sons, fathers, brothers, and husbands. My purpose in dwelling on these problems is not to cast a negative light on Yup'ik society but to try to illuminate a locally identified problem of tragic proportions.

Mortality rates for Yup'ik males differ in several ways from those of other minorities in the United States, as well as from that of the nation as a whole. Male Yupiit are much more likely to die of suicide, homicide, and accidental deaths than members of virtually all other minority groups, or of American men as a group. The sole exception is homicide. While homicide rates among Alaska Native males are close to three times the national average, they are lower than the rates for African American males (taken from Marshall 1992, Berman and Leask 1994).

Incarceration rates for Yupiit are also high (roughly comparable with those for African-Americans). Most of the crimes for which Yupiit are incarcerated were committed under the influence of alcohol and/or drugs. In the Bethel trial district more than 95 percent of crimes may be so categorized (Craig McMahon, Bethel magistrate, interview 1991). Typically, violent crimes are perpetrated against family members, close relatives, and friends when the perpetrator is intoxicated. There is little economic crime (thefts, burglaries), and almost no violent economic crime (armed robbery, car-jacking). What economic crime there is usually involves stealing some form of transportation—boats, outboard motors, four-wheelers and snow machines. Frequently this is the rural equivalent of joyriding, and the vehicles are recovered.

Another kind of male dysfunction, or at least a potentially problematic response, is what might be called an extended adolescence, where men remain unemployed and unpartnered, living in their parents' houses. They tend to be unemployed or underemployed in both the subsistence and wage-labor economies, participating only in those subsistence activities that are either highly productive or that they particularly enjoy, and working for wages only sporadically and briefly. It is common for men in this category to abuse alcohol and drugs: they are heavily represented in the suicide statistics. At most, ten out of sixty-six men who committed suicide in the Y-K Delta between 1985 and 1990 held steady jobs, and sixty-five out of sixty-six were unmarried (Marshall 1992).[8] A similar pattern exists elsewhere in the Inuit area. For St. Lawrence Island, Jolles and Kaningok write, "In Gambell, some young adults live a life suspended between youth and maturity and between a rural Yup'ik life and one imagined to exist in urban centers" (1991:29, footnote 15). Condon (1987) and Rasing (1994) note the same phenomenon in the Canadian Arctic, as does Langgaard (1986) in Greenland. In the village Langgaard describes, both males and females may remain in this kind of extended adolescence, though interestingly, young women still migrate at higher rates than young men.

Female Emigration, Outmarriage, and Nonmarriage

One response by Yup'ik women (and Alaska Native women in general) to the choices and futures they see for themselves in their natal villages is to emigrate.[9] Given the local preponderance of male suicide and accidental death, one would expect a surplus of females in villages. In fact, this is decidedly untrue. The trend is for many more Alaska Native women, including Yupiit, than Alaska Native men to emigrate from smaller villages to urban areas. For Alaska Natives aged twenty to thirty-nine, the median percentage of females was: 45.2 percent in 125 communities of less than 1,000; 51.4 percent in 27 communities of between 1,000 and 9,999; and 55.2 percent in 6 communities over 10,000 population (Hamilton and Seyfrit 1993, from 1990 U.S. Census Bureau data).

This trend is also evident in the Y-K Delta. In an analysis of the six largest villages (those with populations greater than 500), males outnumbered females in this age class in all but one village, and by rates of up to 33 percent, with an average of 15 percent. In Bethel the situation is reversed, with Yup'ik women outnumbering Yup'ik men in this age class by 16 percent, so that the Y-K Delta follows the same pattern, but to an even greater extent (1990 U.S. Census Bureau data, from Marshall 1992). In addition to in-state migration, there is also out-of-state migration. While there are no hard figures, it is possible to estimate numbers of Native women who have emigrated out-of-state in excess of Native male migrants. Based upon birth and mortality figures, not only have approximately 1,000 Alaska Native women in the twenty- to thirty-nine-year-old age bracket migrated from smaller communities to large ones, but an additional few hundred more Alaska Native women than Alaska Native men have migrated out-of-state (Hamilton and Seyfrit 1994).

A phenomenon allied to emigration, in that it also reduces the number of possible marriage partners for Native men, is that of outmarriage. Statewide figures for 1990 show roughly equivalent numbers of Native women marrying Native men (364 total) and non-Native men (370 total, combining the categories "white" and "other"). For Native men, the situation is very different. They married Native women (364 total) at roughly twice the rate at which they married non-Native women (193 total), but overall, they married at a lower rate than Native women (557 versus 744) (taken from Hamilton and Seyfrit 1994).

This pattern of Native female outmarriage is not new. A 1975 study in Fairbanks showed Native women marrying non-Native men at five times the rate at which non-Native women married Native men (Milan and Pawson, in Levin 1991:3). Alaskan marriage statistics from 1980 to 1984 show Native women marrying out at two and one half times the rate of Native men. However, like the previous data, this is only a partial listing, as it shows only formal marriages that occurred in Alaska (Levin 1991). While there are no data available on this issue for the Y-K Delta, this disparity is obvious even to the most casual observer, and might be as high as five to one if the data were complete.

There has always been the demographic potential for female outmarriage, in the historic and contemporary surplus of non-Native males. Now, as in the past, fewer non-Native women than men immigrate to Alaska. Currently in Alaska, non-Native males exceed females in all age classes below sixty-five, with more than 10,000 more non-Native males than non-Native females in the twenty- to thirty-nine-year-old age class. For comparison, there is a total of about 15,000 Alaska Native females in this same age class. The disparity between numbers of non-Native females and non-Native males is even more exaggerated in communities with a population of fewer than 1,000 (Hamilton and Seyfrit 1994, from 1990 U.S. Census Bureau data).

The third option Yup'ik women seem to be taking is not to marry. As mentioned before, this is a major change from older patterns. This is possible, in part, because it is now much easier to survive as a single person without the complementary labor of a spouse. Not only may extended kin and friends supply the raw materials of fish and game, which defined the husband's role, but also women themselves are performing some of these formerly male roles where males are absent, unwilling, or incapable. One Yup'ik woman I interviewed stated her perceptions of this independence: "I don't need my husband, I don't need my father, I don't need my brother. I can make it on my own, and I think a lot of [Yup'ik] women feel that way" (field notes of an interview, July 1991). It is important to note that being unmarried does not necessarily keep a woman from raising a family, usually with the help of extended kin, or from having relationships with men.

Emigration, Cultural Change, and Individual Choice

The changes that have occurred in women's roles and opportunities can be divided into two categories. In condensed form, the changes that tend to increase women's options are predominantly external to the home and to marriage (apart from the fact that marriages are no longer, with rare exceptions, arranged.) These options include the chance for an education, for employment, and for increasing one's status through employment. The changes that have tended to limit women's options are all internal to the home and to marriage. These include lifelong marriages, greatly increased rates of violence and physical abuse,[10] and spousal alcoholism and drug abuse. The net effect is not only that women have the tools to leave their village but also that their leaving provides a way of taking their expanded options with them while leaving many limitations behind. They have been able to transfer into new jobs and settings that they perceive will enhance their life.[11] One Yup'ik woman described a confrontation with a young Yup'ik man over her marriage to a non-Native:

> I can remember too, one year in between school and summer jobs, when I went home for a visit during the summer. And [my husband] and I's [sic] marriage had already been announced, or people knew that we were going to get married. It had been planned at a future date.
>
> I went home and my brother and his friends were doing the usual stuff, drinking and just making fools of themselves. Two of his friends were there with him. They're all in the same situation. They've been out of school for five years. They're at home. They're still living with their parents. They're drinking and making it hard on everybody else.
>
> And one of the guys comes up to me. We're arguing about bootlegging and things like that. They told me that I shouldn't talk like that, because I could really get hurt. It started off from there.

Then the other guy says, "I can't believe you're marrying a *Kass'aq* [Euro-American]." I said, "I can believe that." I said, "I'm going to school, I'm here for a break. I'm going back to a job, I'm here for a break. I'm getting all of these things for myself and making this kind of life for myself. You're here, you're sitting, you're drunk. You live in your mom's home. You expect me to come back and marry you?" And that really shut him up, you know. (transcript of an interview, 1991)

Emmett (1982), writing about migration from a Welsh village, noted clear parallels in the selective power of gender ideology:

These forces [to stay in the village] act differently upon men and women. For a woman it is more difficult than a man to achieve a career . . . if she does climb she will have other and perhaps fewer reasons than a man to regret doing so. Working-class life has fewer rewards for women than for men. Men are more vulnerable to the appeal of the home culture because it contains an appeal to masculinity. Current models of masculinity give high value to the possession of physical strength and the ability to do manual work. Current models of femininity, especially for young women, give no points for red hands, or making do on little money. (1982:212)

In some general sense, many Yup'ik women may have a different image of their future than do many Yup'ik men, including perhaps what they want in a spouse. A recent study of Yup'ik high-school students in the Bristol Bay region found that 50 percent more young women than young men expected to leave the region after high school, and that, for recent graduates, women were two and one half times more likely to be living outside the region—25 percent versus 10 percent (Hamilton and Seyfrit 1993). These expectations may be realistic. Women are more likely to have the skills and credentials to make such a move. Further, moving increases their options for potential partners.

For Yup'ik men, the situation is very different. The private gains they have made are local, sited within marriage, and are nontransferable. The loss of status and prestige relative to women and to the new ideological models of success cannot be circumvented by migrating; neither can the shortage of potential female partners. Deciding whether to stay in a village with few potential partners or to move to an urban area where there is a surplus of non-Native males marrying both Native and non-Native women at higher rates is a problematic choice. Further, moving to an urban environment may be more difficult for Yup'ik men than for Yup'ik women. Traditional and contemporary Yup'ik male gender roles do not provide employment skills sought in urban settings. Typically greater male involvement in substance abuse also makes the transition from "dry" villages, where the availability of alcohol is restricted, to "wet" urban areas where it is not, difficult for many men.

This difference between public gains and private losses may also help explain the difference between the Yup'ik situation and colonial situations elsewhere where men are favored at the expense of women. In the Yup'ik area, colonization has favored men at the expense of women's autonomy in the private sphere, but it has favored women over men in the public sphere. Further, in those agricultural settings where women are the producers, men are usually encouraged to exploit women's labor and production, so that excess goods will be generated. Such goods are both literally and figuratively "grist for the colonial mill" (Buenaventura-Posso and Brown 1980). In the Yup'ik case, where men are defined as the cultural producers of natural products, there is little surplus to extract, besides fish (primarily salmon) and furs, with trapping currently in decline because of low fur prices. The fishing industry employs only a small fraction of the available population, and that only seasonally and part-time. And even here, if fisheries were managed for maximum efficiency per producer, they could be operated with a fraction of the current permit holders. The overall picture in the Y-K Delta is of a colony that "needs" the colonized only to run the proliferating bureaucracies, but not for the usual "work" (agricultural, mineral, or manufacturing) upon which colonies are more usually based.

OUTMARRIAGE REEXAMINED

It has been argued (Bloom 1973:446 in Levin 1991:69) that the reason for Alaska Native female outmarriage is "dissatisfaction with her low standing in the Native culture provid[ing] impetus for migration in the hope of marrying a non-Native man." There are at least two problems with this statement. First, it collapses potential differences in the status of women in disparate Native cultures. At such a level of generalization, the statement is difficult to address, let alone prove or disprove. And second, it opts for a monocausal explanation for preferential Native female migration when the situation is undoubtedly more complex, with a variety of historically situated "pushes" to leave smaller communities and "pulls" to migrate to larger ones.

In the Yup'ik case, outmarriage may be a way of avoiding certain restrictive and destructive family roles potentiated by alcohol. Some outmarrying Yup'ik women have said that they have a better chance of avoiding these problems by marrying out (see also Bell [1980:245] for a similar feeling among one group of Aboriginal women in Australia). For at least some Yup'ik women this is not the preferred marriage but a kind of second choice based on a lack of potential Yup'ik husbands who are sober and responsible. "I've told [my non-Native husband], and I told him that he should really understand where I'm coming from, and that he shouldn't take this badly, but, if I had met a Yup'ik person who was just like him, that I would have married him [that Yup'ik man]"[12] (transcript of an interview, 1991).

Non-Native researchers also sometimes attribute male rage and hopelessness to the pronounced gender imbalance in some age classes.[13] This unfairly blames the victims of violence and reduces a feedback loop to a causal relationship.[14] Hamilton and Seyfrit suggest some of the complexities involved:

> Disproportionate female outmigration . . . leaves young men with less chance of finding stable partners, forming a family, and settling down. Instead, some face an extended period of low responsibility, with associated risks of accidents, substance abuse, suicide and encounters with the law. . . . Young girls meanwhile experience increasing attention from adult men, contributing to problems of abuse, teen pregnancy, early alcoholism and fetal exposure, high-risk sexual activity and self-destruction. Pressure from a male majority could add to the incentives for women and girls to leave. (1994:24)

THE CONTINUING SYMBOLIC IMPORTANCE OF SUBSISTENCE

Subsistence remains symbolically important for men as the historic marker of male success and role fulfillment. In this way it resembles the sustained interest of the British upper class in estates long after the industrial revolution and colonialism created more profitable ways to make money. Analogously, subsistence provides a public way of demonstrating and validating status and success. Its importance in this arena may be in part because Yupiit do not, in general, derive their sense of identity from their wage-work: wage-work is something one does for money. Only rarely does it provide an identity in the way it does for many middle-class Euro-Americans. Similarly, Bodenhorn notes that for North Slope Inupiat, "Jobs were not talked about as 'careers,' nor were they associated with individual identity as is so frequent on the continental United States. Jobs provide money; who you 'are' is decided by other factors" (1989:55). Jolles, too, suggests that for the Siberian Yup'ik of Gambell on St. Lawrence Island, "non-traditional work, at least so far, is not an important source of identity. Identity remains associated with successful performance of subsistence duties" (1993:4).

Given this continuing sense of achieving identity through subsistence, it is perhaps not surprising that I have been unable to find Yup'ik men who have both permanently emigrated from the area and who neither return periodically to do subsistence nor hunt and fish where they reside. While there may be such men, this pattern is clearly uncommon. Much more common is to-and-fro migration, with men alternating between city and village, or making periodic returns to rural areas to hunt and fish. Among these men, as among Yup'ik men working full-time in Bethel, subsistence is still a major topic of interest and conversation. It seems likely that this interest is heightened precisely because they are doing less subsistence. They have even more need to speak of hunting and fishing because they are in fact only rarely hunting and fishing. For such men, subsistence discourse may be vital in validating their image of themselves because this image is so infrequently validated through activities and products.[15]

Subsistence has a similar symbolic importance to women. Many women I interviewed (and talked with) enunciated the importance of subsistence in their lives or, more often, took that importance as an unquestioned assumption, exactly as most Yup'ik men do. In interviews, they stated that subsistence was a favored topic in their conversations with other women. This was confirmed in conversations I observed in public and domestic spaces. Given the gender separateness in Yup'ik society, it is expected that in many situations men will talk with men and women with women. Such conversations may occur in shared space (a kitchen, a tent, public benches at the airport). In this situation, women may tacitly ignore men's conversations and vice versa.

Yup'ik women living permanently or semipermanently in urban Alaskan settings also maintain interests in subsistence. Some of those with whom I discussed these issues are married to non-Natives, some to Yupiit; some return most summers, if not every summer, to put up fish; others do not. For those who return, subsistence seems as important as it is for any other Yup'ik woman. Typically, they focus on processing, the avoidance of waste, and the distribution of what they have processed and of what was distributed to them. They also generally participate in "female" harvesting activities such as berrying and jigging for pike. However, contrary to what I might have thought, even women who do not return regularly still seemed to have a significant subsistence focus.

This focus is on their urban locale, and involves berry picking, gathering, and gardening. There is still a sense of connection to the land and also of producing food for their family, and of sharing. In the absence of male production women's attention seems more focused on what they themselves can produce. There is also positive reinforcement for these interests in the broader non-Native Alaskan context. Gardening, berrying, and preserving food are all admired activities, although not exclusively marked as feminine or Native.

The symbolic importance of subsistence seems heightened for those women whose allegiance to a positive Yup'ik identity might be most easily questioned. This includes women who have married out and/or migrated, as well as those who are professionals. My sense is that few such women are actually trying to shed their ethnicity, though some may be. Having made their life choices, however, their ethnicity and ethnic allegiance may be questioned. Such women may have a greater need for markers that show both the world and themselves that they *are* Yupiit, and that this identity is valued. One woman interviewed talked about the importance of subsistence in reminding herself (and others) of who she was.

She pointed with her eyes to a picture on her office wall of king salmon blankets hanging up to dry at her fish camp: "Sometimes when I'm in here, I look at that, and it's real important to me, because I know no one else could do that" (field notes of an interview, July 1991). I do not believe she meant by this literally that no one else could prepare king salmon blankets, but that the knowledge and skill necessary to cut and successfully dry king salmon blankets was emblematic of adult Yup'ik womanhood. In her professional work setting, which was often personally and culturally alienating, the picture both marked and reassured her of who she was. It made salient an identity which, in that setting, was potentially obscured.

It was in fact doubly powerful because much of its message was covert. To "read" the picture successfully required an embedded local knowledge of Yup'ik values and practices. To comprehend the message, the "reader" had to see not "fish drying" but "king salmon blankets in the initial stages of drying," and to recognize this as a statement of adult Yup'ik female competence.[16] Thus, it is in some ways a message to, and fully understood by, only those who might most tellingly question her cultural allegiance. It is both a sign and a pictorial shibboleth, fully read only by those who share that embedded knowledge and (probably) those values.

GENDER DIFFERENCES, DISCOURSE SIMILARITIES

Given the significant differences (and the potential for different futures) for contemporary Yup'ik women and men, it is not surprising that differences exist in the kinds of issues (of ideology and identity) addressed through discourse, including subsistence discourse. However, such differences seem generally to be differences of degree rather than of kind, and are largely obscured by the differences between individuals. Yup'ik women and men are in many ways confronted with the same overall situation, and while a Yup'ik woman in a particular nontraditional occupational role may find her ethnicity more in question than her gender, these identities are neither clearly separable nor, in practice, separated (this point will be elaborated further in chapter 7). The balance of discourse may be tipped more toward ethnicity for women and toward gender for men, but both men and women must in some way address both issues. This overlap, when combined with the variation in the ways these issues are present and relevant in the lives of particular Yupiit, obscures many of the gender differences that one might otherwise expect. In the end, Yup'ik women and men use subsistence discourse in similar ways to both similar and dissimilar ends. This discourse arena is, after all, a public (and private) stage where identities are constructed and maintained, not a track to which they are attached.

6

Yup'ik Gourmands: Food and Ethnicity

SETTING A WINTER NET UNDER THE ICE FOR WHITEFISH

This year there was an early freeze-up. By the second week in November the most adventuresome are driving small cars on the river. The real go-getters have already had their nets in for a week or more, but I prefer to wait and take fewer risks. There is little snow, and getting to the river is a slow, bumpy process, but once there the going is smooth and fast. In the sled are the two ice chisels, a shovel, an axe, numerous pieces of rope, the nets, a curved pole with two large blunt hooks attached to the end, and the wooden pieces used to move the rope from hole to hole under the ice. This piece consists of a ten-foot piece of one-by-six-inch pine with a hole drilled through it at either end. To one hole is attached a four-foot piece of heavy twine with a white salmon net float at the end. The other hole serves as a pivot point, with a bolt holding it between the two forks of a wishbone-shaped piece. This is made from three one-by-sixes, with the outside pieces about five feet long, and the middle one a foot and a half shorter to form a space for the longer piece with the float.

My fishing partner and I drive carefully along the river, but I am still almost passed by my sled, which tips over once. Nothing is lost however. We head to our usual spot, a shallow eddy which has been productive in the past. When we arrive there is one other net about one hundred yards away, but otherwise the spot is empty. We begin with a discussion of where we have set in previous years and where we should set out nets this year. We end up choosing two spots about fifty yards apart.

We begin by making test holes to find out where the bottom begins to shallow out; a net placed there could float up and freeze in, or the end might get covered with overflow as the river drops over the course of the winter. The ice is only about six inches thick, so it is easy to make the holes. Still, there are a lot of them required, seven for the sixty-foot net, four for the thirty-foot. We make each hole roughly one end and one-half by three feet, with the long axis running the same way as the line of holes.

Then the fun begins. The float stick and wishbone handle are attached and pushed into hole number 2. They are then pivoted around until the float stick is under the ice, pointing towards hole number 1, and the wishbone-shaped handle is still sticking up out of hole number 2. We are lucky, and the float pops up out of hole number 1. My friend ties a lightweight rope to the float and I pull the wishbone handle and float stick out of hole number 2 far enough that I can point it back towards hole number 3. The rope has been feeding into hole number 1 as it is supposed to, but the float doesn't pop up at hole number 3. My friend fishes for the float with the curved stick, and with a little readjustment of the float stick on my part, pulls out the rope and float. He unties the rope from the float, pulls out a few feet and lays an ice chisel on it to keep it in place. Meanwhile, I move my contraption down to hole number 4 and point the float stick toward hole number 3. He fishes for the float, gets it easily, and ties the rope to it. I pull out the handle and float stick, point it toward hole number 5, and continue the process.

Thin clear ice, little or no current, and warmer temperatures often make this process relatively easy in the fall. Replacing even a short net in midwinter can take long hours of chopping through four feet or more of ice, and makes fishing for the float much more difficult as well. Any work that requires bare hands has to be done quickly, and all the equipment gets heavily coated with ice.

When ropes are set for both nets my friend goes to chop some poles while I lay out and ready the nets. Two long and two short poles are cut for each net. The short poles are set at an angle pointing outward from the ends of the net, socketed in shallow holes chopped just inside of the last large holes. These poles will stabilize the larger poles. The float line of the net is tied to the rope, and the net is pulled under the water. At the shore end it is tied to the bottom of one of the longer poles, and the end of that pole is pushed into the hole. At the far end of the holes, the other end of the float line is tied to the other long pole, the bottom part of which is also pushed under the ice. These long poles are tied to the smaller support poles in such a way as to spread and tension the float line as much as possible, in order to prevent it from floating up too far and getting frozen in as the ice thickens. If there is snow, it is shoveled over the holes at the end of the net to slow down the formation of ice.

　While I load the gear onto the sled, my friend takes the long rope and checks the first net we set to see if possibly, by some chance, we might have a fish. I stand and watch expectantly as he pulls out the net, still attached to the pole at one end. It pulls out smoothly, sliding over the ice like an extremely long and wet shirtsleeve coming out of the washer. Then, almost at the end of the net, as I start to turn away, there is a little blurp of water, and a whitefish starts flopping around on the ice, tangled up in the net. "All right!" my friend says as he frees the fish. It is a nice-sized broad whitefish, maybe three pounds, delicious either raw and frozen, aged, dried, or cooked. We reset the net, then finish loading the sled. We had gotten a bit of a late start, and the day fades into twilight as we head home.

CHECKING THE NET

It's a late afternoon in early December—fifteen degrees Fahrenheit and windy, when the boys and I head out to check the net. We are all warmly dressed. The children (aged five and three) have on fur parkas, hats, mittens, and felt-lined boots. I'm wearing a snow-machine suit, heavy sweater, beaver hat, and sealskin mittens over insulated leather gloves. There is a sleeping bag and a plastic sled in the back of the car in case we have to walk back, though the river is like a highway at this time of the year.

　Once on the river I pick up speed, though occasionally it's difficult to know on which side cars coming the other direction are going to pass. Once I slow almost to a stop to allow someone his choice.

　It's getting dusky when we arrive. The boys play around in the snow and dig with the shovel for a few minutes, then retire to the car, only occasionally honking the horn. There is only about a foot of fresh ice, but it still takes a while to free both ends of the net. I tie on the long rope, then roust the boys out of the car to see what we have. First, at the shallow end of the net, there is nothing, then a couple of hump-backed whitefish, then a big loche, thrashing eel-like, a dead sheefish, several more whitefish of both common kinds, another sheefish, this one freshly dead, its gills still red, and another loche, dead for days and slimy. "It's just like Christmas," I tell the boys.

　I stop to turn on the car lights and pick the net as quickly as I can. The frozen mesh has the consistency of chicken wire, and my hands need frequent warming, and glow bright red with suffused blood. The boys get cold or lose interest in the fish and retreat to the car. I pull the net back under the ice, deeper now than when we first set it, retie the poles, and load fish and gear into

the back of the car. We stop to drop off fish at a couple of friends' houses, and
get home at full dark. One of the fish is our dinner. The others I sort into those
alive when caught, for cooking; and those not, for eating frozen. These go into
the freezer for slack times or to give later as gifts.

EATING FOR PLEASURE VERSUS EATING TO SURVIVE

Non-Natives have typically written about Inuit as being survival-focused. They are seen as food-focused only insofar as food is the prerequisite for survival. The image of Inuit eating raw flesh and fat is centuries old. "But [Inuit] are contented by their hunting, fishing and fouling, with raw flesh and warme blood to satisfie their greedy paunches, which is their only glory" (Hakluyt 1589:228, in Fienup-Riordan 1990:13).

In short, little that is sympathetic has been written about Inuit foods. In this virtual vacuum of documentation it is difficult to reconstruct the historic and contemporary attitudes of various Inuit groups toward food. The paucity of accounts by Inuit only increases our uncertainty. Furthermore, it is difficult to judge either positive or negative descriptions of Inuit foods by non-Inuit. Negative descriptions may simply be confirming cultural stereotypes, and the rare positive descriptions may merely be attempts to counter them. Positive descriptions may also reflect machismo on the part of a writer who is secretly less than impressed by Inuit cuisine.

Against this background, I was enthralled when I first read Peter Freuchen's description of eating *giviak* (auk aged in a seal poke).

> It tasted good the moment I got it into my mouth. But I had to be taught how to eat this remarkable dish. As long as it is frozen, you just chew away. You get feathers and bones in your mouth, of course, but you just spit them out. Frozen meat always has an enticing taste, and as it dissolves in the mouth, you get the full aroma of the raw fermented bird. It is incredible how much you can get down, unbelievable how hard it is to stop. If you happen to come across a fully developed egg inside a bird, it tastes like a dream. Or the liver, which is like green cheese. Breast and drumsticks are cooling and refreshing. It was late before we were full, and there was about half the *giviak* left. This was put up on one of the bunks to thaw for later use.
>
> When we had had some sleep, we started the second part of the feast. The *giviak* was now so much thawed that the little auks tasted entirely different, and it was possible to eat them in a new way. Whole

birds could now be pried loose from the compressed mass, and with this the case, great elegance can be demonstrated while enjoying them. A man with *savoir-vivre* holds the birds by the legs with his teeth. Then he strokes it with both hands, thus brushing off the feathers that have already been loosened by the fermentation. He brushes his hands together to remove all feathers, whereupon he turns the bird and bites the skin loose around the beak. This can be turned inside out and pulled free of the bird without letting go of its legs. The eater then sucks the whole skin into his mouth and pulls it out again, pressing his teeth slightly together. In this manner he gets all the fat sitting inside the skin. Taste is, as we know, an individual matter, but this one—I dare guarantee—can become a passion.

When the skin is free from fat, you bite it free around the bird's legs and swallow it in one piece. The breast is eaten by biting down on each side of the bone, and the bone can then be thrown away. This bares the innards, and you can enjoy the various parts one by one. The blood clot around the heart has coagulated and glues the teeth together, the liver and the gall bladder have a spicy taste, while the bitter aroma of the intestines reminds one of a lager beer. When these parts are consumed, the rest—wings, backbone, and pelvis—is taken into the mouth and thoroughly chewed. (1961:104–5)

In another place he talks about Knud Rasmussen's technique of drumming up special delicacies.

It was Knud's special art—during a meal—to start reminiscing about gigantic feasts of yore. Then his eyes assumed a dreamy look while he softly mumbled something about tail of narwhal, well fermented, rotten eider ducks, or other beautiful treats.

Immediately, somebody or other jumped up and demanded to be allowed to show that also in this place such palate-caressing articles could be prepared. Knud expressed a little doubt—but no more than to make it a challenge. The result was always that the man and a couple of his friends ran off to fetch the delicacies. They might otherwise have been set aside for the visit of a dear relative or some such purpose. (1961:100)

Freuchen's positive descriptions are very much the exception. In general, explorers, travelers, and missionaries were appalled by many native foods, particularly aged or fermented foods as well as those foods consumed under famine conditions. I wonder if these attitudes are a variation of the issues Sahlins discusses in *Stone Age Economics* (1972). Sahlins focused on the apparent differences between the attitudes of explorers

and the indigenous inhabitants. His insight was that most early ethnographers and travelers among hunter-gatherers were applying agricultural-
ist notions to nonagricultural systems. Agriculturalists must survive on
stored crops between one harvest and the next. Profligacy courts starvation. For most hunter-gatherers, however, storage is of limited effectiveness, because stored foods spoil. On the other hand, there are few
seasons in which it is impossible to catch or gather more food. For
hunter-gatherers, the most effective way to store food is through relationships, by feeding others when one has plenty, and being fed when
one does not. The situation is slightly different in the Yup'ik area, where
some types of food could be stored through the winter, but even there,
people still depended upon hunting and fishing on a more or less year-
round basis.

In particular, Native habits of feasting when there was food, and
accepting fasting when there was not, seemed improvident to Euro-
American observers. Exemplifying this, the otherwise generally sensitive
E. W. Nelson wrote, "All the Eskimo are forced by the harsh nature of
their climatic surroundings to provide a supply of food for the winter,
but they are careless and improvident in many ways. They frequently
consume nearly all of their stores during midwinter festivals and live in
semi-starvation" throughout the early spring (1899:268).

In Sahlins's presentation, explorers seem concerned or even obsessed
with the possibility of starving, because, unlike the Native people, they
do not believe more food will be caught. Whenever supplies begin to run
short, they seem to think that they will starve (though see Stefansson
1921 for the opposite reaction). This focus on their own impending starvation, and on the poor quality of food they and others ate when supplies
were low, blinded them to the extent to which Inuit sought out, prepared, and enjoyed delicacies when food was plentiful. Explorers focused
on the starvation diet and not on the memorable feasts that were (and
are) also part of Inuit lives.

In the explorers' defense, it is true that many Inuit groups have oral
histories of starvation in the not-so-distant past. Yup'ik elders caution
that it is important that children be taught to eat not only preferred
foods but also spoiled and disgusting food, so that, as adults, they will
be able to eat such food, if necessary, to survive. There were famines,
but it may have been the explorers, rather than the Inuit, who were
famine focused.

It is also true that Europeans and Euro-Americans found that the
processing of many Inuit foods violated their food categories. It may
have been easier for some explorer-ethnographers to rationalize the prep-

aration and eating of such foods by saying that it was the result of having little or no choice and that ecological conditions precluded other treatment of the food.

In fact, Inuit food often was and is fermented to perfection, much as a Camembert cheese is carefully ripened before consumption. "In a climate which does not readily turn all meats into inedible spoiled garbage, as would occur in some parts of the Lower-Forty-Eight, the Eskimos must try very hard to get their meats to 'cure,' or 'age,' which is what I suppose the foreigners mean when they describe *rotten* food" (Senungetuk 1971:68, emphasis in the original).

The nineteenth-century Moravian missionary John Kilbuck, in the following quotation, combined the environmental rationale and the recognition that people do actually like the resulting aged food:

> If from any reason, as sickness or overwork, a woman is unable to cut up and dry all the catch of the husband—the salmon are buried and cured by the secret process of the underground force. —The people of the coast are particularly addicted/given to the practice. —It seems to agree with them too. —When asked how they could eat such stinky stuff—with a bland smile—they reply "We don't eat the smell!" (in Fienup-Riordan 1988:11)

The Yupiit are actually making a pun here, on the name for aged salmon heads: *tepa* (smell). Kilbuck makes the same pun elsewhere, and in fact the same phrase is still current in Bethel. "The heads of the salmon are buried, immediately—and reaching a certain stage of fitness—are eaten. This is a summer dish, a most dangerous one too, for when exposed to the air it becomes poisonous as many deaths from it prove. The smell *[tepa]* is enough to kill ordinary mortals" (ibid.). Here Kilbuck brought another facet of Western governmentality to bear on traditional Native food processing, by claiming it to be a public health hazard. He raised the fear of botulism, not well understood at that time as arising from anaerobic, rather than aerobic, conditions (Fienup-Riordan 1988:461). Conversations with Public Health Service doctors in the Bethel area show that this prejudice against aged foods is still widely held. Although it is true that there are occasional deaths from botulism in the area, this is almost invariably the result of improper handling or storage of the food.[1] Public health officials and medical personnel do attempt to educate local people on this problem, and stress that older techniques are safe(r). However, the overall effect of public health campaigns is to discourage the preparation and consumption of aged foods. This is in part because such personnel rarely completely disguise their distaste for the idea of fermented meat and fish, or their fear of botulism. In comparison, recent reports of high salmonella counts in commercially sold chickens have focused on prompt and thorough cooking, rather than discouraging consumption. Similarly, cheeses made from raw (unpasteurized) milk are common in Europe, although the possible health risks are well documented, and, at least in England, such cheeses carry warning labels.

Jones's (1983) book is unique in its treatment of aged foods. It focuses on the proper preparation of aged foods traditional to the greater Kotzebue area, and celebrates, rather than discourages, their preparation and consumption.

YUP'IK "COOKING"

Inuit cooking is often set at the opposite end of the culinary scale from Chinese and French gourmet traditions. The presumed primativeness of Inuit is mirrored in the assumption that their foods are at the nature (raw) end of the nature: culture dichotomy. In China, however, there is also a long history of famines during which people ate whatever they could find to stay alive. Early European explorers found that many Chinese foods violated their categories of what was edible. The two cultures had different ideas about whether something was a pet, a vermin, or a foodstuff. However, most of the cooking techniques, including temperate fermentation, were familiar, as were the basic foodstuffs (Chang 1977). Thus the two cultures found common culinary ground.

The same recognition of common methods has not often been afforded to Native Alaskan techniques such as freezing, low-temperature fermentation, and the eating of certain foods without cooking, the equivalent of "Caribou Tartar." Joseph Senungetuk describes an Inupiaq view of "frozen" foods.

> To explain this [increased palatability and flavorfulness], let me offer a new word: *koowahk*. This is actually an old Eskimo word, meaning *meat in a frozen state*, having ice crystals between the layers of muscle, so that there is a separation between water and meat. Also, I shall extend the descriptive range usually ascribed to the various ways in which meat may be prepared, from "raw" and "cooked," to still another state. Frozen meat or fish has already undergone a change in texture and palatability. (1971:64)

An essential point of such techniques is that final preparation is not the same as "cooking." Final preparation may consist solely of reducing the meat or fish to manageable-sized portions. The lengthy preparations (culturally equivalent to "cooking") have usually occurred much earlier. Dried king salmon is "cooked" in the lengthy period when the fresh fish are cut, salted, dried, and smoked. There are opportunities to affect the flavor and palatability of the fish significantly at all stages. Each person cuts her salmon somewhat differently. The salting process can affect drying time and flavor. Some people use a saltshaker, most use brine, and some spread the kidneys on the fillet before salting. The weather can make a significant difference as well, influencing drying and smoking time. Finally, how the fish is hung in the smokehouse, how long and with what kind of wood it is smoked, and how dense the smoke is, all have an effect on the final taste.

In comparison with this previous labor, final preparation is negligible (see also Sharp 1981:231 for a parallel situation with the Chipewyan). People often cut the dried, scored fillets up at the table as needed. The same is true of *qassayaaq* (frozen raw whitefish aged before freezing and served frozen: Jacobson 1984:316), where the making, refurbishing, and lining of the storage pit in the earth and the rough cleaning of the fish all occur weeks prior to consumption, when the frozen fish are cut up at the table. To ignore this is tantamount to asking a French peasant, "How do you cook milk?" while discounting or not noticing the entire cheese-making process. Similarly, focusing on how Yupiit cook, as opposed to how they transform wild meat and fish into food, including things such as fresh seal liver and silver salmon head cartilage, which come ready to eat, misses much of the essential activity.

I refer to the French and the Chinese because these are both cultures that are associated with sensuous, even sybaritic, food traditions. In common with these traditions, Yup'ik people will often talk about memorable meals, or the way that a certain person prepares a particular food with the equivalent of a "wok signature." I remember the reverence with which one woman's seal intestine soup was remembered—properly prepared, it resembles *al dente* homemade noodles in seal broth. Such attitudes extend particularly to strongly aged "spicy" foods, which, like strong cheeses, are not universally liked, but are loved by their partisans.

A friend once talked with relish about a kind of aged meat that "is so strong it makes your eyes water when you stand over the cooking pot to stir it. It also smells really strong, but it tastes wonderful." Because it also causes terrible flatulence, and one's skin smells of it for days, he and his family would eat it only if they knew that non-Natives were not likely to be around for a few days.

Some traditional Yup'ik foods are fermented and then frozen to prevent further fermentation, much as wine is bottled when the yeast has turned the sugars to alcohol, but before vinegar eels can turn the alcohol to vinegar (see Jones 1983). People also recognize that it may not be possible to stop the fermentation process fully, and, as with a slightly ammoniating Brie cheese, foods may be eaten after they have "peaked," so that they are not wasted. Whereas in the past Native people were sometimes faced with no options other than to eat questionable food items or go hungry, the contemporary availability of store-bought food, as well as larger larders, now gives people other options. A general decrease in botulism cases may result from this greater latitude in avoiding possibly spoiled foods.

An additional reason for the lack of knowledge about Yup'ik cuisine is that Yupiit themselves are acutely aware of non-Native attitudes toward raw/fermented/frozen meat and fish and of Yup'ik food in general (compare Brody 1975:164). As noted, Yupiit are often reluctant to eat such foods in the presence of non-Natives or to serve them to non-Natives.

> My own personal experience in villages is that many times people are very concerned about you getting what they think you want. It took me a long time to learn some of the great eating out here, because of [Yup'ik] people's reluctance to give a White Man things that they consider to be not White Man's food. I could end up with a cheeseburger and someone from upriver sitting across the table from me [would] be eating *egamaarrluk* [partially dried fish, boiled for eating]. And when I finally learned how to eat *egamaarrluk*, well, needless to say, my desire to eat *egamaarrluk* was much greater than my desire to eat a cheeseburger. (transcript of an interview with John White, July 23, 1991)

More than once I have had the experience of stopping in on a Yup'ik family for some business-related reason and surprising them in the act of eating frozen or fermented foods. Their response was typically embarrassment that I, a non-Native person, had "caught" them eating such foods, while I felt chagrined because I had caused their embarrassment. Typically, as a guest, I would then be offered food, often *akutaq* (a food often liked by non-Natives). Once eating, however, I was (or felt) free to start eating the "forbidden" food as well, praising its preparation and taste. The combination of eating with gusto (even if I had just eaten) and speaking Yup'ik was usually sufficient to repair the situation, and the meal would continue. In some villages, the rumor that I liked Native foods was sufficient to have people inviting me in for meal after meal. It is not clear to me how much of my hosts' pleasure was that we could speak Yup'ik together, even if I couldn't always follow everything, and how much was the pleasure of being able to extend proper hospitality to an "other" and have it enjoyed.

CHANGING ATTITUDES AND DIETS

It is clear that younger people (at least in villages) are still eating significant amounts of wild foods. Given the age structure for most villages (typically half the population is under fifteen), continued high consumption of subsistence foods means that children are eating wild foods in quantity. There does seem to have been a shift from purchasing raw materials—flour, sugar, salt, tea, and coffee—to purchasing prepared foods in addition to raw materials. This is the difference between buying bags of flour and buying cans of premade spaghetti. It is in the snack and supplemental category that the largest volume of food and drink is purchased by and for younger people: sodas, candy, and snack items. However, the emotional connection with Native foods remains strong. For example, every time the Rural Student Services at the University of Alaska Fairbanks holds a Native foods luncheon, there is a tremendous turnout of Native students hungry for a taste of home.

A Yup'ik man once mentioned that, in choosing between the two different bowls of *akutaq* on the table, many younger people would prefer the one made of vegetable shortening and salmonberries with sugar. Older people, on the other hand, would uniformly choose the other one, called *tenguggluk*, made from cooked tomcod livers mashed with cranberries, a sort of semi-liquid pâté. He suggested that younger people were attracted to sweetened forms of *akutaq*, unlike their elders, whose tastes were formed prior to the ready availability of sugar.[2]

FOOD AS AN IDENTITY MARKER

Food often functions as an identity marker in the Y-K Delta (see Bodenhorn 1989:114 for analogous statements about North Slope Inupiat). Yupiit often ask non-Natives who eat Yup'ik foods a diagnostic question: do they also eat the local "aged" specialty, such as fermented flipper, aged whitefish or salmon, or aged salmon heads? These questions seem to have two levels of meaning. On the surface, they are informational queries about whether one eats a variety of Yup'ik food, or merely the ones most congenial to non-Native tastes. Often, when I have replied that I have eaten, for example, fermented whitefish, but am unable to consume a large quantity of it because it upsets my stomach, people will say, "Oh yeah, it does that to me too." They may add that their sister, brother, or mother can't eat it at all for this reason.

On a deeper level, a positive answer or an expressed willingness to try such foods seems to answer the unstated proxy question "How do you *really* feel about Yupiit," or "Do you really know what we're about?" It is interesting that people feel free to ask you in a public situation if you eat "stink heads." However, if you dropped in on these same people when they were eating "stink heads," they would likely be embarrassed. I would suggest that the difference is between talking about a marker and coming face-to-face with it in a situation where it may be imbued with exclusionary power. Here again, discourse about an activity (the eating of aged foods) may substitute for the activity itself. It is also true that some of the people who ask if one eats those aged foods, particularly younger people, don't eat them themselves. This preference, as well as issues of accommodation, may partially explain the trend for younger Yupiit to take as markers of ethnicity those foods that are most congenial to Euro-American tastes, such as dried salmon and sweet berry *akutaq*. Interestingly, the foods most typically served at Native food potlucks, including those at the University of Alaska, do not violate Western food categories. This may be in response to both the food preferences of younger people and the difficulty of acquiring fermented foods in urban settings. Primarily, though, I imagine these seemingly tacit restrictions are a function of the potlucks' public nature. Avoiding possibly negatively sanctioned foods avoids negative sanctions.

Food also functions to mark identity in feasting and hosting. Relatives, friends, and elders are invited to feasts at which rare or difficult-to-acquire items are often served. Once after church I went along with others in the village (it had been a blanket invitation) to someone's house for a feast. We were served dried chum salmon, mink soup, and *akutaq* with tea and pilot crackers afterward. When I stopped in to visit someone else on my way home, they immediately got up and put their coats on when I relayed the menu. They said that had they known that mink was being served they would have gone earlier. Similarly, at *Slaaviq* (see Fienup-Riordan 1990:94–122), people may serve otter or goose, which their hosts have been saving for this special occasion, exactly like the treats that Rasmussen cajoled out of his hosts (above). Both raw and prepared foods are the most common kinds of gifts given to a departing guest. This might include a couple of ducks, a container of *akutaq*, some frozen berries, a frozen whitefish or two, a piece of moose meat, or some cooked greens. Such gifts nourish the relationships between people.

Finally, food appears as an identity marker in day-to-day eating. Food provides a link with the past, and this past defines what a "home-cooked meal," or a dish "just like my mother (or aunt) used to make" consists of. Like one's native language, one's natal foods remain a lifelong attachment. For most people, they signal comfort and correctness in the world. In the greater Yup'ik area, the attachment to food seems more durable than the attachment to the Yup'ik language itself. There are areas, such as along the lower Yukon River, where few or no younger people speak Yup'ik, but where the food tradition has continued largely unabated. Kwachka (1990) argues that one reason for the rapid rate at which Alaskan Native languages are becoming moribund is that, as for some other hunter-gatherers, subsistence and the food provided through subsistence form a boundary marker that is clear enough that the particular language spoken is superfluous. In this sense, then, subsistence foods are, like language, another possible marker of ethnicity.

There are also situations in which talk about Native foods serves as a proxy for Nativeness, particularly in the absence of such foods, as, for example, for Native students at the University of Alaska, Fairbanks. It is very common to hear such students reminisce at length about the food at home, the things they are particularly missing. In part this is a discussion about homesickness in an alien place, but it is also a discourse (in English or Yup'ik) about identity, about who they are, in the absence of its enactment in other practice. So, in the end, not only may Native foods be used to mark Native-ness but also talk about Native foods can fulfill this function in the absence of the foods themselves. While commensality is common, this discourse on Native foods is much more so: one may talk with many people with whom one will never share a meal.

7

Subsistence Discourse as Practice

PTARMIGAN HUNTING BY SNOW MACHINE

It is a bright day in March, sunny and windy. I snow-machine over to my partner's house and arrive just as he is finishing getting ready. We put our daypacks around the snow-machine handlebars, our shotguns in our laps, and take off. There is some new snow, which makes the ride easier in spots, but also promises the possibility of bogging down where it has settled deeply.

*We decide to hunt along the Gweek River (*kuik *means "river") above Bethel, and head out along the line of bluffs parallel to the Akiachuk trail. My friend spots the first flock of ptarmigan, and gets one before they spook. We follow them, hoping to get another chance when they land, but they eventually fly out of sight. Our general approach is to ride along the ridges and rims of little valleys and cul-de-sacs, or travel with one of us on each side of the brush lining a waterway. Often it is possible to ride in the drifted snow along the edges of the brush, but sometimes the only option is to bump along on the tundra.*

I get bogged down a couple of times, which usually necessitates dragging the snow machine back a couple of feet so that the track can get a better purchase. Such riding is rather more work than one might think. You are always leaning, pulling, and bouncing up and down. When not hunting I often travel in a kneeling position to absorb the pounding in my legs instead of my back, but I prefer to hunt with the gun resting across my lap, where it is readily available.

When we see ptarmigan we try to drive within range and shoot. Sometimes they wait for us; often they don't. Yupiit say that ptarmigan are more flighty and easily spooked on bright days. We see flocks on the average of once or twice an hour. After a while my friend's snow machine begins to run more and more raggedly, and eventually he stops to change to hotter-running spark plugs. Other than that we have no problems. We stop for lunch in a grove of willows that provide some shelter from the wind, but still, like most cold-weather meals, it is an abbreviated affair. We talk of game, of other hunts, and where we might try next. We hunt for another hour, then return home via the river, as my friend wants to check the density of ice nets above Bethel. We end up with a total of eight ptarmigan between us.

INTRODUCTION

In the previous chapters it has become clear that subsistence is the subject of passionate feeling, constant discussion and illusion, and highly embedded symbolic meanings. This chapter attempts to account for the complexities of subsistence and subsistence discourse as situated practice. In line with practice/structuration theory, "structures" or "dispositions" can be understood as the basis for the repetitive patterning of action. Such structures are not only the primary constituent of what is usually called "culture" but they are also the basis of most other observed commonalities within groups of people, including, for example, shared contextualization conventions or the particular roles assumed by individuals in dysfunctional families. Older assumptions about the basis of such commonality, of "shared-ness," are problematic for a number of reasons. First, they tend to divert attention from practice and interaction. Instead, they tend to reify groups and then impute teleology to them; that is, they postulate "culture" or "class" as "things" in and of themselves and capable of being causal agents. This reification also frequently obscures the reality that membership in such groups can be an epiphenomenon of situated practice, the result of negotiation and strategization rather than ascription.

PRACTICE/STRUCTURATION THEORY

The major theorists in this field have been Pierre Bourdieu (1977, 1990; Bourdieu and Passeron 1977) and Anthony Giddens (1979, 1984). Bourdieu has favored the term "practice theory," while Giddens prefers "structuration theory." Fundamentally, practice/structuration theory explicates the repetitive patterning of action; why we do what we do, with variation, over and over again.

> By the duality of structure, I mean the essential recursiveness of social
> life, as constituted in social practices: structure is both medium and
> outcome of the reproduction of practices. Structure enters simultane-
> ously into the constitution of the agent and social practices, and "exists"
> in the generating moments of this constitution. (Giddens 1979:5)

> The structures constitutive of a particular type of environment . . .
> produce *habitus, systems of durable, transposable dispositions,* structured
> structures predisposed to function as structuring structures, that is, as
> principles of the generation and structuring of practices and representa-
> tions. . . . (Bourdieu 1977:72; emphasis added)

Giddens writes:

> The notion of the duality of structure . . . involves recognizing that
> the reflexive monitoring of action both draws upon and reconstitutes
> the institutional organization of society. . . . In structuration theory
> "structure" is regarded as rules and resources recursively implicated in
> social reproduction; institutionalized features of social systems have
> structural properties in the sense that relationships are stabilized across
> time and space. (Giddens 1984:xxxi)

At issue here is the constitution of culture. In the past, culture has been
seen as a thing in and of itself that had agency; that wanted, needed, and
did things. Instead, Bourdieu and Giddens argue that culture consists of
shared routinized behavior, habits writ large, with the caveat that such
routines are not necessarily simple, unsophisticated, or conscious. These
routines (part of what Bourdieu and Giddens mean by *structures*) are usually embedded in social practices, are learned through repetition, and
they form a basis for future action. Because one has done something one
way in the past, one is more likely to repeat the same action in similar
situations in the future. This is true of a vast range of things from something as mundane as how to tie one's shoes (which is almost completely
routinized for most people), to how to conduct a meeting or a symphony.
In these latter cases, the "conductor" brings an entire history of experiences to bear on any given instance. Bourdieu and Giddens argue that
responses grow out of past experience, which they call past practice.
Because such experiences are most densely shared with individuals from
a similar background, such individuals will be likely to act in a similar
fashion in a similar situation.

In practice/structuration theory, then, the concept of culture as a
learned system of rules and norms is replaced by the concept of structures (Giddens) or of dispositions (Bourdieu). Instead of rules being

learned, structures are sedimented in individuals, and while future practice may be guided partly by "how one is supposed to be"—for acknowledged norms can be used strategically—it is more often guided by "what
one has done before." The shift is from "rules" to "precedents."

Unfortunately, neither Giddens nor Bourdieu provides a satisfying
theory of how "culture"—some shared system of structures and practices—is either learned, maintained, or changed. In part this is because
both theorists take a top-down approach, focusing on what Giddens calls
"societal structures" and what Bourdieu calls "class habitus."

Bourdieu does say that "Practical estimates give disproportionate
weight to early experiences," but he never successfully addresses the
question of how dispositions are learned (1977:78). Giddens suggests that
one should study interaction: "Analysing the structuration of social systems means studying the modes in which such systems, grounded in
the knowledgeable activities of situated actors who draw upon rules and
resources in the diversity of action contexts, are produced and repro-
duced in interaction" (Giddens 1984:25). However, beyond this exhorta-
tion neither he nor Bourdieu provides much except definitions. The actual microlevel learning, the seat of all this recursiveness, is a kind of
black box.

My extension of these theories is twofold. First, having disposed of
the idea of culture as a thing and having located all structures in individuals, the next step is to recognize interaction as the source of structuration and explore how this occurs. Further, if the structures of habitus are
learned through interaction, and only instantiated in individuals, then I
suggest that there must be parallel structures shared with smaller groups,
what might be called "subcultural" and "family" habitus. Indeed, this
progression extends to the individual as well—that is, "individual" habitus, those structures shared fully with no one else. I contend that similar
structures inform all levels, and that a more powerful version of practice/
structuration theory may be created through combining it with family
systems theory, a particular kind of small group psychology, and by
extending certain insights from sociolinguistics.

This approach has a number of advantages. Focusing upon shared
structures as a basis for commonality leads to a clearer and more useful
theoretical position. Such a focus not only locates such structures within
individuals but also, I would argue, leads directly to a consideration of
interaction, by foregrounding the question of how structures are engendered, maintained, and changed. In addition, although sedimentation (a
word less tainted with auxiliary associations than "learning") obviously
occurs in a variety of ways—including through the repetitive practice

of habitual tasks (Connerton 1989) and the practices of governmentality (Foucault 1979)—even these often occur through, and are mediated by, interaction.

Thus we are brought back to a focus on interaction, particularly linguistically mediated interaction. This is a return to the primacy of "talk," but with the caveat that the issue is not what people say, or even how they say it, but the reasons behind why they say what they say. This focuses on discourse as practice. And only by reference to intense local ethnographic, linguistic, and sociolinguistic knowledge can we understand the strategic moves being made in discourse.

A further advantage of such an approach is that it permits simple and clear comparisons between structures shared within groupings of different sizes such as the members of a "culture," members of a "class," "speakers of a dialect," or the members of a "family" (recognizing that the meanings and even the existence of all the preceding categories are the subject of continuing debate). Still, a "network" approach, which recognizes that commonality exists to the extent that structures are shared by some set of individuals, allows one to generalize between sizes of groups that share those structures. Such generalizations and comparisons can legitimately be made between micro-, mezzo- and macrolevels, so that one could, for example, make theoretically sound comparisons between, say, the effects of systemic racism and familial incest in terms of the interactional structures engendered, or between the selective use of a particular dialect and particular food items for creating a social boundary.

FAMILY SYSTEMS THEORY

Family systems theory provides models for how structures arise and are maintained in dyadic, triadic, and small-group interactions. This theory descends from the work of Gregory Bateson and others working at Stanford in the early 1950s (Bateson et al. 1956, Ruesch and Bateson 1951, Watzlawick et al. 1967). In a seminal work on the etiology of schizophrenia, Bateson et al. (1956) linked schizophrenic behavior not to a cause within the patient, biochemical or otherwise, but to the interactional setting: that is, to the family system in which the person evincing symptoms is enmeshed. In other words, they located the "cause" of the mental illness not in any one of the individuals but in the specifics of the familial interaction.[1] Rather than focusing on the dualism of patient and family (or patient and doctor), they concentrated instead on the duality of their mutual interaction and the structures embodied therein. They posit schizophrenia as a learned response to being placed in a psychological double bind, of being faced in the long-term with only impossible choices. Their description seems very much like an individual version of structuration. The double bind is structured by past (interactional) experience and structures future experience. It is a "structured structure, predisposed to function as a structuring structure" (Bourdieu 1977:72). However, in addition to demonstrating how this structural recursivity might work, Bateson et al. also posit how such a structure may be changed, stating that the therapist can "set up relatively benevolent binds and aid the patient in his emancipation from them" (1972:227). In other words, new structures can be learned and may eventually displace others. Certainly something like this must account for the more ordinary processes of sedimentation that we know as "learning." Bateson's theory is both interactionally based and inherently dynamic. As such it may be extended to explain both enculturation and acculturation.

Bateson et al. were examining a specific type of mental illness (to use the older "patient-focused" language) and were grappling with some of the larger philosophical issues involved. They saw schizophrenia as the outcome of an inability to differentiate between communicative levels. In terms of Bateson's stated goal of making this linkage, the attempt was not particularly successful. However, in the process, Bateson laid the groundwork for Goffman's work with frames of reference (1974), as well as Gumperz's work with contextualization conventions (discussed later).

Bateson's attempt to include mental illness within larger issues of communications theory also gave rise over time to a radically different understanding of mental illness and treatment. The most direct descendant of his work, at least philosophically, is known as the ecological approach to family therapy, also called the family systems approach (Auerswald 1968, Hoffman 1981). The metaphor of the family as an ecological system carries the sense of an ongoing dynamic interaction that has coevolved, with all parts interrelated, and where change in any actor puts stresses on the others. As opposed to more classic systems of psychotherapy, which diagnose and treat the presenting individual, the family systems approach, following the lead of Bateson et al., sees the "mentally ill" individual as a symptom of the family's illness. From this viewpoint, not only will it be difficult to help the presenting individual without changing the family as a whole, but also "curing" the ostensibly sick person will mean that someone else in the family would be likely to manifest the symptoms. Treatment involves an explicit recognition of the durability of the dispositions (roles) inculcated in the family. Change means changing individual habitus, restructuring someone's structured structures through leverage applied by changing other relationships within the family. Through these changes, the family is brought to both a new sense of what is normal and a new logic of interaction.

The family systems approach provides a habituslike notion of durable dispositions at the level of the individual. It is dynamic: it provides a theory of how such dispositions interactively develop and are strengthened over time through repetition. These structures are changeable, though the process is slow and requires (in this case therapeutic) relearning through further interaction. The family systems approach provides a way of connecting power and agency within the family to the creation, embodiment, and continual re-creation of these structures. Finally, in keeping with practice theory, this view of structures does not rest on the problematic dichotomy of the individual and society. What it still lacks is a way to connect larger societal structures theoretically with their recursivity in individuals (see Willis 1977 for an ethnographic example of this connection).

CONTEXTUALIZATION CONVENTIONS AND SOCIOLINGUISTICS

Gumperz and others (Gumperz 1982a, 1982b, 1986; Gumperz and Cook-Gumperz 1982; Jupp et al. 1982; Scollon and Scollon 1982; Gal 1987; Woolard 1985) have shown how key linguistic elements and practices—what Gumperz has called "contextualization conventions"—are used strategically in conversations. These conventions are a way to both capture and discuss how individuals use different levels of communication in conversations, à la Bateson. They allow analysis to shift from what is particular in a situation to what is general and shared. Such conventions can consist of shifts in "code, dialect and style . . . as well as choice among lexical and syntactic options, formulaic expressions, conversational openings, closings and sequencing strategies" (Gumperz 1982a:131). They are acquired "as a result of a speaker's actual interactive experience, i.e., as a result of an individual's participation in particular networks of relationship" (Gumperz and Cook-Gumperz 1982:18), and are often deeply evocative of shared membership.

Gal (1987), focusing on language choice, notes that such choices are implicitly evaluative. "Attitudes toward the languages are, implicitly, evaluations of the groups, activities, and social relations of solidarity or power they index" (693).

In a broader sense these implicit evaluations are made toward any practice perceived by participants as emblematic of a group. Such markers can be either boundary markers—external signs by which others recognize group membership—or internal markers—claims made to shared realms of experience. Both Cohen and Emmett describe the play of such shared conventions in maintaining connectedness and community:

> The sense of belonging, of what it means to belong, is constantly evoked by whatever means comes to hand: the use of language, the shared knowledge of genealogy or ecology, joking, the solidarity of sect, the aesthetics of subsistence skills. This persistent "production" of culture and attribution of value becomes an essential bulwark against the cultural imperialism of the political and economic centers, and thus provides fundamental means by keeping the communities alive and fruitful. (Cohen 1982:6)

> In encounter after encounter, in a very large proportion of the talk, the term "double meaning" is totally inadequate to convey the density of meanings, cross references, awareness of ignorance here, a layer of knowledge there, and double, triple and quadruple layers of knowledge and understanding. Words can seldom be taken at face value. And of course very much of the communication uses no words. . . . Gossip and talk and all the non-verbal communication are used not only to create this oral history of the town. They are used to include and exclude; to pass time and entertain; to judge and constrain others; to confer and deny favors; indeed, as precious currency: the commodity exchanged most; a large part of the raw material from which social relationships are created. (Emmett 1982:207–8)

Power and agency enter into the equation when actors manipulate their differential (and class-based) knowledge of such conventions; they form an important part of one's cultural capital as well (Bourdieu and Passeron 1977).

Gumperz and Cook-Gumperz note that "Like grammatical knowledge, [contextualization conventions] operate below the level of conscious choice" (1982:18). I am interested in examining a particular subset of related usages, those that exist at the boundary of consciousness. This is the area in which the evocative and connotative force of particular usages and references to particular meanings or identities may be strategically manipulated. Like contextualization conventions, such usages have particular meanings that derive from their situated embeddedness. In other contexts, their meaning may be radically different (which further complicates their cross-cultural/intergroup usage). However, when such conventions are shared, they are constantly invoked. Strategically they may be used to validate a variety of memberships. For example, in the same afternoon I may be "asked" to recognize commonality based on my being male, being interested in boats, being an anthropologist, being an academic, being a parent, being Yup'ik-speaking (if not Yup'ik), and being knowledgeable about plumbing. None of these in isolation are primary identities, but they all represent ways through which I might acknowledge comembership with someone, in some setting. They are all identities (real or fictive) that I might be expected to claim, and hence, to which someone else can make a claim of comembership.

Such claims can also be thought of as claims to jointly agreed-upon meanings, with the proviso that the most important element is not the particular restricted "dictionary" meaning but the evocative force of the label. The semantic meaning is much less important than the constellation of images that are evoked. Is an item "junk," with one set of uses, values, and meanings, or is it an "antique" with a different set (see Thompson 1979)? Is someone unemployed or a vagabond? In the most simplistic cases, verbal sparring or bantering over these differences may be both conscious and explicit. Often, and more interestingly, such sparring over evocative meaning is only implicit. As mentioned above, the identities referenced need not be real or available to be filled: the same procedure may be used to refer to fictional or semi-fictional identities as well (see Example 3 in this chapter).

It may be useful to call such structures "co-occurrence structures," where one person is consciously, semiconsciously, or unconsciously using co-occurrence rules to build images in the mind of the other, with the caveat that "In dealing with conversational exchanges we do not and need not treat the psychological issue of what an individual has in mind, but rather we focus on how intent is interpreted by ordinary listeners in a particular context" (Gumperz and Cook-Gumperz 1982:17). In cross-cultural or multicultural settings listeners and speakers often differ in background and hence in how they interpret each other's strategic moves. Discussion and action are based on what is heard—culturally filtered and interpreted—rather than on what is said.

These co-occurrence structures may be explained most easily by examining a graded series of examples. The following examples are arranged in a progression of increasing complexity. They run from discrete and abstracted situations to those in which participants have widely differing agendas and communicative styles. The first two examples represent fragments of conversations I have heard. They are, however, reported, rather than transcribed from actual transcripts. They are simplified both by being extracted from their embedded situation and by being abstracted by my necessarily partial memory of the actual event. Example 3 is taken from a novel. In its published context this passage exemplifies a certain kind of communicative skill, the ability to shift frames of reference. Again, it is a simplification, but of a more complex situation. Finally, Example 4 is an actual transcript of an extended cross-cultural interaction in a formal setting. Even here, however, transcription necessarily obscures subtleties of detail that are preserved on the audiotape. Videotaping would have preserved even more detail. However, any attempt to capture the practices embedded in an ongoing process necessarily involves abstractions, because of the complexity of such situations, for several reasons.

Any "strategic move" embedded in an actual situation is potentially understandable on a number of levels. Participants strategize simultaneously on a number of different levels and for a variety of different purposes. Also, most such moves are largely implicit. This very implicitness means that they can be refuted only through further practice. Attempts at direct explication can and usually will be denied: "That's not what I meant."

EXAMPLE 1. Two Euro-American males are in the middle of a conversation about baseball. Person A says, "I'm for the Mets, myself. My family always has been. Guess we like to root for the underdogs."

Person A is hinting that attacks against the Mets may be taken not only as a personal challenge but also as a challenge against his whole family. By saying "my family," that is, that such support is shared by a larger reference group, he is suggesting that supporting the Mets is not a preference, or a personality characteristic, but a shared, at least subcultural, feature. Further, he makes it an explicitly moral stance. Somehow, in terms of images, rooting for the Mets links one with the oppressed and downtrodden. Through such moves, person A has made it more difficult for person B to disagree with him. Person A's assertion is now linked with a host of other issues and images, some tacit, some explicit. What began as a simple choice has been embedded in a matrix of issues. Should person B support some other baseball team, he would probably need to parry this implication of moral superiority, as well as the implication that person A's support was not, at least generally, a shared cultural feature but was an idiosyncratic preference.

EXAMPLE 2. A group of office workers, mostly strangers, orders lunch. People will be paying some attention to what others order. Each person's order can be "read" as a statement of personal preference, as well as in a variety of strategic ways. Is ordering an avocado-and-Cheddar sandwich a statement about one's vegetarianism, with various moral and political implications possibly attached, or is it only what that person feels like eating? Is ordering rare roast beef a counterstatement? Does the salmon-quiche eater support commercial fisheries, believe in the efficacy of omega-3 fatty acids for preventing arterial sclerosis, or wish to show a non-macho image? These are all possible and largely nonexclusive readings. Whether any of these possible issues and images are ever explicitly raised or clarified through future practice depends largely on participants' future interactions. If they continue to interact, and if that interaction becomes important on a personal, social, intellectual, or financial level, then it is likely that strategic plays of these sorts will be made. What one orders for lunch can potentially be made to represent larger images of self—of one's politically correct vegetarianism or masculine carnivorousness. Such images can form a basis for alliance, as well as inclusionary and exclusionary practices.

EXAMPLE 3. In this example, taken from John Steinbeck's *Cannery Row*, Mack and the boys, a group of indigent, sometime-sardine-cannery workers, are waiting for dark so that they can catch a mass of frogs from a pond. The frogs are to be sold to Doc, a marine biologist who sells biological specimens, so that Mack and the boys can buy whisky to throw this same Doc a party.

A man dark and large stalked near and he had a shotgun over his arm and a pointer walked shyly and delicately at his heel.

"What the hell are you doing here?" he asked.

"Nothing," said Mack.

"The land's posted. No fishing, hunting, fires, camping. Now you just pack up and put that fire out and get off this land."

Mack stood up humbly. "I didn't know, Captain," he said. "Honest we never seen the sign, Captain."

"There's signs all over. You couldn't have missed them."

"Look, Captain, we made a mistake and we're sorry," said Mack. He paused and looked closely at the slouching figure. "You're a military man, aren't you, sir? I can always tell. Military man don't carry his shoulders the same as ordinary people. I was in the army so long, I can always tell."

Imperceptibly the shoulders of the man straightened, nothing obvious, but he held himself differently. "I don't allow fires on my place," he said.

"Well, we're sorry," said Mack. "We'll get right out, Captain. You see, we're workin' for some scientists. We're trying to get some frogs. They're workin' on cancer and we're helpin' out getting some frogs."

The man hesitated for a moment. "What do they do with the frogs?" he asked.

"Well, sir," said Mack, "they give cancer to the frogs and then they can study and experiment and they got it nearly licked if they can just get some frogs. But if you don't want us on your land, Captain,

we'll get right out. Never would of come in if we knew." Suddenly
Mack seemed to see the pointer for the first time. "By God that's a fine-
lookin' bitch," he said enthusiastically. "She looks like Nola that win
the field trials in Virginia last year. She a Virginia dog, Captain?"

The captain hesitated and then he lied. "Yes," he said shortly.
"She's lame. Tick got her right on her shoulder."

Mack was instantly solicitous. "Mind if I look, Captain? Come,
girl. Come on, girl." The pointer looked up at her master and then
sidled up to Mack. "Pile on some twigs so I can see," he said to Hazel.

"It's up where she can't lick it," said the captain and he leaned
over Mack's shoulder to look.

Mack pressed some pus out of the evil-looking crater on the dog's
shoulder. "I had a dog had a thing like this and it went right in and
killed him. She just had pups, didn't she?"

"Yes," said the captain, "six. I put iodine on that place."

"No," said Mack, "that won't draw. You got any Epsom salts up
at your place?"

"Yes—there's a big bottle."

"Well you take a hot poultice of Epsom salts and put it on there.
She's weak, you know, from the pups. Be a shame she got sick now.
You'd lose the pups too." The pointer looked deep into Mack's eyes
and then she licked his hand.

"Tell you what I'll do, Captain. I'll look after her myself. Epsom
salts'll do the trick. That's the best thing."

The captain stroked the dog's head. "You know, I've got a pond
up by the house that's so full of frogs I can't sleep nights. Why don't
you look up there? They bellow all night. I'd be glad to get rid of
them."

"That's mighty nice of you," said Mack. "I'll bet those docs would
thank you for that. But I'd like to get a poultice on this dog." He turned
to the others. "You put out this fire," he said. "Make sure there ain't a
spark left and clean up around. You don't want to leave no mess. I and
the captain will go and take care of Nola here. You fellows follow along
when you get cleared up." Mack and the captain walked away together.

Hazel kicked sand on the fire. "I'll bet Mack could of been president of the U.S. if he wanted," he said.

"What could he do with it if he had it?" Jones asked. "There
wouldn't be no fun in that." (1945:51–2)

In this vignette Mack continually shifts frames, and, in shifting the
frames, the larger structures of co-occurrence that go with them. He

does this by a series of strategic moves that, in their presentation of a more positive image, the landowner accepts.

Each such shift changes the appropriate structures of co-occurrence, that is, the proper way to treat coparticipants within this new frame. The initial frame is of a landowner confronting trespassing vagrants. The appropriate action in this frame is for the landowner to evict them, at gunpoint if necessary. Mack's initial shift is from this civilian frame, where their interests are opposed to those of the landowner, to a military one, in which they are explicitly subordinate to the landowner, but where there is an implicit potential for the alignment of interests. Throughout Mack keeps making their subordination and compliance clear, constantly reassuring the landowner that he is in charge.

The next shift creates a situation of aligned interests, in curing cancer and then in the health of the dog. Mack offers to perform a service for the landowner, while at the same time presenting him with a still more favorable self-image, the owner of a champion pointer. At this point Mack's control of the situation becomes explicit. He contradicts the landowner's treatment, then invites himself up to the farmhouse to treat the dog. However, it is all done in the name of solicitousness. In this frame, they are like pseudo-war buddies who hunt together, and take care of each other's dogs. Also, Mack and the boys have been by this point revealed to be not indigents but laborers in the work of curing cancer. In this setting, where curing cancer elevates the position of Mack and the boys, the landowner wants to both reciprocate for Mack's diagnosis and forthcoming curing of the pointer, and ennoble himself, by contributing to a potential cure for cancer. He invites them to hunt frogs by the house, and he invites Mack into his home.

Mack's artistry hinges on two techniques. First, he continuously makes it clear that the landowner is in charge. Through his use of respect markers—"Captain" and "Sir"—as well as the repeated apologies, he de-escalates potential conflict. That is, his actions "soften," rather than "harden," the landowner's position.

Second, Mack gains the landowner's complicity in these shifts, offering with the major shifts a more positive (even though false) image. It is delivered almost in the nature of a contract. That is, if the landowner will go along with the frame shift, Mack will believe him to be a former military officer and later, the owner of a champion pointer. The landowner colludes in the frame shift, because it also offers him (as well as Mack and the boys) the possibility of being someone else, someone richer, wiser, more experienced. They are using shared cultural knowledge to construct jointly a conversational setting which they both know to be untrue.

EXAMPLE 4. The situation becomes increasingly complex when cultural difference is included, and participants are trying to understand each others' strategic moves. The following example (taken from Morrow and Hensel 1992) is drawn from field notes and official tapes of public meetings of the Kuskokwim River Salmon Management Working Group, a comanagement forum intended to bring commercial and subsistence fishermen, processors, and managers together at the negotiating table. Fifteen to thirty people attended these meetings, held two to three times a week throughout most of the summer, at the U.S. Fish and Wildlife Service office in Bethel, Alaska.

It is necessary to preface this transcript with a few comments to facilitate reading. The speakers will be referred to by their roles. In order of appearance, they include: the cochair and Western Alaska Salmon Coalition representative, non-Native (Chairman); a fisheries biologist, non-Native (Biologist); a commercial fisherman and audience member, Yup'ik (Fisherman); a representative of the Kuskokwim Fisherman's Cooperative, Yup'ik (Co-op Representative); an Elder representative, Yup'ik (Elder); and a representative of the Kuskokwim United Fisherman's Marketing Association, Yup'ik (KUFMA Representative). All are male; the Chairman, Biologist, and Fisherman are in their forties, the KUFMA Representative is perhaps in his fifties, and the Elder and the Co-op representative are in their sixties to seventies.

These negotiations are frequently characterized by opaque exchanges. Interpretation is problematic because of linguistic as well as cultural differences. Many speakers would have been more eloquent in Yup'ik, but the language of this public forum was English. In fact, the use of Yup'ik during sessions was discouraged. When one participant tried to translate a portion of the proceedings for another, the chair presumed that the two were caucusing and asked them to postpone their discussion. The Co-op representative in particular is difficult to understand. Nonetheless, a knowledge of Yup'ik and of Yup'ik-influenced English makes it possible to understand most of what he says. That participants were required to use English, that an interpreter was not provided, and that clarification was never requested all reflect the political dimensions of the Native/non-Native relationship.[2]

To appreciate the nature and difficulty of these interchanges, it is useful first to read the dialogue aloud, before reading the annotations, keyed by Roman numerals. The Co-op Representative's speech is easier to understand if the repeated expression "on that" is omitted (in his usage, this functions as a speech marker roughly equivalent to a vocal pause such as "you know").

A very simple transcription system has been used. A few words that were particularly emphasized are italicized; hyphens mark false starts; and words unspoken but clear from context are inserted in brackets. The dialogue is divided into paragraphs signaled by a pause plus a slight change of topic. Overlapping speech (which was rare in this formal setting) is indented at the point of overlap.

Much is happening in these exchanges, and commentary on a variety of aspects would be possible, but the focus has been narrowed to highlight issues of miscommunication and misread strategic moves. The larger setting is that the group is intent on using this rare opportunity to influence the Commissioner. From the perspective of the non-Natives (as evinced on other parts of the tape), there is apparent agreement on how they should approach the Commissioner. Their testimony will be most effective if there is unanimous agreement among the board and audience that there is a severe shortfall of chum salmon caused by overfishing in the False Pass area. Their strategy is first and foremost to stress the lack of fish. Secondly, they stress the personal and financial costs to local people of this situation. Finally, they are prepared to "take a tough stand" on closing the fishery, if necessary, that is, to make it clear that they can make the hard decisions, even if the Commissioner cannot or will not. This is a direct challenge to his machismo. If he is a "real man," he will match their tough stand with a tough stand of his own (against the False Pass fishery). They expect that the Yupiit will reinforce this stand.

July 8, 1991

> [The Commissioner of the Alaska Department of Fish and Game is hearing testimony on overharvesting of Kuskokwim-bound salmon by fishermen in the False Pass area. There is a larger than usual attendance and sometimes palpable tension. The topic of discussion is the wording of a motion to delay or close the next fishing period.]

Chairman: Other discussion on the motion? Yeah, [Biologist]?

Biologist: Mr. Chairman, yeah ah- Perhaps my recommendation needs a small bit of clarification. I essentially agree with what [name of a previous non-Native speaker] just said and that was- that was- I was saying that we needed to back off until we had clear evidence of- that things were better than they are now.

Chairman: [Fisherman]. You have anything new? (I)

Fisherman: Well, I just wanted to make a clarification. I thought I
heard you state in your recommendation that, you
know, we may be looking to closing it up until Coho
management—(II)

(INAUDIBLE)

Biologist, very emphatically: *yes*, that's a possibility. (III) If things don't
ever *improve*,

Chairman: [Elder].

Elder: Ah, I- I just want to say that, ah, you know, I think
there's fish out there, you know. Ah, ever since I start
fishing, you know, I start fishing from way back, and
if there's no fish yet, even you set your net out, you
don't catch *any*, but there's- in this last period I didn't
get a lot of fish, but there's steady stream of fish, you
know. You get- on a drift you get three, four of them.
If there's no fish, you wouldn't get any, so there's fish.
(IV) And one thing- one thing you got to remember is
we had North wind, you know, and the water was
clear. (V)

And the fish aren't dumb, you know. They- they
can elude the net any way they want to, because
they've seen it, because they- that they're- you know,
just like us, they live in that water. And they see everything what's down there, so you know- you know. (VI)

I told you before [Biologist], you don't swim with
the fish and see where they *go*, you know, but I think
we shouldn't- like you said- we shouldn't close this
fishery. Just say that through your study that it- the
fish aren't passing through. (VII)

I think we should all, you know, pitch in together
and see, what- what- goes before we decide what we're
going to do with the fishery, you know, the river, for
this year. (VIII) And I- Just like you say, there's spots
of fish where the subsistence fishermen get their fish.
It's true, but ah- it doesn't happen all over the river.

Like this morning, one of my boys went out fishing. In five minutes, less than five minutes he got over

one hundred chums, you know, reds and chums. So that's- that'll tell you. (IX)

When you said at first that through subsistence users' reports, you know, you're just putting it, you know, putting your stamp on it, and you know it's there, but we want to tell you that, you know, *we know*, because we live here way before you came here. We eat, and our kids grow up on it, you know, and we *know*. (X)

It could be, the chum, you know, they could hit if this North wind is not blowing all the time, you know. That's all I want to say is that one.

The other thing, you know, I didn't have a chance to talk to that commissioner. You know what, you know- I've been into meetings into Anchorage, hearings [on the] False Pass [fishery]. You know, we're just little people over here, what they call us, little people. We don't have much money to flash around over there in Anchorage. The guys from down there, you know, they come in with a gold watch, gold ring, you know, and they've got vests and they walk around with a cigar in their mouths, and they- when somebody talks, people listen [to them] (XI) [BRIEF PAUSE WHILE TAPE TURNED]-hurts all of us, you know. It doesn't add up, you're not with us, you just said. You know I don't talk much, you know, when they're at a meeting, but I listen.

You- you said you're- you're not going to take some actions. But I think you know, you're talking about kids, because we don't make over five thousand dollars fishing. And those guys down there make over two to three hundred thousand dollars, you know, fishing. You know, we've got kids just like anybody else, we try to feed them. And what statements you have made, it has lots of weight to the guys that's listening here.

I know, because I work with my people for a long time. I don't- like I say, I don't say much, but I *listen*. I know what's going on. I know what kind of person, you know, when they talk, what kind of person they are. That's all I have to say. Thank you. (XII)

Chairman: Thank you, [Elder]. [Co-op Representative]?

Co-op   Yeah, Mr Chairman, what I'm thinking on that one, I
Representative: know what I- when I'm little boy, these are the kids on
that. They go wrong. The fish is running down there,
and the water is very clear. Right now on that the people, he need money. I come down to meeting to help
our people. Now the North wind, is not much fish.
The south, uh, South wind he tell us truth about this
winter. They're a coming. He take all that *Akulurak*
fisherman down there, they call on that False Pass, and
when I little boy he talking about that one, and the fish
is coming through to that, to here to *Kusquqvak* [one
channel of the Kuskokwim River above Bethel], spread
it out on those in a pie, and he tell us many times.
(XIII) Right now on that, the fish he'll be- the wind he
get change, he get more fish there coming up to our-
help people on that, ah, this coming Friday, on that
what I'm thinking. (XIV)

Maybe nobody go with me, I think about that
one. The people he really need for that one. I kind of
depending on those other children. (XV)

And the governor, he tell us when we hurt, the
people, "help your people," the council, to help them
on those job. One job, that's only just fishing on that,
that's only for the people without job on that, just only
can get it, it's for the winter, and for stove oil and for
grub for the winter.

Right now, on that, the fish they're a'coming.
Who's going to take them? (XVI) We can not to boss
to the fishing down there, coming on this way get thick
one. South wind he tell us about this winter and the
fall. But they're get, the fish they're a'coming then. Eh,
but we know, I talking not about that *Kass'aq* [non-
Native] way, I talking about their Eskimo way, right
now, about their- this winter in the north. He tell us
about north is not much fish. In the east, in the east and
those they're sometimes on that South wind. Before
those coming in the fish, there before get break up.

When the South wind, old timers they tell us
about, "oh, yeah, that- that's a good on that- that's a

good sign, the fish he coming toward to the Kuskokwim River." Never change when I little boy, I'm get
old timer right now, never change.

He tell us about like this on that. Some day, no
temptature [*sic*]. No temptature [*sic*] he talking about.
Some day when he break up, the ice, before it get
breakup. The fish running underneath king salmon, before it get breakup. After that, it'll bring to the starvation. I never forget those words from the old timers
and old, old lady tell me the truth. Thank you. (XVII)

Chairman:	Thank you [Co-op Representative]. Any other discussion on the motion?
KUFMA Representative:	Mi—
Chairman:	—[KUFMA Representative].
KUFMA Representative:	Yeah, I follow up them guys, [Elder] and [Co-op Representative]. (XVIII) There's some fish out there in the river. Last- since the spring, the water is clear all the time, and when I fill up the bucket and couple of hours, just like rainwater.

Right now, since couple of days, it's clouding up,
from upriver. I- it's gonna- I think it's going to help
the fish. More fish next period. It's clouding up now,
couple days in the water—I watch them pretty close
for fish. I think some of them [the others who have testified?] watching too. I follow up that [suggestion], this
coming Friday, open up the fishing. That's all. (XIX)

Chairman: Anybody else? [PAUSE] I'll take my crack at it. We've
been talking about there not being enough chum
salmon ever since the first period. Everybody's had a
reason to say that there's some there, but every time
we put the fleet out there, we're hard pressed to harvest fifty thousand fish. Everybody that comes to this
table, there's a point where they've got to make a decision that there's not enough fish, because one of the
things that we have to decide here is when there's not
enough fish. I've made the decision right now, based
upon what the fleet has shown us, that I think we've
got to get more fish in the river before we fish again.

I don't support this motion, but I'll support a motion that we meet again on Friday to review any new information. (XX)

That's all I have. Is there any other discussion on the motion? If there's no other discussion of the motion, the chair will hear the motion.

SUMMARY OF STRATEGIC MOVES IN EXAMPLE 4

The Chairman recognizes the Fisherman with the implication that the Fisherman's remarks may be redundant (I). There were prior exchanges between them. The Fisherman then counters the Biologist's assertion that things may never improve. He is the first to state an assertion that all other Yupiit giving testimony will reinforce: fish will come; they are just not here yet. The Biologist counters with an even stronger negative assertion (III). This is followed by the Elder's strong assertion that there are fish (IV). He gives reasons why the fish seem to be less abundant (V). He next gives a reminder that the fish are aware and responsive (VI). In his reminder there is a clear concern with the power of words: "Do not say that the fish are not there; just say that they are not passing through the biologists' test points" (VII). He then appeals to solidarity and consensus (VIII).

In his next statements, the Elder again challenges the statement that there are no fish, pointing out various signs that controvert this statement (IX). He upbraids the biologist for his disregard of users' reports, "rubber-stamping" them when they should be given more weight than the biologist's data (see following discussion) (X).

In the next section of his testimony, he states that the words of people with economic clout and a flashy style are taken seriously; Native words are disregarded (XI). It is interesting to note that the Commissioner was wearing a gold-nugget-studded watch and ring. There is at least an implication that the Commissioner's visible markers link him with the high-volume non-Native fishermen of the False Pass area rather than with low-volume mostly Native fishermen of the lower Kuskokwim River. The Elder states repeatedly that he is aware of the power of words and uses his speech reservedly (in contrast to the Commissioner). He suggests that his speech should be validated especially because he listens much more than he speaks. The Commissioner should be careful about what he says, and make decisions that will benefit "the little people" (XII).

In the initial parts of his testimony, the Co-op Representative may be suggesting that the Commissioner and the other non-Natives are like children in their inexperience (XIII). He (an "old timer") speaks with the authority of age and local knowledge, which has stood the test of tradition. He repeats reasons for the temporarily low catches. Gesturing in the direction of False Pass, he describes a pie-shaped wedge in the air, which represents the route of the fish. He reiterates that fish are sentient and respond to human need (XIV). The situation is made worse for the Yupiit because they must depend on those who are like children to make important decisions for them. Again, he does not expect to be heeded (XV). Following up on the Elder's statements about the sentience of the fish, he says that the fish are coming in response to the peoples' need. When they come, they must be taken; a decision to close the fishery will allow them to pass, and they may be offended and not return in the future (XVI). The Co-op Representative says further that a time has been foreseen when fish will not come, and impending starvation is predictable from certain weather conditions. Present conditions, however, indicate that this is not that time (XVII).

The final Yup'ik speaker, the KUFMA Representative, corroborates previous speakers and moves that the fishery be opened that Friday (XVIII). He refers to the testimony of other Yupiit who have testified, a standard Yup'ik way of demonstrating consensus and validity (XIX).

The Chairman, in his concluding statement, declares that the evidence shows that there are not enough fish and that it is the group's responsibility to admit this. He does not support the KUFMA Representative's motion.

The arguments made by non-Natives can be understood only within the framework of Western scientific reasoning. Their underlying image is of biological systems affected by direct human intervention. The biological system is a given, though knowledge of it may be incomplete. In the system of fish, fishermen, and regulatory agencies, the point at which effective pressure can be applied is via the regulators. Their goal is to combine persuasion and coercion effectively to motivate the Commissioner to change the situation.

This agenda directly conflicts with the Yup'ik strategy and Yup'ik ideology (see the discussion in chapters 1 and 2). A fundamental part of the Yup'ik agenda is to avoid paying too much attention to the resource.

Undue attention to resources in trouble hastens their downturn and eventual demise. . . . Wild resources are known to make themselves scarce to remind humans of their equal footing with them, especially when humans make inordinate commotion over wild resources. When resources face difficult times, it is considered more appropriate to deliberate and act on what human behavior and interaction should be changed to improve the situation. (Pete 1991a:3)

This is one reason why the Yupiit appear to play down the "lack" of fish. The issue of not making a commotion over a resource in trouble is also part of the larger issue of speaking appropriately and respectfully. None of the Yupiit want to say, or to have it publicly said, that there are no fish. To do so would be to admit publicly to an extreme moral failing. Animals and fish come to those who treat them properly, and who live their lives correctly. If the fish avoid someone, it is clear evidence of a major moral fault.[3] If the fish avoid everyone, then either the individual failing is of massive dimensions, or everyone is to blame. With this in mind, the arguments of the Yupiit become much clearer.

Most importantly, no one wants to say there are no fish, only that they haven't come yet, or that the wind is influencing them so that they are not yet catchable. This recasts the situation so that it does not conflict with Yup'ik values and also becomes potentially understandable within the Western scientific paradigm. I am not suggesting that the Yupiit who testified necessarily have internalized an understanding of this paradigm. They have all, however, had significant experience with the sort of arguments non-Natives will accept and reject.

There was a more classically Yup'ik example of argumentation given in testimony at the Alaska Board of Fish hearings in Bethel, in February 1992. Paul John, an older Yup'ik man, scolded the Board through the following story, which I will paraphrase. Mr. John described two Yup'ik hunters. One was very successful, always catching lots of game. The other was less successful. However, the successful hunter had a lazy and sloppy wife, who wasted food and did not take proper and complete care of the game her husband caught. The unsuccessful hunter had a very diligent wife, who was always careful not to waste a scrap. Over time the successful hunter began to catch less and less, while the formerly unsuccessful hunter caught more and more, until he surpassed the one who had been more successful. Mr. John told Board members that they were like that bad wife. By clear implication, their moral attributes and actions were responsible for declining catches.

The fact that the Alaska Department of Fish and Game test nets are not catching many fish is not diagnostic from the perspective of the Yupiit. No one knows where the people who fish the test nets are from, or their moral status. These test fishermen may in fact be the children that the Co-op Representative says "go wrong." The fact that the subsistence fishermen *are* catching fish, and the test net fishermen are not, immediately raises the issue of the test net fishermen's moral status. When the Elder Representative says that one of his sons caught over one hundred reds and chums in five minutes earlier that morning, part of what he is saying is that "*We* are not morally compromised." Clearly, subsistence reports by local people to whom the fish come should be given more weight than reports by non-Native seasonal workers whom the fish (apparently) avoid.

This discussion also relates to other discussions (in other meetings) about the whole enterprise of running a "test fishery." Under Western scientific ideals of replicability, the test netting is conducted in as comparable a fashion as possible. The same spots are fished each time, so that choice of fishing spot or knowledge of fish habits will not influence the data. This means fishing where there are almost never fish, as well as where there are likely to be fish. This has been difficult for Working Group members to understand. Why should someone fish where there aren't going to be fish? They have suggested that some local people be hired to go out at regular times and catch as many fish as possible in a timed drift. I wonder if in fact some of the resistance to the test fishery is that trying *not* to catch fish is an anathema. Attempting and succeeding in not catching fish merely advertises one's moral failings. In addition, it may be seen by Yupiit as playing with or mocking something that is very serious, with possible negative consequences for everyone.

Even when Yupiit raise questions that fit at least partially within the scientific paradigm, the situation has been so polarized that their concerns are unlikely to be heard. In the following exchange, a Yup'ik man in the audience raises a reasonable point about replicability, which is treated as another wrongheaded attack against the test fishery. His point is attended to only when it is restated by a non-Native and placed within "scientific" discourse through the use of contextualization cues which mark that discourse. The speakers include: a member of the audience, Yup'ik (Audience Member); a second fisheries biologist, non-Native (Biologist 2); the Chairman; and myself (Chase Hensel).

July 5, 1991
[Meeting of the Kuskokwim River Salmon Management Working Group, at the U.S. Fish and Wildlife Service building in Bethel, Alaska.]

Audience Member: Is there any way you can move that ah, test fishery, from there because I've got, you've got two

	sloughs below that comes out above your ah, above your ah, sonar and fishing site and I'm pretty sure all the fish go through those Straight Slough and Steamboat Slough.
	Lot of, hell of a lot of them [chum salmon] at Kalskag, that Straight Slough's getting wider and deeper every year, you know.
Biologist 2:	Mr. Chairman
Audience Member:	And a lot of them probably passing there.
Biologist 2:	Could respond?
Chairman:	Yeah
Biologist 2:	Just the only point about that, if we would move, right now we have test, test fish data from 1984,
Audience Member:	I mean for next year.
Biologist 2:	Yeah so from 1984 through this year. If we would move that test fishery at all, the ahm, the catch per unit efforts [CPUE] that we look at would not be comparable with historic data.
Audience Member:	Well you try it next year, see how much, how much more you'll probably, you'll get lot of fish
Biologist 2:	But we wouldn't have anything to compare it with.
Audience Member:	That's a lot of fish, there's a couple sloughs there go through, lot of fish goes through.
	[PAUSE AND INDISTINCT BACKGROUND VOICES]
Chairman:	Chase
Chase:	I don't know that, it didn't sound like you [Biologist 2] were considering his point. You're saying that your results need to be comparable. He's saying the river is changing, the course is changing, so it's no longer comparable, so, you may want to consider that in your CPUEs, that they may already be biased.

At the next break, Biologist 2 commented that he appreciated my point (as opposed to Audience Member's point), that he had not understood it in that way. It is significant that I also felt constrained to argue within the Western scientific paradigm, and did not add that the Audience Member's desire to have the test fishery where the fish *are* might be for reasons of Yup'ik ideology as well.

There is a similar misalignment in the culturally appropriate way to approach those who are more powerful. The Yup'ik approach to the Commissioner in Example 4 is one of supplication. They stress that they are just "little people," although morally virtuous. They are, after all, catching fish steadily, if not in great numbers. Additionally, they guard their talk and pay proper attention to the power of words. Traditionally, in Yup'ik culture, those with the most power (as demonstrated by hunting success) were supposed to distribute more, particularly to the poor and elderly. My understanding of the proper stance for the three older Yupiit who gave long statements is that they tried to state the clear power inequities with the expectation that the person with the power would fulfill his side of the social contract and distribute largesse. Both the Elder and the Co-op Representative also began and ended their presentations by validating and legitimating their testimony, giving the reasons why they are "culturally authorized" to speak, that is, why they in particular are in the supplicant role.[4] It is not unlikely that they are frustrated by the Commissioner's apparent unwillingness to fulfill his "culturally assigned" role, as the giver of what has been requested.[5]

In the end, what happens is that the non-Natives keep saying that "There are no fish," and the Yupiit keep saying "Don't say that there are no fish." Everyone is confused. Presumably the non-Natives wonder why the Yupiit who are comanaging the resource in this organization are undercutting the effectiveness of the presentation. The Yupiit wonder how grown men can be so careless with their speech, and so willing to declare publicly that they (and everyone else) are morally bankrupt. The disjunction is amplified because the Yup'ik speakers' strategies are mapped onto their second language. Undoubtedly some markers that could potentially help clarify the situation, such as possible deference markers used with the Commissioner, are lost. However, many of these disjunctions stem from such fundamental differences in worldview that they would be very difficult to clarify, much less resolve, even with expert translation.

Comments in previous meetings support the notion that the Yup'ik refusal to say that "there are no fish" is interpreted by the Fish and Game Representative as some combination of ignorance (benighted Natives) and greed (rapacious fishermen). Both images are current in non-Native culture, particularly in the professional culture of wildlife managers and biologists (see Morrow and Hensel 1992). Since communicative debacles like this are extremely common, particularly in resource management, meetings of this sort are ideal for the creating and hardening of stereotypes, which Gumperz and Cook-Gumperz state as a general rule: "What starts as isolated situation-bound communication differences at the individual level may harden into ideological distinctions that then become value laden, so that every time problems of understanding arise they serve to create further differences in the symbolization of identity" (1982:3).

In the end, the strength of the contextualization conventions is such that each group seems to talk by each other, as evinced by both the Chairman's sighs[6] and the Co-op Representative's comments that "maybe nobody go with me." There are numerous instances in which participants seek to influence each other, but they are largely unsuccessful.

SUBSISTENCE DISCOURSE AS PRACTICE

Treating subsistence discourse as practice allows one to account for aspects of this practice that a more strictly economic approach would ignore. People's strategic moves are frequently multivalent. A single exchange can simultaneously reference several levels of meaning and image, and participants may or may not be aware of such moves. Situations where one is only semiconscious of how one is manipulated in an interaction are common; that is, one feels manipulated, but is unable to pinpoint exactly how or where the manipulation has occurred.

The primary strategic uses of subsistence discourse among Yupiit and non-Natives include the exchange of information, negotiating gender and ethnic identities, and negotiating relative status and success in role fulfillment. Of these, exchanging information is potentially the least convoluted, although such exchanges often form the framework for other strategic moves.

Subsistence information flows relatively freely, although there are situations in which someone may hope to tell less than he or she learns. For example, people are notoriously reticent about the location of good berry patches. Likewise, people may be reluctant to specify where they are planning to commercial fish or hunt ducks, lest they increase their (local) competition. The general attitude, however, is that information should be shared. People do not conceive of themselves as being in direct competition for resources in a system of limited goods (though they may be in competition for status and prestige). Instead, all are targeting streams of fish and game, pulses that pass through the water and land, most abundant in one place today and elsewhere tomorrow. Not only does sharing information increase everyone's chances but also most such information is so quickly disseminated that there is little point in withholding it. If it is important news, such as the catching of the year's first king salmon, everyone is likely to hear it several times from several sources. In addition, the newsworthiness of such information declines rapidly over time; knowing where a band of caribou was two days ago is much less interesting than hearing where it was this morning. Sharing information is also important because it tends to increase everyone's safety. If an emergency occurs, people will know where other groups may be and thus where help may be found. If a group doesn't return, searchers know where to begin looking for them.

NATIVE, NON-NATIVE, HOW NATIVE? ETHNICITY ON A CONTINUUM OF PRACTICE

It is clear that people not only recognize and understand who they are through what they do but they also enact who they are through discourse about these practices. This discourse is also simultaneously a way of situating themselves along this continuum, of validating the complexities of who they are through discoursing on the complexities (and disparateness) of what they do.

When Janet Shantz said that her involvement in subsistence "puts me in touch with the Yup'ik part of me," she was recognizing the complexity of ethnicity in this setting, where parts of one's life may seem either more, or less, Yup'ik.

Interviewees also recognized changes in themselves through practice; that is, through their response to the actions of others. Paul Longpre and his guest were both surprised by his response to his guest's "playing" with the moose. At that point Longpre realized that he had been acquiring more than just hunting "skills," that there was an ideological component that he had acquired as well. And again, his story may also be seen as a claim to a particular kind of "understanding" from me. He wanted me to accept that there were ways in which his own identity had become more complex.

Interviewees also talked about how they (and others) recognized who they were through their own actions. For example, in Shantz's description of her mother feeling "as if her mom's hand was on her hand," Shantz's mother learned more fully who she was and what she could do, through this experience. Her friend (who helped Shantz's sister put up salmon, and made those most complex cuts for the first time) also was both recognizing and demonstrating who she was through practice. Further, Shantz's telling of these incidents was also practice, a way of situating herself, her sister, and her friend.

A similar sense of the complexity of discourse, practice, and identity is apparent in other interviews as well. The woman with the photo of her fish camp on her office wall was making a very complex statement indeed. It is clear that both her professional career and her "Yup'ik-ness" are important to her. Her subsistence practices seemed, among other things, to be a way of achieving a balance in her life. And certainly her talk to me about her subsistence practices was also strategic, in that it was asking me to recognize the complexity of her identity as well.

Negotiating Gender and Ethnic Identities Through Subsistence Discourse

Subsistence discourse is used to negotiate gender and ethnic identities, both in the sense of what is appropriate behavior for each category, and what that category consists of: that is, both what it means to be a laudable male in Yup'ik terms, and whether, or to what extent, one *is* a laudable *male*, in Yup'ik terms. These are two sides of the same coin. The same practice that is valorized (for example, hunting success) also reinforces the category (either male or Yup'ik) that it exemplifies.

The situation is further complicated by the way in which gender and ethnicity are intertwined in this situation of a bicultural continuum. Also, because appropriate gender roles are ethnically defined, and ethnicity is partly signaled through gender role appropriateness, gender and ethnicity are not, except in the abstract, independent. The intertwining of gender and ethnicity is further complicated by the local conception of ethnicity in practice not in terms of discrete categories of Native versus non-Native, but along a continuum. That is, although the conceptual categories of Native/non-Native are distinguished, ethnicity itself consists of the enactment of practices that mark an individual as Native to some degree, not simply Native or non-Native in a given context. This is further complicated by the fact that while non-Native gender roles are currently politicized, Native ones are much less so. For Yupiit, doing a task generally assigned to the opposite gender (for instance, a man cutting fish, a woman checking nets) generally does not call one's gender into question, though the action will usually be justified (lack of "appropriate" personnel to cut fish or check nets). This flexibility in Yup'ik gender roles has strong historic roots: successful mastery of cross-gender roles has always been admired.

Fulfilling non-Native roles, as opposed to Yup'ik ones, occasions a more complex response, as was noted in chapter 5. For Yup'ik men, such actions seem to call their gender identity as *males* into question; for

Yup'ik women, their identity as *Yupiit*. So, for example, the actions of a feminist Yup'ik woman may be seen as bringing her Yup'ik-ness into question, much more than her gender: that is, she may be accused of acting non-Native, rather than non-female.[7]

In practice, there are a variety of ways in which non-compliance with traditional gender roles is justified. For example, one may justify an action by citing the example of a laudable person, i.e. "George does it that way," or by referring to changing norms. One Yup'ik man I interviewed cuts fish with his wife. He justified his behavior as a reasonable accommodation to the realities of his work schedule, since he and his family had only the weekends both to catch and process their fish. In his description and explanation of his practice, he held up his behavior as normative, at least for Bethel. Stepping back from the conversation, it is possible to see that he was referencing a complex blend of gender and ethnic identities, including implicit allusions to my own (non-Native, male) practices; that is, his talk about his fish-cutting practices was also practice.

Similar strategic uses of subsistence discourse are common between non-Natives, to show (and imply) local knowledge and involvement. In response to a question by one non-Native (Person B) about what he had been doing, for example, another (Person A) replied that he had been busy "getting his fish up." In the local context, this raised the whole co-occurrence structure of putting up a large quantity of fish, most likely in a traditional Yup'ik fashion. This requires having, or at least having access to, a fish camp, or at least a smokehouse and drying racks, a boat, motor and nets, plus significant local knowledge, or at least knowledgeable help (which again implies local connections). During questioning by person B, however, it turned out that A was smoking the odd salmon in a small electric smoker and freezing the result, an enterprise requiring considerably less local knowledge and involvement. Person A sought to raise a co-occurrence structure of dense local knowledge and involvement, when in fact the actual activity was relatively minor and the knowledge was gained through print (he had followed a set of written instructions that had come with the smoker, as opposed to apprenticing himself to an experienced fish processor). In this example, the participants could have been either male or female.[8]

The fish-smoker was clearly unsuccessful in his gambit, probably at least partly because of the "size" of his claim. Had he said he had been "catching a few salmon," or "smoking a few fish," exactly "how many" might have gone unquestioned. It is even possible that B might have thought he was intentionally, that is, ironically, understating his involvement, and given him credit for more involvement.

A similar claim—in this case to local (Yup'ik) values—was made in an interview. Part of the following transcript of an interview with a non-Native status hunter appeared in chapter 2. In the first exchange the interviewee mentions giving his unwanted fish to "the old folks," although he says these words more softly. Taking food to older people is a commonly stated Yup'ik value. It is both an act of generosity and an act of exchange. The thoughts of older people are powerful, and in reciprocity (expressed as thankfulness) they will think about and positively influence the giver's future successes. Even though the interviewee was engaging in what Yupiit would consider aberrant behavior (catch and release fishing), he was still claiming that part of his action was locally correct. In this regard, he was purposefully situating himself as following Yup'ik values. Here is his description. (In the following transcript, significant points are marked with roman numerals.)

> My fishing is mostly catch and release. Last year I probably caught three or four hundred rainbows [trout] and I think I brought five or six of them home.
>
> I probably ate a couple of dozen while I was up there. Most of what I catch goes back into the river, unless it's going to die anyway. Quite often by the end of the trip I've got a dozen or so fish that are dead, and so I'll stop in Kwethluk or whatever and drop them off [SOFTER] to the old folks. (I) And that goes all through summer. September I go moose hunting. (transcript of an interview, 1991)

At this time, his claim to virtuous distribution passed by me completely unquestioned. It is not uncommon for non-Natives to establish relationships with older Yupiit. It seemed quite commonplace that he had adopted this local practice. Later in the interview I returned to this point in my attempt to understand the balance of subsistence products flowing into and out of his household:

> C: Something else that occurs to me, because you were talking about dropping off the trout in Kwethluk, are there other things that I might think about, where you're catching more than you need, or distributing things? (II)
>
> A: Ahmmm [PAUSE, SIGH]
>
> C: I guess I'm getting more of a picture of a household economy which might be that trout go out, and strips and pieces of moose and caribou come in. I mean, in terms of exchange stuff. (III)

A: No, to be honest with you, I give the trout, yeah, it is an exchange type situation. However, usually the people I give the fish to are not the people I get things from. Most of the moose and strips and stuff that I get come from personal friends of mine, whereas most of the stuff that I give away goes to the older people, old folks, they . . .

C: Do you have a couple of families that you know when you're coming through Kwethluk and you? (IV)

A: No, not particularly. When I'm coming down, and I see someone standing on the bank, at their fish camp, I'll stop at their fish camp and say, "Hey, you want them?" If they say "no," I'll stop at the next one. If by the time I get to Kwethluk I haven't gotten rid of them, then I'll go in and find somebody, first, and just keep going along until I find somebody who's willing to take them off my hands, because I won't use them.

My question on the nature of the household economy (II) did not clarify the nature of the exchanges, so I restated his statements as I understood them. He then used my term (exchange) but still did not explain what the exchanges were. I was unable to understand in what way these were exchanges, since they were not characterized by reciprocity. Most typically, person A brings or sends a locally available resource to person B in another area who reciprocates at the appropriate season with something available in B's area. This interviewee, on the other hand, was describing two unconnected half-exchanges. Gifts of fish went to some "older people" in Kwethluk and gifts of meat came to him from coworkers.

I was confused by his response. In my experience, because gifts validate relationships, it is actually quite difficult to give gifts to Yupiit without reinforcing existing relationships or establishing new ones. For example, in the early 1980s, while conducting a bilingual survey in a village near Bethel, I had a very pleasant interaction with an older Yup'ik man. After we had eaten and discussed the questionnaire as well as other subjects, he gave me a gift of a wooden pestle (berry masher), which he had made. The following Saturday, after my son and I had checked our ice-fishing net, we drove down to his village and gave the old man and his wife a sheefish. In the course of a fairly brief visit we learned that one of their children had died around the same time my son was born. They understood that this must be why we had brought the fish. My son was actually their son (reborn), so of course he (we) would bring them fish. And they started calling him by their former son's name (a different Yup'ik name than the two he already had). This experience demonstrated the way that gifts establish relationships in Yup'ik terms. It also made it clear that one does not take food to merely any older person, but to appropriate ones, related to the giver in particular ways, which were (potentially) recognized, as well as strengthened, through the gifts.

In this light, I wondered what his relationship with these "older folks" was, so I asked question IV. At this point his story unraveled. Though he had until then described his actions in terms that referenced Yup'ik ideals, he finally admitted to a distribution pattern as aberrant as his fishing in terms of those ideals.

It was simply bad luck that his story of giving his extra fish to the "older folks" was revealed as a false claim. I happened to be doing research on subsistence, and so followed up with a series of questions that eventually brought the contradictions to light. The only clue I had, however, was how odd it seemed to me that his fishing would so clearly violate Yup'ik values, while his distribution validated them. Typically, the transfer of values and practices requires intense local involvement. If he were involved to such an extent in local relationships, his catch and release fishing would, I assumed, have come under scrutiny, and been questioned by Yupiit. He would likely have recognized (or have been helped to recognize) that the two practices (as he described them) belonged to different spheres of discourse. As such, they should be kept separate, as being appropriate to two different audiences. That is, he should have talked about catch and release fishing to non-Native audiences, and "giving the fish to the older folks" to Yup'ik ones.[9] I would imagine that many such claims to local knowledge and "insider" status are successful, even though this one was not.

Status and Role Fulfillment

As mentioned above, subsistence discourse is often the primary way in which one's perseverance, luck, and success are made manifest. One-upmanship in telling hunting exploits is not uncommon among non-Native men. Non-Natives often talk of the size of "the one that didn't get away," as well as "the one that did." Among Yupiit, personal exploits are much more frequently related in a way that illustrates a point under discussion, such as animal behavior or an innovative response to potential danger. Often they are told for their humorous aspects and at the teller's expense. Boasting is considered inappropriate, and even the occasional individual who seems to be bragging about his or her exploits will usually follow one of these scripts, though still managing to cast him- or herself in the role of super-hunter, fisher, or gatherer.

Conversational Plays to Ethnicity and Identity

In discourse, then, references to subsistence activities and products are often used as proxies for "Native-ness" and "rural Alaskan non-Native-ness." This is less of an issue among Yupiit: it comes to the forefront in cross-cultural interactions and in interactions between non-Natives.

In cross-cultural and non-Native to non-Native conversations, subsistence is widely used as a proxy for Yup'ik culture and Yupiit. This discourse provides a way of interactively negotiating potential congruency in worldview. On the shallowest level, what is being discussed are attitudes toward Yup'ik culture and Yup'ik people in general. In cross-cultural interactions, Yupiit use the manner in which non-Natives refer to subsistence to gauge whether or not they are likely to be respected. In other words, "Are your attitudes toward me (my kind of person) sufficiently respectful that I don't risk damaging (at least temporarily) my sense of self?" (Goffman 1963).

On a deeper level, negotiations examine the extent of congruency in worldview. It has often been clear to me that, in interactions with Yupiit I didn't know or had just met,[10] one aspect of the questions about my subsistence activities was that such questions represented a kind of testing. I was being queried (indirectly) about my attitudes as well as my activities. They were using discourse as practice to try to understand how my practice was situated and what worldview was reflected.

One non-Native, Martha Scott, described to me the process she underwent in recognizing that she was never going to understand subsistence fully in the way that Yupiit did, but that this was not a prerequisite for successful interactions and friendships. What was important was respecting the meaning and importance of subsistence to Yupiit.

M: I've never really had a Yup'ik person articulate that [difference in understanding] to me. I've only witnessed that by hanging around.

I mean the subsistence way of life is just kind of like the threads in their [her Yup'ik friends'] clothes, and that's not the way it is for me. I understand that. And I think for a long time that I wanted to, how would you say this? I can sympathize but I can't empathize, because I don't know what it's like.

C: But for a long time you thought that you were?

M: I thought I could when I first got up here. This is nature, this was their God when they danced, this was all part of everything. I get that, intellectually. I can read *Eskimo about Bering Strait* [Nelson 1899]. I can get Nelson's stuff, and I got it, and you think you get it.

But I came to the realization several years ago that I don't get it. That I get it as much as I can, but I'll never really get it.

And that's a really important thing that Yup'ik people have taught me, because it's taught me that it's OK to be the way I am and live here. I thought maybe it was a prerequisite to live here that I had to get it. And somehow part of me had to be more Yup'ik or something like that, but it doesn't have to be.

My friends totally accept about me that there's some things that I'm not going to understand, and when you do that, Chase, you really accept yourself in a visitor status. And I sit really fine with that, my heart is fine with that, but that's really hard for a lot of people. Yup'ik people have helped me be more of myself and feel comfortable being myself here. (transcript of an interview, July 12, 1991)

Given these potential multiple meanings for subsistence, many non-Natives are quite careful to qualify negative remarks. When they make a negative evaluative comment about subsistence, they are careful to restrict its application to a particular person or practice, rather than to generalize to all persons and/or subsistence in general. In the context of the Y-K Delta, blanket disparaging comments often serve as a marker for paternalistic or racist attitudes.

Conclusion

I have argued that in this bicultural situation ethnicity is largely achieved rather than ascribed. That is, while individuals have concepts of "being Yup'ik" and "being non-Native," the locally important aspects of these identities consist in how and in what manner one fits within that identity. Ethnicity per se is less important than how one's actions and discourse situate one within that bicultural continuum. This view results from two related sources.

First, there has been a long history of intermarriage. The offspring of such marriages seem to have been relatively free to choose their ethnicity, particularly when there had been intermarriage in previous generations as well. In local terms, ethnicity was and is judged less on the basis of genetic heritage than on practice, the extent to which one "acts Yup'ik" or "acts white."

Second, traditional Yup'ik views of categorization see categories as inherently flexible and indeterminate. This view has reinforced local attention on the enactment (rather than the assignment) of ethnicity. But there are implications beyond the local applicability of this model.

Places like Bethel, where members of two or more cultures meet in an ongoing maelstrom of change, are becoming omnipresent. Viewing ethnicity as achieved rather than ascribed allows a more critical understanding of such settings because it focuses our attention on actual practices rather than on an a priori system of categorization. This allows the potential for examining the situated enactment of ethnicity.

An important aspect of this study has been to show how Natives and non-Natives use roughly similar practices and related discourse to maintain different identities. Where traditional ethnographies generally focused only on the exotic group, I have sought to illustrate how both groups use discourse and practice. Traditional ethnographies also typically examined only the effects of the hegemonic culture on members of the subordinate culture: I have instead tried to show this process as bidirectional. At least some non-Natives are strongly affected by Yup'ik beliefs and worldview, as well as by Yup'ik practices. Furthermore, this system of Yup'ik practices and beliefs becomes a powerful referent for many non-Natives. Even non-Natives whose hunting and fishing practices are incongruent with Yup'ik ones may attempt to cast their practices in Yup'ik terms.

One of the important issues being negotiated through attempts to regulate subsistence is the extension of governmentality into the Yup'ik area. I have argued that such regulation is really a contest over biopower, that is, over worldview and ideology in definitional terms.

I have also tried to show some of the complex links between language, gender, ideology, and differing gender development paths under colonialism. Although I began this study with a sense that subsistence practices and discourse were more important to Yup'ik men than to Yup'ik women, I was soon disabused of this notion. I came to recognize that Yup'ik men and women have been unequally affected by Western "development," and that differential outmarriage and emigration are sequelae of both this differential history and cultural patterns that favor women's involvement in the labor force. This gender difference in history and what I have called "pre-adaptation for Western work" are also important for those aspects of one's identity that are highlighted through practice. For at least some Yup'ik men and women there is a slight difference in which aspects of their identities are publicly expressed and validated through subsistence discourse. For men, subsistence most importantly validates gender identity and role fulfillment, and secondarily ethnicity. For women the situation is reversed: subsistence most importantly validates ethnic identity, and secondarily gender identity. It may be that these identities, masculinity for men and ethnicity for women, are most easily called into question in this setting.

Finally, in the broadest sense, I have tried to show how people use co-occurrence structures strategically in conversation. I have suggested that this topic can be approached most fruitfully by intense attention to a particular discourse arena.[1] Rather than trying to understand such strategic moves in the abstract, it is more profitable to use a practice-based approach, and to attempt to understand the communicative force of such moves within their embedded context. Such an approach necessitates intense ethnographic knowledge. In the context examined here, this discourse and the practices from which it derives saliency are a primary vehicle for discussing attitudes about ethnicity. They are used as proxies when negotiating potential congruencies in worldview, as well as when making evaluative comments about groups or individuals.

These markers are able to represent larger issues of worldview because they act like the wider anthropological equivalents of linguistic co-occurrence conventions, what I have termed co-occurrence sets or co-occurrence structures. Such sets call up larger images with them. These larger images are like structures (in the sense that Giddens and Bourdieu use the term). They are learned interactively and are held in common by recognizable subgroups (and larger groups); they guide interaction and are amenable to strategization. As such, they provide a way of linking individual action with macro-level practice theory.

In terms of future research into discourse as practice, I am currently engaged in examining cross-cultural interactions as a site of structuration; that is, examining the kind of accommodative communicative structures engendered over time in cross-cultural interactions. This is particularly interesting because, although the experiences of co-conversants are largely shared, the insights, realizations, and learned accommodations are not. Some individuals are cognizant of, and make a wide variety of accommodative shifts in, interaction; others know very little and/or make very few such accommodations. Since habitus level structures are inadequate to explain the diversity of outcomes in terms of structures learned, something else must be posited. I suggest that it is subcultural-, family-, and individual-level structures that at least partially structure the acquisition of these communicative structures. Hopefully, such research will yield more evidence of the similarity of structures at all levels, from individuals to the largest groups. It has the potential to clarify the link between individual interactive learning and culture-level communicative structures.

Notes

Introduction

1. The use of the ethnonym "Eskimo" is problematic. On the one hand, it is commonly used self-referentially by Alaskan Yupiit and Inupiat and is arguably the most widely recognized referent for Inuit peoples. However, in Canadian and Greenlandic contexts the term "Inuit" is preferred, with "Eskimo" seen as having clear racist/colonialist connotations. There are, however, two problems with using the word "Inuit" (lit. The People) in the Yup'ik context. First, it is not in common usage, since Yupiit generally use "Eskimo" instead, reserving "Inuit" almost exclusively for political contexts. Second, it is a cognate with the base word for Yup'ik, so that Yupiit Inuit (or Yup'ik Inuit) sounds awkward (The Real People-People). So, in an uneasy solution, I have chosen to use the term "Yupiit," except when referring more widely to Inuit peoples, where I use the word "Inuit."

2. The use of the terms "Native" and "non-Native" is also complex. In Southwestern Alaska, "Native" is commonly used to mean "Alaska Native," "Yup'ik," or "the Yup'ik language" (as in "to speak Native"). The negation, "non-Native," semantically maps onto the Yup'ik word *Kass'aq*, "white person, Caucasian" (Jacobson 1984:190), and in fact the words "white" or "white man" are often used. There are widely used terms in Yup'ik referring to Asians, African Americans, and non-Inuit Native Americans, and these distinctions generally carry through into local English usage. Members of such groups will likely be specified rather than lumped together with Euro-Americans as "non-Natives."

3. The exceptions involve federally regulated species, such as sea mammals, where hunting is restricted to Alaska Natives, and user conflicts on federally regulated lands, where preference may be (and legally can be) given to Native users.

4. Economics does play a role in subsistence, as the following note and quotes show. The financial expense involved in pursuing a particular activity is certainly one factor that participants consider, but, except in extreme cases, it is not the sole determining factor. Focusing exclusively on "the bottom line" tends to blind researchers to questions of situated meaning.

5. With the exception of Example 4 in chapter 7, false starts and vocal pauses have been deleted from transcripts, as were such interviewer's vocalized encouragements as "uhm-hum" and "eh-heh." Insertions are shown in brackets.

6. Most hunters share expenses, so that hunting is still more cost-effective than buying food from the store. This is true, in most cases, even when chartering airplanes to hunt caribou. One reviewer suggested that because of Arvin Dull's professional position, he may be expected to contribute more money than others in a hunting party. That is, it may be less cost-effective for him to hunt, precisely because he can afford to cover a disproportionately large amount of the costs.

7. There is some trade in subsistence products such as salmonberries, whole seals, seal skins, seal oil, and dried salmon, both informally and through local stores. However, overall quantities involved are relatively small, and this trade seems more limited by lack of supply than lack of demand.

8. The only exception were the statements of one couple who had left the area, and whom I was unable to contact.

Chapter 1

1. Overflow is water that has flowed out over the ice. It is often obscured by a thin layer of new ice over it. Depending on the thickness of this ice, it may hold a fox but not a snow machine, or a snow machine but not a car. In the Delta, overflow most commonly forms when the ice is frozen to the bottom or shore and does not float up when the water level changes due to tide or melt-water.

2. This was part of the Distant Early Warning system, created to give advance notice of nuclear attack.

3. There is some pressure in Bethel, primarily in the school system, to use the word "multicultural" instead of 'bicultural' to describe the local situation. Realistically, however, there are few if any other distinct cultures with sufficient members to maintain some cultural identity.

4. Writing in 1887, E. W. Nelson (cited in Ager 1982:49) thought that over-harvesting with firearms was responsible for the disappearance of caribou, al-

though similar shifts by caribou herds and massive population crashes have been observed since, calling this assertion into question.

5. This use of the term "men's house" seems warranted in the Yup'ik area. Kilbuck noted that "except to bring in the meals and at festivals—women are not allowed in the *kashigi [qasgiq]*—and it is deemed improper for a woman to sit on the benches [men sit, work and sleep on the benches, boys and women sit on the floor]" (Kilbuck, in Fienup-Riordan 1988:21). However, see Bodenhorn (1990:67) for a discussion of the complexity of this issue in the Barrow area (Northwest Alaska). She notes that in interviews with elderly Inupiaq women, they called the analogous structure a community house or ceremonial house; Bodenhorn argues that the space could be used for a variety of purposes, with its use determining what it "was" at that time. This is analogous to a patch of lawn that is sometimes a soccer field, sometimes a football field, and includes a baseball diamond.

6. Interestingly enough, in the cases of which I am aware, the individuals involved do not seem to have suffered from sex role confusion. They later married and took up sex-appropriate gender roles while maintaining skills of the opposite gender as well. My impression is that a clear distinction was made between their sex and social gender. Their enactment of social gender consisted of performing gender-appropriate activities. It did not entail a denial of their sex. A girl might be dressed like, and encouraged to hunt and fish like, a boy, because she was named after, say, her grandfather, and used to be male. This in no way precluded her from later fulfilling culturally appropriate female roles. Such cross-gender naming is common in many Inuit societies.

7. Bodenhorn, in her paper "I'm Not the Great Hunter, My Wife Is" (1990), directs attention to the overtness with which some North Slope Inupiaq hunters recognize the vital nature of women's contribution to hunting. Yupiit also recognize that as primary processors and distributors, mothers, wives, and daughters are in a critical position. I suggest that the actions of others (members of the family, the village, and the surrounding area) have the potential to harm a hunter's relationship with classes of animals, such as someone decreasing a fish run by traveling over the water after a recent death in the family. Processors have the potential to affect a hunter's relationship with classes of animals and with individual animals that the hunter would hope to catch over and over again. Although women had this kind of responsibility for their effects on game, among Yupiit, hunters, not their spouses, are considered to be those actively involved in the pursuit of game.

8. Proper treatment included sharing what was caught and seeing that nothing was wasted. It also included keeping the animal and products—such as its meat and fur—clean, and correctly disposing of the bones.

9. This section is taken from Hensel and Morrow 1983. The coastal data were partially supplied by Mary Pete, Alaska Department of Fish and Game, Division of Subsistence, Bethel, Alaska.

Chapter 2

1. Exceptions include the high-seas interception of salmon and herring, as well as at least one incident of massive commercial interception of salmon in the Kuskokwim Bay (Lenz 1985:95).

2. For example, the Glacier Bay National Monument has been closed to subsistence fishing since the mid-1950s, although commercial and sportfishing, as well as tourist activity, have been allowed to continue. The guns and game of at least some subsistence users were confiscated, and they were discouraged from returning to the Monument. Given that the subsistence users were Tlingit Indians, and that the tourists and sportfishermen were and are non-Native, many Tlingit feel that such actions were racially motivated (Nora Dauenhauer, Sea Alaska Heritage Foundation; Robert Schroeder, Alaska Department of Fish and Game, Division of Subsistence, personal communication, July 1989).

3. In the late 1980s, students in a high-school cultural heritage class in Stebbins made beluga nets. Elders from the village advised and guided students in the construction, site selection, and deployment of these nets. One student caught a beluga in his net (Mary Pete, personal communication, April 10, 1991).

4. Fur clothing, particularly fancy parkas with intricate fur mosaic trim, sometimes functions both as ethnic markers and as status markers. Meade (1990) discusses the importance of traditional parka designs as markers of regional group membership within the Yup'ik area, as well as the symbolism of some of the designs.

5. The introduction of commercial twine for making king salmon gill nets has also increased the availability of this species for drying.

6. The use of sugar for preserving blueberries is well attested from Inupiaq areas farther north (Jones 1983:85).

7. Wolfe (1987) shows that the important unit for subsistence research is not the individual household but the larger grouping of related households that catch, process, and share subsistence products. Focusing on individual households gives the impression that some households are super-producers and others super-consumers. This is true, but it is an artifact of the analytic framework being imposed, of examining production and consumption in terms of dwellings rather than in terms of multi-household units that share production, processing, and consumption. In these larger groups the most active members do more of the hunting and processing, and the older, younger, and infirm members produce and process less. Those employed full-time may also be less active, contributing cash to cover expenses, and participating in subsistence activities after work and on weekends. Furthermore, as individuals age and grow into and out of subsistence careers, there are also changes over time in who the most active subsisters are.

8. As a general rule, the greater the fat content of a fish, the more difficult the fish is to dry without the fat turning rancid or mold developing.

9. These are berries that have been covered with snow over the winter, and are revealed as the snow melts.

10. Although gardening is an important focus for some people in Bethel, the climate requires gardeners to be knowledgeable, diligent, and lucky if they are to harvest very much. This interviewee has been heavily involved in setting up community gardening plots and in a project to provide low-cost "seed" potatoes. Gardening seemed to be more of a focus for her than for other people interviewed.

11. In jury selection for a recent trial in Bethel, several prospective Yup'ik jurors from nearby villages listed their hobbies as hunting and fishing. However, they gave this answer when replying to a standard list of questions, one of which asked for "hobbies" (Phyllis Morrow, personal communication, July 1, 1991). My supposition is that, given the option of replying "none," or supplying something that fit the Euro-American questioners' expectations, they chose the latter course.

12. This name appears variously on the United States Geological Survey (USGS) maps as "Chukwoktulik" and "Chukfaktoolik." There were at least two settlements with this name.

13. At the same time that such stories are told less often in family contexts, they are told and read more often in school, in bilingual programs. They still form a stock of referents for most Yupiit, in the same way that the Bible did for many nineteenth-century Americans.

14. In part this could be a function of big *land* game being viewed by non-Natives as more "appropriate" food (most beeflike), and of the federal prohibition against non-Native marine mammal hunting. Additionally, many non-Natives view marine mammals as tasting "fishy," that is, they violate non-Native taste categories (Mary Pete, personal communication, April 10, 1992).

15. In Yup'ik stories, ritual pollution is usually discussed in terms of cleanliness. The main sources of possible contamination are the dead and women in general, but particularly menstruating and postpartum women. Animals will avoid unclean hunters and hunting gear. In general, observances are less strict than they were in the nineteenth century. Extensive seclusion at first menses is becoming uncommon, but many women still avoid traveling over water during their menstrual period, to avoid offending the fish and thus bringing misfortune on the village.

16. Verbalized anti-hunting sentiments are fairly rare in Bethel.

17. This notion of hunting as competition seems to have been shared by rural Euro-American subsistence hunters as well, and presumably reflects shared notions about human/animal interactions.

18. The Barrow "Duck-in" of 1961 resulted when a number of Inupiaq men, including the local state legislator, were arrested for spring waterfowl hunting. In protest, some 300 Inupiaq Eskimos, including 138 holding dead eider ducks they claimed to have shot, gathered in the local community hall. Faced with having to arrest much of the community, including elders, the authorities backed down (Chance 1990:146–7).

19. A floatplane can land safely with holes in its floats, but it must be dry-docked and repaired before it can take off again. Since agents are unlikely to risk being stranded, or possibly having their plane sink, they are not likely to land.

Chapter 3

1. A distinction should be made between two kinds of situations. Situations truly open to Native and minority participation are those in which Natives and members of other minorities may participate fully, without changing who they are and how they interact. Much more common are situations in which Natives and members of minority groups can participate onlt if they are willing and able to "act white" (often at the cost of violence to their own sense of self), and can operate successfully within shared non-Native typifications.

2. Both local English and Yup'ik (language) have terms to negatively sanction those who overidentify with the opposite group. *Kass'amirte-* is a verb stem meaning "to act like a white person; a derisive description applied to a Yup'ik person trying to act like a white person" (Jacobson 1984:190). "To go Native" is a derisive term applied to non-Natives who are perceived to be trying to act as if they were Yup'ik. Their opposites neither exist nor make sense. There are no common lexicalized terms in either language for cultural hyperperformance of one's own group identity, although one occasionally hears negative comments about the hidebound traditionalism of some member of the other culture. Each group recognizes and, to varying degrees, stigmatizes its own members who act like the "other," and negatively sanctions "others" who hyperperform the stereotype they hold of that "other."

3. People in Bethel are interested in the categories as well, primarily where membership is ambiguous. In general, though, they are less interested in gross categorization than in how someone's actions fit within that category, although the concepts of category and fit are in dynamic tension.

4. This is a stock-in-trade of situation comedies, where the comedian is put in the position of trying to convince skeptics that he or she is actually sane and not a criminal or a deviant, etc., or that there is a logical reason for cross-dressing, wearing prison clothes, no clothes, etc. Much of the humor is in the drawn-out and difficult process of asserting an identity different from the apparent one.

5. Negative stereotypes are also open to strategic manipulation. For example, guilt may be a point where leverage may be applied.

6. As noted in the introduction, I am using the term "Inuit" here because it is preferred over the term "Eskimo" in Canada and Greenland, though not necessarily in Alaska, where it is commonly used by Natives and non-Natives.

7. This is less true once one leaves the United States. In Europe, such activities do seem to reflect upon all Americans.

8. Colonialism can be defined, at least partially, as the extension of control from one region of the world into another for the purposes first of profit and

second of prestige and political power. Generally, colonial control substitutes extractive activities aimed at a world market for indigenous activities aimed at subsistence and local markets. The results are broadly similar regardless of whether the (generally raw) materials extracted are rubber, coffee, tea, spices, copra, guano, gold, or copper (see Thomas 1994 for a discussion of such similarities and differences). Alaska has "hosted" a number of "rushes" or "stampedes" for furs, whales, gold, salmon, and, most recently, oil.

9. Overt recognition of this envy is found in a current joke. "What is the favorite Alaskan wine? I want subsistence rights, too."

10. An additional claim often made to justify such expropriation is that Natives are "pampered," by ANCSA, by preferential programs such as the Alaska Native Health Service, and so on. In this way, both a positive image (corporate Native) and a negative image (feckless dependent) are combined to justify expropriation.

11. Although Bethel supports many churches, non-Natives are certainly no more religious than their counterparts in the rest of the country.

12. I would say, based on my interviews and eleven years of residence in Bethel, that non-Natives who immigrate to the Y-K Delta tend more toward the pothunting end of non-Native ideology, although this is often mixed with certain aristocratic beliefs such as fair chase. Perhaps because it is more difficult to return to urban Alaska or the lower forty-eight states with large quantities of fish or game, hunters and fishermen who visit the region but live elsewhere seem to be primarily status hunters. In a Bethel court case a few years ago, trophy hunters flew in and shot a moose, even though the weather was too warm to preserve the meat, so that it spoiled. Many status fishers fly in to catch and release fish on rivers such as the Kanektok, Goodnews, or Togiak. It is with those hunters and fishers, whose ideology is most at odds with Yup'ik beliefs, that major conflicts have arisen (Wolfe 1988, Morrow and Hensel 1992, Fienup-Riordan 1990).

Chapter 4

1. This also likely reflects differing cultural attitudes toward safety versus autonomy. For example, Yup'ik children generally learn to handle sharp knives correctly and deftly at a considerably earlier age than is typical of non-Native children. There is a basic cross-cultural disagreement on exactly what is "age-appropriate behavior" with cutlery. While a functionalist might argue that this is a practical response to the Yup'ik past, where people lived in small spaces in which large quantities of fish and game were frequently being processed with sharp implements, and there was no "away" place to put things, I would argue that it has more to do with a Yup'ik sense of autonomy. Since the dead are reborn, growing up is at least partly relearning, as opposed to learning things for the first time, and the sense of respect for an adult's space and options is extended to those same adults now reborn, to the extent possible. Hence neither

guns nor knives are necessarily kept as out of the way in many Yup'ik households as in many non-Native ones.

2. All of these techniques share the need for some surface upon which to cut the fish; for knives, generally ulus (locally made semilunar knives); for sharpening stones or files; and for a variety of containers for holding and transporting fish and waste and for washing up.

Chapter 5

1. This chapter and the following one differ from previous chapters in that they focus primarily on Yupiit, and the Yup'ik side of historical Yup'ik/non-Native interactions, as characterized primarily by Nelson (1899), but also by Edmonds (1967), Zagoskin (1967), and Kilbuck in Fienup-Riordan (1988).

2. Child-rearing patterns also facilitate women working. Even very young children may be placed in the care of a relative while a woman is working (Robin Barker, personal communication, July 4, 1991).

3. It is important to note that while Native women do succeed in college at significantly higher rates than Native men, overall Native graduation rates are still very low in comparison with non-Natives.

4. This excludes categories of relatives who may safely be alone together, including husbands and wives, parents and children, grandparents and grandchildren, parallel aunts and uncles and their nieces and nephews, and both cross and parallel cousins. It does not a priori include those two generations apart, such as elders and youth, neighbors, and so on.

5. In part of the Yup'ik area, the verb *kemni-* (to be lightheaded, drugged), is used for both alcoholic excess and steambathing (Jacobson 1984:198).

6. In interviews and conversations with judges, prosecutors, public defenders, and staff and administrators for the Department of Corrections, all agree that there is a sense in which the state of Alaska is incarcerating thousands of Alaskan Natives to keep them from drinking. When sober, most (though not all) such prisoners present little danger to society or themselves. They rarely become violent except when drinking or abusing other substances.

7. One way in which problem individuals have, at least until recently, been handled by such villages is "blue ticketing" (from the carbon copy of the one-way ticket issued to malefactors), that is, banishing troublemakers who move to Bethel or Anchorage. This is an old pattern: ostracism was a traditional way of dealing with antisocial individuals. A community's ability to blue-ticket successfuly was and is a clear sign of its continuing functionality.

8. It is interesting in terms of subsistence underemployment that there is local recognition that taking up sled dog racing is one way for a young man to escape drinking and substance abuse. Keeping sled dogs requires not only a tremendous amount of direct care—feeding, harnessing, training, unharnessing, cleaning up—but perhaps an equal amount of indirect time spent catching fish for dog food, cooking dog food, repairing sleds, harnesses, tug and gang lines,

etc. The local sense is that it leaves little idle time to get in trouble, as well as entailing daily responsibilities throughout the year.

9. The differentially high migration of women from indigenous communities seems to be a circumpolar pattern, although as yet most evidence is anecdotal (though see Langgaard 1986:310 for the then extant situation in Greenland).

10. Domestic violence rates in the Y-K Delta vary between villages. In some villages, rates exceed national norms. In other villages they are suspected to be approximately equal to national norms (Shinkwin and Pete 1983). Because domestic violence is such a serious problem nationwide, some women may leave a situation that they perceive as worsening, marry out, and still end up in abusive relationships. They are particularly at risk if they have moved to the lower forty-eight states and lack the support of an extended kin network. In addition, Fogel-Chance notes from her research among North Slope Inupiaq women in Anchorage, Alaska, that marriage to a Euro-American "was associated both with a move to the city and divorce," so marriage to a non-Native may offer only a temporary solution to these problems (1993:101).

11. Child-rearing skills represent a kind of cultural capital as well, since it is not uncommon for young women to move to an urban area initially to act as a "nanny" for an older sister or other relative.

12. It is interesting to note that the woman's non-Native husband is a very active hunter and fisherman—on a par in his activity level with many active Yup'ik men with a similar schedule of summers free of wage-work. Although she was not able to find a Yup'ik man to be the kind of husband she wanted, she was able to find a non-Native husband who would be both a hunter and a wage earner.

13. For example, in 1991 an anthropology graduate student came to Bethel to research ways in which female emigration and the related gender imbalance in some age classes were causing male rage, substance abuse, and violence.

14. There are interesting parallels with Scheper-Hughes's description (1979) of decline in a rural Irish village. These include changing gender roles and differing expectations by men and women, female outmigration, male alcohol abuse, and high rates of (generally) male insanity.

15. One population of temporary migrants I have interviewed (and talked with informally at length) are Yup'ik college students in Fairbanks. Many not only return during the summer and at peak subsistence seasons but also hunt, fish, gather, and trap in nearby areas while going to college.

16. Not unexpectedly, there was more that could be read into the picture. The competence marked was that of a riverine setting, not a coastal one; and the solidity and seeming permanence of the fish-drying racks also implied her embeddedness in some kind of economically and socially functioning family unit.

Chapter 6

1. Most contemporary cases of botulism in Alaska result from the improper use of modern airtight containers as substitutes for traditional non-airtight mate-

rials and containers. Actions such as replacing the traditional grass lining of an aging pit with layers of plastic, or putting aging food in a lidded plastic bucket, may create ideal conditions for the growth of botulism-causing bacteria.

2. This may also reflect a general human trend toward the enjoyment of more "bitter" foods as one ages (Nelson Graburn, personal communication, April 11, 1992).

Chapter 7

1. While the biochemical basis for some kinds of mental illness has become increasingly clear, other recent research has shown that the biochemical connections between brain and body form an extremely complex and powerful system of feedback loops, and that to speak of mind and body as separate or separable is inaccurate. For the present, experience—particularly trauma—remains important as a potentiating factor.

2. Susan Gal offers a now classic discussion of the relationship between language choice and political-economic identity. Her work demonstrates that "acceptance of the authority and prestige of the state language depends on the political-economic position of the minority group with respect to the state and regional economy" (1987:649). In terms of the gross hegemonic force of English, this is certainly true in the Yup'ik-speaking area. Discourse analysis, a rather nontechnical example of which is presented here, yields other, micro-level insights. These suggest that social interactional practices, of which a preference for positive phrasing is one example, develop within a speech community and subsequently play an important role in the developing patterns of discourse between members of differing speech communities. Social identity in a cross-cultural context is constantly created and adjusted through these discourse patterns.

3. Animals may also avoid a hunter, or be unusually difficult to kill, because of a recent or imminent death in the hunter's family. That is, either someone in the hunter's family has recently died, or will die in the near future. Many Yupiit avoid hunting for up to a year after a death in the immediate family.

4. This is the opposite situation of the one mentioned in the introduction. There the problem was one of being unable to record interviews with Yupiit because they wished to avoid the possible interpretation that they were claiming expert status. Here, these three older Yup'ik men *are* authorized to speak. They begin and end their presentations by clearly stating why this is so (see also Underwood 1986 for similar examples among the Sioux). They are conduits of inherited wisdom, who "listen" and "never forget," and they are richly experienced from their own lives. They speak "to help the people," not from self-aggrandizement.

5. Gumperz and Roberts (1991) argued that native speakers of East Indian languages had similar expectations in interactions with British officials, even though interactions occurred in English.

6. The chairman seemed more confused than judgmental about the miscommunication and tried to encourage agreement through his own example: "One of the things that we have to decide here is when there's not enough fish. I've made the decision right now . . ." He could not comprehend why (Yup'ik) others wouldn't join him in that decision. I should add that such confusion is somewhat understandable. Although I attended the meeting, and felt at the time that participants were talking past each other, it was only after working with tapes and transcripts that Phyllis Morrow and I began to understand the more subtle aspects of this interaction.

7. In comparison, in contemporary Euro-American culture it is likely to be one's gender that is called into question. For example, most men who knit, sew, or crochet (all prototypically feminine activities) feel compelled to offer some explanation for why such activities are actually not inappropriate. A man who crocheted doilies could explain such behavior by saying that this was part of his stroke recovery program, to help him regain fine motor control. Such deviance must be justified if it is not to taint one's gender identity.

8. Although there are many exceptions, there is a degree of truth to the assertion that, in terms of many gender roles, Alaska attracts proportionally more nontraditional women and traditional men, particularly in the rural areas. A tag line on a local radio show was "Bethel, where the men are men, and the women are too." Another way of phrasing this is that women and men are attracted to Alaska for similar reasons, because of perceived opportunities for independence, and to hunt, fish, ski, hike, boat, and camp. Such activities are so stereotypically male-identified as to seem slightly anachronistic (from an urban point of view). They are therefore attractive to "traditional" non-Native men. They are decidedly nontraditional for women and consequently attract those "tough Yukon women" who are the subject of admiring (and ironic) Alaskan songs and stories.

9. Although such giving is not inappropriate for non-Natives, it is an unexpected action. In this context it seems strongly Yup'ik influenced.

10. Because I am male, and given general patterns of Yup'ik cross-gender behavior, more of my interactions with strangers have been with men than with women. However, my own interactions with women, as well as secondhand reporting from women, support the notion that this pattern is quite common among women as well.

Chapter 8

1. Ideally, such a discourse arena should be a locus of group concern, be widely contested, and be readily available, that is, it should be a conversational staple.

References

Active, John
 1992 "Yup'iks Hang On as State Rewrites Nature's Rules." *Anchorage Daily News*, April 1, 1991:B9.

Ager, Thomas
 1982 "Raven's Works." In *Inua: Spirit World of the Bering Sea Eskimo*, edited by William Fitzhugh and Susan Kaplan, pp. 38–56. Washington, D.C.: Smithsonian Institution Press.

Alaska Department of Labor
 1991 *Alaska Population Overview 1990, Census and Estimates*. Juneau, AK.

Anderson, Cindy, Charles Burkey, Doug Molyneau, and R. Kim Franscisco
 1994 "Report to the Alaska Board of Fisheries: Kuskokwim Area, 1994." *Regional Information Report no. 3A94–30*. Alaska Department of Fish and Game, Division of Commercial Fisheries Management and Development, Arctic-Yukon-Kuskokwim Region. Bethel, AK.

Auerswald, Edgar H.
 1968 "Interdisciplinary Versus Ecological Approach." *Family Process* 7(2):202–15.

Barker, James H.
 1993 *Always Getting Ready/Upterrlainarluta: Yup'ik Eskimo Subsistence in Southwest Alaska*. Seattle, WA: University of Washington Press.

Barth, Fredrik
 1969a Introduction to *Ethnic Groups and Boundaries: The Social Organization*

of Culture Difference, edited by Fredrik Barth, pp. 9–38. London: George Allen and Unwin.

1969b "Pathan Identity and Its Maintenance." In *Ethnic Groups and Boundaries: The Social Organization of Culture Difference*, edited by Fredrik Barth, pp. 117–34. London: George Allen and Unwin.

Basso, Keith H.

1979 *Portraits of "the Whiteman": Linguistic Play and Cultural Symbols Among the Western Apache*. Cambridge: Cambridge University Press.

Bateson, Gregory, Don D. Jackson, Jay Haley, and John H. Weakland

1956 "Toward a Theory of Schizophrenia." *Behavioral Science* 1(4):251–64.

Bell, Diane

1980 "Desert Politics: Choices in the Marriage Market." In *Women and Colonization: Anthropological Perspectives*, edited by Mona Etienne and Eleanor B. Leacock, pp. 239–69. New York: Praeger.

Berman, Mathew, and Linda Leask

1994 *Violent Death in Alaska: Who Is Most Likely to Die?* Anchorage: University of Alaska, Anchorage, Institute of Social and Economic Research, *Alaska Review of Social and Economic Conditions* 29(1):1–12.

Bodenhorn, Barbara

1989 " 'The Animals Come To Me, They Know I Share': Inupiaq Kinship, Changing Economic Relations and Enduring World Views on Alaska's North Slope." Ph.D. diss., Cambridge University.

1990 " 'I'm Not the Great Hunter, My Wife Is': Inupiat and Anthropological Models of Gender." *Etudes/Inuit/Studies* 14(1–2):55–74.

1994 "Gendered Spaces, Public Places: Public and Private Revisited on the North Slope of Alaska." In *Landscapes: Politics and Perspectives*, edited by Barbara Bender, pp. 169–203. Oxford: Berg.

Bogojavlensky, Sergei

1969 "Imaangmiut Eskimo Careers: Skinboats in Bering Strait." Ph.D. diss., Harvard University.

Boserup, Ester

1970 *Women's Role in Economic Development*. London: George Allen and Unwin.

Bourdieu, Pierre

1977 *Outline of a Theory of Practice*. Cambridge: Cambridge University Press.

1990 *In Other Words: Essays Towards a Reflexive Sociology*. Palo Alto: Stanford University Press.

Bourdieu, Pierre, and Jean-Claude Passeron

1977 *Reproduction in Education, Society and Culture*. London: Sage.

Brody, Hugh

1975 *The Peoples' Land: Eskimos and Whites in the Eastern Arctic*. Harmondsworth: Penguin.

1986   *Maps and Dreams: Indians and the British Columbia Frontier*. London: Faber and Faber.

Buenaventura-Posso, Elisa, and Susan E. Brown
1980   "Forced Transition from Egalitarism to Male Dominance: The Bari of Colombia." In *Women and Colonization: Anthropological Perspectives*, edited by Mona Etienne and Eleanor B. Leacock, pp. 109–33. New York: Praeger.

Chance, Norman A.
1990   *The Inupiat and Arctic Alaska: An Ethnography of Development*. Case Studies in Cultural Anthropology. New York: Holt, Rinehart and Winston.

Chang, K. C., ed.
1977   *Food in Chinese Culture: Anthropological and Historical Perspectives*. New Haven, CT: Yale University Press.

Coffing, Michael W.
1992   *Kwethluk Subsistence: Contemporary Land Use Patterns, Wild Resource Harvest and Use, and the Subsistence Economy of a Lower Kuskokwim River Area Community*. Technical Paper no. 157. Alaska Department of Fish and Game, Division of Subsistence.

Cohen, Anthony P.
1982   "Belonging: The Experience of Culture." In *Belonging: Identity and Social Organization in British Rural Cultures*, edited by Anthony P. Cohen, pp. 1–17. Manchester, Eng.: Manchester University Press.
1986   "Of Symbols and Boundaries, or does Ertie's Greatcoat hold the Key?" In *Symbolising Boundaries: Identity and Diversity in British Cultures*, edited by Anthony P. Cohen, pp. 1–19. Manchester, Eng.: Manchester University Press.

Collins, Henry B.
1982   "The Man Who Buys Good-For-Nothing Things." In *Inua: Spirit World of the Bering Sea Eskimo*, edited by William Fitzhugh and Susan Kaplan, pp. 28–37. Washington, D.C.: Smithsonian Institution Press.

Comaroff, John L.
1987   "Of Totemism and Ethnicity: Consciousness, Practice and Signs of Inequality." *Ethnos* 52(3–4):301–23.

Condon, Richard G.
1987   *Inuit Youth: Growth and Change in the Canadian Arctic*. New Brunswick, NJ: Rutgers University Press.

Connerton, Paul
1989   *How Societies Remember*. Cambridge: Cambridge University Press.

Cruikshank, Julie
1979   *Athapaskan Women: Lives and Legends*. Mercury Series, Ethnography Service Paper No. 57. Canada: National Museum of Man.

1981   "Legend and Landscape: Convergence of Oral and Scientific Traditions in the Yukon Territory." *Arctic Anthropology* 18(2):67–93.

Dreyfus, Herbert L., and Paul Rabinow
1982   *Michel Foucault: Beyond Structuralism and Hermeneutics.* Chicago: University of Chicago Press.

Edmonds, H. M. W.
1967   "Report on the Eskimos of St. Michael and Vicinity." *Anthropological Papers of the University of Alaska,* 13(2):1–143.

Eidheim, Harald
1969   "Where Ethnic Identity is a Social Stigma." In *Ethnic Groups and Boundaries: The Social Organization of Culture Difference,* edited by Fredrik Barth, pp. 39–57. London: George Allen and Unwin.

Emmett, Isabell
1982   "Place, Community and Bilingualism in Blainau Ffestiniog." In *Belonging: Identity and Social Organization in British Rural Cultures,* edited by Anthony P. Cohen, pp. 202–21. Manchester, Eng.: Manchester University Press.

Fall, James A.
1990   "The Division of Subsistence of the Alaska Department of Fish and Game: An overview of its research program and findings 1980–1990." *Arctic Anthropology* 27(2):68–92.

Fanon, Frantz
1968   *Black Skins, White Masks.* London: MacGibbon and Kee.

Fienup-Riordan, Ann
1983a   *The Nelson Island Eskimo: Social Structure and Ritual Distribution.* Anchorage, AK: Alaska Pacific University Press.
1983b   *The Effects of Renewable Resource Disruption on the Socioeconomic and Sociocultural Systems of the Yukon Delta.* Anchorage: Alaska Council on Science and Technology.
1988   *The Yup'ik Eskimos: As Described in the Travel Journals of John and Edith Kilbuck.* Kingston, Ontario: Limestone.
1990   *Eskimo Essays.* New Brunswick, NJ: Rutgers University Press.
1991   *The Real People and the Children of Thunder: The Yup'ik Eskimo Encounter with Moravian Missionaries John and Edith Kilbuck.* Norman, OK: Oklahoma University Press.

Fitzhugh, William W., and Susan Kaplan
1982   *Inua: Spirit World of the Bering Sea Eskimo.* Washington D.C.: Smithsonian Institution Press.

Fogel-Chance, Nancy
1993   "Living in Both Worlds: 'Modernity' and 'Tradition' among North Slope Inupiaq Women in Anchorage." *Arctic Anthropology* 30(1):94–108.

Foucault, Michel
  1979 *Discipline & Punish: The Birth of the Prison.* New York: Vintage-Random House.

Freeman, Milton M. R.
  1985 "Effects of Petroleum Activities on the Ecology of Arctic Man." In *Petroleum Effects in the Arctic Environment,* edited by F. R. Engelhardt, pp. 245–73. New York: Elsevier Applied Science Publishers.
  1988 "Tradition and Change: Problems and Persistence in the Inuit Diet." In *Coping With Uncertainty in the Food Supply,* edited by I. de Garine and Geoffrey A. Harrison, pp. 150–69. Oxford: Clarendon.

Freuchen, Peter
  1961 *Book of the Eskimos.* Cleveland: World Publishers.

Gal, Susan
  1987 "Codeswitching and Consciousness in the European Periphery." *American Ethnologist* 14(4):636–53.

Garfinkel, Harold
  1967 *Studies in Ethnomethodology.* Englewood Cliffs, NJ: Prentice-Hall.

Geertz, Clifford
  1973 *The Interpretation of Culture.* New York: Basic Books.

Giddens, Anthony
  1979 *Central Problems in Social Theory: Action, Structure and Contradiction in Social Analysis.* Berkeley, CA: University of California Press.
  1984 *The Constitution of Society: Outline of the Theory of Structuration.* Berkeley, CA: University of California Press.

Goffman, Erving
  1959 *The Presentation of Self in Everyday Life.* Garden City, NY: Doubleday.
  1963 *Stigma: Notes on the Management of Spoiled Identity.* Englewood Cliffs, NJ: Prentice-Hall.
  1974 *Frame Analysis.* Cambridge, MA: Harvard University Press.

Graburn, Nelson H. H.
  1971 "Traditional Economic Institutions and the Acculturation of Canadian Eskimos." In *Studies in Economic Anthropology,* edited by George Dalton, no. 7:107–21.

Gumperz, John J.
  1982a *Discourse Strategies.* Cambridge: Cambridge University Press.
  1986 "Interactional Sociolinguistics in the Study of Schooling." In *The Social Construction of Literacy,* edited by Jenny Cook-Gumperz, pp. 45–68. Cambridge: Cambridge University Press.
  1992 "Contextualization and Understanding." In *Rethinking Context: Language as an Interactive Phenomenon,* edited by Alessandro Duranti and Charles Goodwin, pp. 229–52. Cambridge: Cambridge University Press.

Gumperz, John J., ed.
  1982b *Language and Social Identity*. Cambridge: Cambridge University Press.
Gumperz, John J., and Jenny Cook-Gumperz
  1982 "Introduction: Language and the Communication of Social Identity."
         In *Language and Social Identity*, edited by John J. Gumperz, pp. 1–
         21. Cambridge: Cambridge University Press.
Gumperz, John J., and Cecilia Roberts
  1991 "Understanding in Intercultural Encounters." In *The Pragmatics of In-
         ternational and Intercultural Communications*, edited by Jan Blom-
         maert and Jef Verschueren, pp. 51–90. Amsterdam: John Ben-
         jamins.
Hamilton, Lawrence C., and Carole L. Seyfrit
  1993 "Female Flight? Gender Balance and Outmigration by Native Alas-
         kan Villagers." Paper presented at the 9th International Congress
         on Circumpolar Health, Reykjavik, Iceland, June 22, 1993.
  1994 "Coming Out of The Country: Community Size and Gender Balance
         Among Alaskan Natives." *Arctic Anthropology* 31(1):16–25.
Hawkes, Ernest W.
  1913 "The 'Inviting-in' Feast of the Alaskan Eskimo." *Geological Survey
         Memoir 45*, Anthropological Series 3. Ottawa: Department of
         Mines.
Hensel, Chase
  n.d.   "Cutwater Bows and Shearwater Sterns: An Analysis of Some Alas-
         kan Kayaks." ms.
  1992 "Where It's Still Possible: Subsistence, Ethnicity and Identity in
         S.W. Alaska." Ph.D diss., University of California, Berkeley.
         Ann Arbor, MI: University Microfilms.
Hensel, Chase, and Phyllis Morrow
  1983 *Pitengnaqsaraq*. Bethel, Alaska: Lower Kuskokwim School District Bi-
         lingual/Bicultural Department.
Heritage, John
  1984 *Garfinkel and Ethnomethodology*. Cambridge: Polity.
Hewitt, Roger
  1986 *White Talk Black Talk: Inter-racial Friendship and Communication
         Amongst Adolescents*. Cambridge: Cambridge University Press.
Hobsbawm, Eric, and Terence Ranger, eds.
  1983 *The Invention of Tradition*. Cambridge: Cambridge University Press.
Hoffman, Lynn
  1981 *Foundations of Family Therapy: A Conceptual Framework for Systems
         Change*. New York: Basic Books.
Ives, Edward D.
  1988 *George Magoon and the Down East Game War: History, Folklore and the
         Law*. Urbana, IL: University of Illinois Press.

Jacobson, Steven A., comp.
1984 *Yup'ik Eskimo Dictionary.* Fairbanks, AK: Alaska Native Language Center.

Jolles, Carol Zane
1993 "Changing Roles of *Sivuqaq* Women: Clanswomen in the Public sphere." Paper prepared for the 7th Conference on Hunting and Gathering Societies, Moscow, Russia, August 1993.

Jolles, Carol Zane, and Kaningok
1991 "*Qayuutat* and *Angyapiget:* Gender Relations and Subsistence Activities in Sivuqaq (Gambell, St. Lawrence Island, Alaska)." *Etudes/Inuit/Studies* 15(2):23–53.

Jones, Anore
1983 "*Nauriat Niginaqtuat*": Plants That We Eat.* Kotzebue, AK: Maniilaq Corporation.

Jorgenson, Joseph J.
1990 *Oil Age Eskimos.* Berkeley, CA: University of California Press.

Jupp, T. C., Cecilia Roberts, and Jenny Cook-Gumperz
1982 "Language and Disadvantage: The Hidden Process." In *Language and Social Identity,* edited by John J. Gumperz, pp. 232–56. Cambridge: Cambridge University Press.

Klein, Laura F.
1980 "Contending with Colonization: Tlingit Men and Women in Change." In *Women and Colonization: Anthropological Perspectives,* edited by Mona Etienne and Eleanor Leacock, pp. 88–108. New York: Praeger.

Kleinfeld, Judith, Jack Kruse, and Robert Travis
1983 "Inupiat Participation in the Wage Economy: Effects of Culturally Adapted Jobs." *Arctic Anthropology* 20(1):1–21.

Krauss, Michael E.
1980 "Alaska Native Languages: Past, Present and Future." *Alaska Native Language Center Research Papers, No. 4.* Fairbanks, AK: Alaska Native Language Center.

Kruse, John A., Judith Kleinfeld, and Robert Travis
1982 "Energy Development on Alaska's North Slope: Effects on the Inupiat Population." *Human Organization* 41(2):97–106.

Kwachka, Patricia
1990 "Language Shift and Cultural Priorities." Paper delivered at the 6th International Conference on Hunting and Gathering Societies, Fairbanks, AK, June 1990.

Langgaard, Per
1986 "Modernization and Traditional Interpersonal Relationships in a Small Greenlandic Community: A Case Study from Southern Greenland." *Arctic Anthropology* 23(1–2):299–314.

Lantis, Margaret
>   1946   "The Social Culture of the Nunivak Eskimo." *Transactions of the American Philosophical Society*, N.S. Vol. 35, no. 3, Philadelphia.

Lenz, Mary
>   1985   *Bethel, the First 100 Years, 1885–1985: Photographs and History of a Western Alaska Town*. Photographs by James H. Barker. Bethel: Bethel Centennial History Project.

Levin, Michael J.
>   1991   "Alaska Natives in a Century of Change." *Anthropological Papers of the University of Alaska* 23(1–2):1–217.

Luhrman, Tanya M.
>   1989   *Persuasions of the Witch's Craft: Ritual Magic in Contemporary England*. Cambridge, MA: Harvard University Press.

Marquez, Gabriel Garcia
>   1970   *One Hundred Years of Solitude*. Translated by Gregory Rabassa. New York: Avon-Bard.

Marshall, David L.
>   1992   *Native Accidental Deaths and Suicides in Southwest Alaska, 1979–90*. Alaska Department of Health and Social Services, Juneau, AK.

Mather, Elsie
>   1985   *Cauyarnariuq*. Anchorage: Alaska Humanities Forum; Seattle, WA: University of Washington Press.
>   1995   "With a Vision Beyond Our Immediate Needs: Oral Traditions in an Age of Literacy." In *When Our Words Return: Writing, Hearing and Remembering Oral Traditions of Alaska and the Yukon*, edited by Phyllis Morrow and William S. Schneider, pp. 13–28. Logan, UT: Utah State University Press.

McIntosh, Peggy
>   1988   "White Privilege and Male Privilege: A Personal Account of Coming to See Correspondences Through Work in Women's Studies." Working paper 189, Wellesley College Center for Research on Women.

Meade, Marie
>   1990   "Sewing to maintain the Past, Present and Future." *Etudes/Inuit/Studies*, 14(1–2):229–39.

Milan, Fredrick A., and Stella Pawson
>   1975   "The Demography of the Native Population in an Alaskan City." *Arctic* 28(4):275–83.

Moore, Henrietta, L.
>   1988   *Feminism and Anthropology*. Cambridge: Polity.

Morrow, Phyllis
>   1984   "It is Time for Drumming: A Summary of Recent Research on Yup'ik Eskimo Ceremonialism." *Etudes/Inuit/Studies* 8(suppl.): 113–40.

1990 "Symbolic Actions, Indirect Expressions: Limits to Interpretations of Yup'ik Eskimo Society." *Inuit Studies* 14(1–2):141–58.

1991 "What Drives the Birds?: Molting Ducks, Freshman Essays and Cultural Logic." In *The Naked Anthropologist*, edited by Philip De Vita, pp. 58–69. New York: Wadsworth.

Morrow, Phyllis, and Chase Hensel

1992 "Hidden Dissension: Minority-Majority Relationships and the Use of Contested Terminology." *Arctic Anthropology* 29(1): 38–53.

Nadel, J. H.

1984 "Stigmata and Separation: Pariah Status and Community Persistence in a Scottish Fishing Village." *Ethnology* 23:101–116.

Nelson, Edward W.

1899 "The Eskimo about Bering Strait." *Eighteenth Annual Report of the Bureau of American Ethnology.*

Nelson, Richard K.

1969 *Hunters of the Northern Ice.* Chicago: University of Chicago Press.

1978 *Hunters of the Northern Forests: Designs for Survival Among Alaskan Kutchin.* Chicago: University of Chicago Press.

1983 *Make Prayers to the Raven: A Koyukon View of the Northern Forest.* Chicago: University of Chicago Press.

Ogbu, John

1978 *Minority Education and Caste: The American System in Cross-cultural Perspective.* New York: Academic.

Oswalt, Wendell

1963 *Napaskiak: An Alaskan Eskimo Community.* Tucson, AZ: University of Arizona Press.

Pete, Mary C.

1991a "Subsistence Herring Fishing in the Eastern Bering Sea Region: Nelson Island, Nunivak Island and Kuskokwim Bay." Technical Paper no. 192. Alaska Department of Fish and Game, Division of Subsistence.

1991b "Subsistence Herring Fishing in the Nelson Island and Nunivak Island Districts, 1990." Technical Paper no. 196. Alaska Department of Fish and Game, Division of Subsistence.

1991c "Subsistence Herring Fishing in the Nelson Island and Nunivak Island Districts, 1991." Technical Paper no. 211. Alaska Department of Fish and Game, Division of Subsistence.

Rasing, Wilhelm C. E.

1994 *"Too Many People": Order and Nonconformity in Iglulingmiut Social Processes.* Nijmegen: Katholieke Universiteit.

Ray, Dorothy Jean

1967 *Eskimo Masks: Art and Ceremony.* Photographs by Alfred A. Blaker. Seattle: University of Washington Press.

Reiger, John F.
　　1986　*American Sportsmen and the Origins of Conservation*, rev. ed. Norman,
　　　　　OK: University of Oklahoma Press.
Ruesch, Jurgen and Gregory Bateson
　　1951　*Communication, the Social Matrix of Psychiatry*. New York: Norton.
Sahlins, Marshall D.
　　1972　*Stone Age Economics*. New York: Aldine.
Scheper-Hughes, Nancy
　　1979　*Saints, Scholars and Schizophrenics: Mental Illness in Rural Ireland*. Berke-
　　　　　ley, CA: University of California Press.
Schneider, Jane, and Annette B. Weiner
　　1989　Introduction to *Cloth and the Human Experience*, edited by Annette B.
　　　　　Weiner and Jane Schneider, pp. 1–29. Washington, D.C.: Smith-
　　　　　sonian Institution Press.
Scollon, Ron, and Suzanne Scollon
　　1980　*Interethnic Communication*. Fairbanks, AK: Alaska Native Language
　　　　　Center.
　　1982　*Narrative, Literacy and Face in Interethnic Communication*. Norwood,
　　　　　NJ: Ablex.
Senungetuk, Joseph E.
　　1971　*Give Or Take A Century: An Eskimo Chronicle*. San Franscisco: Indian
　　　　　Historian Press.
Shaeffer, Pete, Delano Barr, and Greg Moore
　　1986　*A Review of the Game Regulations Affecting Northwest Alaska*. Kotzebue
　　　　　Fish and Game Advisory Committee.
Sharp, Henry
　　1981　"The Null Case: The Chipewyan." In *Woman the Gatherer*, edited by
　　　　　Frances Dahlberg, pp. 221–44. New Haven, CT: Yale Univer-
　　　　　sity Press.
Shinkwin, Anne, and Mary Pete
　　1983　"Homes in Disruption: Spouse abuse in Yup'ik Eskimo Society." ms.
Stefansson, Vilhjalmur
　　1921　*The Friendly Arctic: The Story of Five Years in Polar Regions*. London:
　　　　　Macmillan.
Steinbeck, John
　　1945　*Cannery Row*. New York: Bantam Books.
Tanner, Adrian
　　1979　*Bringing Home Animals: Religious Ideology and mode of Production of the
　　　　　Mistassini Cree Hunters*. London: C. Hurst.
Thomas, Nicholas
　　1994　*Colonialism's Culture: Anthropology, Travel and Government*. Cam-
　　　　　bridge: Polity.
Thompson, Michael
　　1979　*Rubbish Theory: The Creation and Destruction of Value*. Oxford: Oxford
　　　　　University Press.

Tinker, Irene, Michele Bo Bramser, and Mayra Buvinic
    1976 *Women and World Development.* New York: Praeger.
Underwood, Charles Fred
    1986 "The Indian Witness: Narrative Style in Courtroom Testimony."
           Ph.D. diss., University of California, Berkeley.
Watzlawick, Paul, Janet Beavin Bavelas, and Don D. Jackson
    1967 *Pragmatics of Human Communication: A Study of Interactional Patterns,*
           Pathologies and Paradoxes. New York: Norton.
Wells, Roger, and John W. Kelly (interpeter)
    1890 *English-Eskimo and Eskimo-English Vocabularies.* Bureau of Education
           Circular of Information No. 2, 1890. Washington D.C.: Govern-
           ment Printing Office.
Willis, Paul
    1977 *Learning to Labor: How Working-Class Kids Get Working-Class Jobs.* New
           York: Columbia University Press.
Wolfe, Robert J.
    1979 "Food Production in a Western Eskimo Population." Ph.D. diss.,
           University of California, Los Angeles. Ann Arbor, MI: Univer-
           sity Microfilms.
    1987 "The Super-Household: Specialization in Subsistence Economies."
           Paper presented at the 14th Annual Meeting of the Alaskan An-
           thropological Association Meeting, Anchorage, AK, March 1987.
    1988 " 'The Fish Are Not to be Played With': Yup'ik Views of Sport Fish-
           ing and Subsistence-Recreation Conflicts along the Togiak River."
           Paper presented at the Annual Alaska Anthropological Associa-
           tion Meeting, Anchorage, AK, March 1988.
Wolfe, Robert J., Joseph J. Gross., Steven J. Langdon, John M. Wright, George
   K. Sherrod, Linda J. Ellana, Valerie Sumida, and Peter J. Usher.
    1984 "Subsistence-Based Economies in Coastal Communities of Southwest
           Alaska." Technical Paper no. 89. Alaska Department of Fish and
           Game, Division of Subsistence.
Woodbury, Anthony C., comp. and ed.
    1984 *Cev'armiut Qanemciit Qulirait-llu / Eskimo Narratives and Tales from*
           Chevak, Alaska. Fairbanks, AK: Alaska Native Language Center.
Woolard, Katherine
    1985 "Language Variation and Cultural Hegemony: Toward an Integra-
           tion of Sociolinguistic and Social Theory." *American Ethnologist*
           12(4):738–48.
Yarie, Sarah Fulton, Thomas Frank, Steve Brown, Lewis Overton, and Pat Pitney.
    1991 "1991 Statistical Abstract," University of Alaska. Fairbanks: Office
           of Institutional Research.
Zagoskin, Lavrentii Aleksieevich
    1967 *Lieutenant Zagoskin's Travels in Russian America 1842–1844,* translated
           by Penelope Rainey, edited and translated by Henry N. Michael.
           Toronto: University of Toronto Press.

Index

Printed in the United States
4973

9 780195 094770